Opening Up

Opening Up

THE HEALING POWER OF CONFIDING IN OTHERS

James W. Pennebaker, Ph.D.

AVON BOOKS ◆ NEW YORK

AVON BOOKS
A division of
The Hearst Corporation
1350 Avenue of the Americas
New York, New York 10019

Published in hardcover by William Morrow and Company, Inc.; for information address Permissions Department, William Morrow and Company, Inc., 1350 Avenue of the Americas, New York, New York 10019.

The William Morrow and Company edition contains the following Library of Congress Cataloging in Publication Data:

Pennebaker, James W.
    Opening up : the healing power of confiding in others / James W. Pennebaker.
        p.   cm.
    Includes bibliographical references.
1. Inhibition—Health aspects.   2. Self-disclosure—Health aspects.   3. Written communication—Therapeutic use.   4. Stress (Psychology)—Prevention.   5. Mind and body.   I. Title.
RC455.4.I54P46   1990   90-33785
158'.2—dc20   CIP

First Avon Books Trade Printing: October 1991

AVON TRADEMARK REG. U.S. PAT. OFF. AND IN OTHER COUNTRIES, MARCA REGISTRADA, HECHO EN U.S.A.

Printed in the U.S.A.

OPM   10   9   8   7   6   5   4   3   2   1

*To my mother, Elizabeth Whiting Pennebaker,
who taught me to laugh with others and at myself*

*And to my father, William Fendall Pennebaker,
who aroused my curiosity about the world*

PREFACE

Have you ever had a secret too shameful to tell?

Have you stopped yourself from disclosing a personal experience because you thought others would think less of you?

Have you ever told a stranger some of your darkest secrets that you have never divulged to your closest friend?

Have you ever lied to yourself by claiming that a major upheaval in your life didn't affect you or, perhaps, didn't occur?

If so, you may be hurting yourself. Not because you have had a troubling experience but because you can't express it.

We are all humans simmering in the same stew. Our lives oscillate from exhilarating highs to devastating lows. We can usually cope with the highs. It's the lows that are a problem. Most of us will face one or more horrible experiences in our lives—death of a loved one, divorce, loss of a job, crime—the list is endless. How we cope with those events will dictate our happiness for months or even years afterward.

This is a book on disclosing your most painful secrets and how it affects your health. My story is that of a researcher rather than a physician or therapist. My students, colleagues, and I have been trying to learn how and why disclosure of our intimate secrets can improve health. In our odyssey, we have tested thousands of people of all ages and backgrounds. Normally, I would have been happy to publish our findings in professional journals and move on to another project. But this work has been different. The nature of confession and inhibition is meaningful to many people's lives right now. Even beyond direct applications, the problems we are grappling with give some insight into human nature.

In writing this book, I have tried to be faithful to potential readers seeking information on traumas as well as to those interested in the areas of psychology and medicine. If you find that you are currently living with some kind of personal upheaval, even if it happened a long time ago, I hope what I have to say will benefit you. As you will see, writing or talking about your experiences may improve both your physical and mental health. I am not selling a miracle cure. Rather, research from our laboratory and elsewhere is uncovering some exciting findings that may help you in your coping.

The second group of people for whom this book is written is made up of individuals interested in the mind, the body, and psychosomatics. For the last several years, the project in which I have been immersed suggests that translating events into language can affect brain and immune function. If you are intrigued by the links between the mind and body, you can join me in speculating why not talking about traumas may be unhealthy and why writing or talking about them can bring about health improvements. In reading this book, please understand that the experiments I discuss are usually more complex than the summaries I provide. I have included a Chapter Notes section at the end of the book that briefly discusses some of the more esoteric issues and provides specific references for further reading.

Throughout the book, I refer to several individuals whom I have studied or interviewed. In all cases, I have changed the names and other identifying information of the people involved, to protect their anonymity. In addition, I have reconstructed some of the direct spoken quotations from my memory or notes of conversations. The gist of each of the stories, however, is true and based on real people.

In addition to the hundreds of people who served as participants in our research, I am deeply indebted to the many others who helped me on this project. I am particularly grateful to my dedicated and loyal students, who devoted months and, sometimes, years of their lives in conducting the experiments on which this project was built. My thinking about confession and health has been most strongly influenced through discussions with my wife, Ruth Pennebaker, and my colleagues Dan Wegner and David Watson. In addition to the invaluable comments from these three individuals, I greatly appreciate the feedback I received on various parts of this manuscript from the following people: Laura Carstensen, Rebecca Eder, Mary Gergen, Maria Guarnaschelli, Joyce Saenz Harris, Bob Ornstein, Roxi Silver, and Carol Tavris.

The research on which this book is based could not have been conducted without the strong support of my colleagues and the administration at Southern Methodist University. I have relied heavily on the advice and friendship of Mike Best and the other members of the Department of Psychology at SMU. I am also indebted to the faculty and students in the Department of Psychology at Stanford University for their ideas and encouragement during my visit in 1989. Finally, this research would not have been possible without grants from the National Science Foundation and the National Institutes of Health.

CONTENTS

1
Confession and Inhibition: The Beginnings of an Approach

Long before the Spanish conquered the new world, Indians of North and South America had elaborate confession rituals wherein tribe members disclosed their transgressions to others. Indeed, rituals of confession are currently prominent among most Eastern and Western religions.

A growing number of Americans pay millions of dollars to therapists and self-help groups so that they can divulge their secret views of the world.

A large percentage of people write about their very deepest thoughts and feelings in diaries or letters but do not disclose the personal sides of themselves to the close friends they see every day.

On airplanes, buses, and trains, people are likely to disclose intimate sides of themselves to individuals they have never met before.

Why do people throughout the world seek to tell their untold stories? Is there some kind of urge to confess? Is it healthy for us to divulge our deepest thoughts and feelings? Or, conversely, is it unhealthy *not* to disclose the private side of our life? I have been fascinated by questions such as these for quite a while. Beginning in the late 1970s, I embarked on a large research project in an attempt to get some answers.

The main discoveries of this project indicate that actively holding back or inhibiting our thoughts and feelings can be hard work. Over time, the work of inhibition gradually undermines the body's defenses. Like other stressors, inhibition can affect immune function, the action of the heart and vascular systems, and even the biochemical workings of the brain and nervous systems.

In short, excessive holding back of thoughts, feelings, and behaviors can place people at risk for both major and minor diseases.

Whereas inhibition is potentially harmful, confronting our deepest thoughts and feelings can have remarkable short- and long-term health benefits. Confession, whether by writing or talking, can neutralize many of the problems of inhibition. Further, writing or talking about upsetting things can influence our basic values, our daily thinking patterns, and our feelings about ourselves. In short, there appears to be something akin to an urge to confess. Not disclosing our thoughts and feelings can be unhealthy. Divulging them can be healthy.

Those are the most basic ideas of the book. But there is much more to the story. Before detailing the nature and implications of confession, let me explain how I got into this business. Several years ago, I became fascinated by three seemingly unrelated phenomena: the joy of talking, the nature of lie detection, and the role of self-understanding in affecting the mind–body link. Piecing together these observations laid the groundwork of an intriguing model of inhibition and confrontation.

I was originally trained as a social psychologist—someone who studies attitudes and social behaviors. After graduate school, I found myself teaching a class of three hundred freshmen about basic psychology at the University of Virginia. Because graduate training emphasizes research skills rather than teaching abilities, I quickly learned that class demonstrations were a wonderful way of hiding one's lack of knowledge about a topic. Further, if the demonstrations were set up right, I could actually conduct research and teach at the same time.

In one of the first class meetings, I split the students into small groups of people who didn't know one another. Once in their assigned groups, the students were told just to talk for fifteen minutes about anything they wanted. As you would expect, they talked about their hometowns, why they had come to college, what dormitory they lived in, friends they had in common, the weather, and related topics—the usual cocktail-party fare.

At the end of fifteen minutes, they all returned to their regular seats and estimated how much of the time every person in the group talked, how much they liked the group, and how much they learned from the group. Two rather surprising findings came from this and subsequent demonstrations. First, the more people talked, the more they liked the group. Second, the more they talked, the more they claimed to have learned from the group. In other words, as a group member, the more you dominate the conversation, the more you claim you have learned about the others.

In general, we would rather talk than listen. Most of us find that communicating our thoughts is a supremely enjoyable learning experience.

Not long after this, I was introduced to the world of lie detection. Up to that time, I had been interested in how students felt when they talked about superficial topics to their classmates. I was now in a position to learn what happened physiologically to people in the real world when they talked about crimes they may or may not have committed.

There is something frighteningly magical about the idea of lie detection. Machines that can accurately read others' private thoughts have been the basis of dreams by police officers, poker players, and parents. A crude approximation of this magical lie detector is the polygraph—an instrument that continuously measures several physiological indicators such as heart rate, blood pressure, breathing rate, and perspiration on the hand.

In law enforcement, polygraph exams and related lie-detection methods assume that when suspects try to deceive their interrogators, their biological stress levels will increase relative to when they tell the truth. Although numerous studies indicate that polygraph techniques do much better than chance at catching truly guilty suspects, they are far from perfect.

Ironically, the real value of the polygraph is in bringing about confessions. A particularly skilled polygrapher uses a suspect's biological responses to various questions as an indicator of what topics provoke the most anxiety. Once the "hot" questions are isolated, the polygrapher may note, "Gee, I really believe what you have told me, but my machine shows a huge reaction when you answered that question. Why do you think this is happening?" In more cases than not, deceptive suspects try to rationalize their physiological responses. In so doing, they often contradict their earlier stories. Finally, the more they are confronted with these contradictions, the more likely they are to ultimately break down and confess to the crime.

Because of my interest in physiological responses to stressors, I was invited to give a series of talks to some of the top-level polygraphers of the FBI, CIA, and other secret agencies with initials of which I had never heard. Fortunately, I spent several late evenings talking with the polygraphers about their job. As a group, these people were unusually bright and insightful. What most impressed me was a remarkably similar experience that many of the polygraphers reported in interrogating some of their suspects—something I call the polygraph confession effect.

A San Francisco–based polygrapher first alerted me to the polygraph confession effect in recounting an exam he had given to a forty-five-year-old bank vice-president who was a suspect in an embezzlement investigation. When initially run through the polygraph exam, the bank vice-president's heart rate, blood pressure, and other physiological levels were quite high. This is normal for both innocent and guilty people, because such an exam is almost always threatening. Nevertheless, the polygrapher suspected that the bank vice-president was lying or holding back information, because his physiological levels went even higher when the vice-president was asked about some of the details of the embezzlement. With repeated questions and prodding, the vice-president finally broke down and confessed to embezzling $74,000 over a six-month period.

In line with standard procedures, after the bank vice-president had signed a written confession, he was then polygraphed again to be certain that his confession was itself not deceptive. When hooked up to the monitoring apparatus, his overall physiological levels were extremely low. His hands were no longer sweaty. His heart rate and blood pressure were extraordinarily low. His breathing was slow and relaxed.

You can appreciate the irony of this situation. This man had come into the polygrapher's office a free man, safe in the knowledge that polygraph evidence was not allowed in court. Nevertheless, he confessed. Now, his professional, financial, and personal lives were on the brink of ruin. He was virtually assured of a prison term. Despite these realities, he was relaxed and at ease with himself. Indeed, when a policeman came to handcuff and escort him to jail, he warmly shook the polygrapher's hand and thanked him for all he had done. This last December, the polygrapher received a chatty Christmas card written by the former bank vice-president with a federal penitentiary as the return address.

Even when the costs are high, the confession of actions that violate our personal values can reduce anxiety and physiological stress. Whereas dominating the conversation in a group may be fun, revealing pent-up thoughts and feelings can be liberating. Even if they send you to prison.

There was a third phenomenon that had a significant impact on my interest in confession and health. It dealt with the nature of psychological insight and the mind-body link. I was probably drawn to the area of psychosomatics by virtue of having asthma as a child. I grew up in West Texas, a very dry and flat part of the world. During my adolescence, asthma attacks became a routine feature of the windy part of winter (as opposed to the windy parts of spring, summer, and fall). Clearly, I reasoned, pollen and dust that had blown in from New Mexico and Nevada were to blame.

In college, I never had any wheezing bouts except when I went home for the Christmas holidays. The pollen and dust again. During my last year in college, however, my parents came to visit me in Florida in late November. The day they arrived, I developed asthma. All of a sudden, the profound realization hit me that there was more to asthma than pollen. Conflicts with my parents were undoubtedly linked to my upper respiratory system. Interestingly, once I saw the parent-asthma connection, I never again wheezed. It was too embarrassing.

Asthma, wheezing, congestion, and other respiratory changes have long been known to be related to psychological conflict. In fact, two pioneers in psychosomatic medicine, Harold G. Wolff and Stewart Wolf, documented effects such as these in a book with the intriguing title *The Nose* (together and separately, they also published books entitled *Headache, The Colon,* and, of course, *The Stomach*). In landmark studies spanning two decades, Wolff, Wolf, and their collaborators developed the stress interview, whereby volunteers would be asked a series of psychologically threatening questions while, at the same time, relevant bodily changes were monitored.

The stress interview serves as a medical version of a lie-detector exam. For most people, there are a limited number of psychological issues that account for most psychosomatic problems. Current stress interviews, for example, routinely touch on issues of loss, rejection, sexuality, parental problems, uncontrollable trauma, and failure. Depending on the person's health problem, the interviewer might measure muscle tension in the neck (for tension-headache sufferers), blood pressure and heart rate (for hypertensives), breathing rate or oxygen consumption (for those with respiratory problems or panic attacks), or one of a few dozen other biological indices.

As Wolff, Wolf, and a generation of psychosomatic researchers soon learned, different psychological conflicts are linked to specific changes in our bodies. One person's blood pressure may increase when he is forced to discuss the death of his parents, whereas another might respond to the same topic with the beginnings of a migraine headache. A third person may not show any biological changes to the death topic but may react selectively to issues surrounding sexuality.

That many, perhaps most, illnesses have a significant psychosomatic component is not surprising. More peculiar is that we rarely see the relationship between psychological events and illness in ourselves. When we do, however, the course of the illness often changes for the better.

Why are we blind to many of the psychological precursors to illness? One problem lies in our abilities to perceive cause–effect relationships. When we see something happen, we naturally look for something that preceded the event by no more than a few seconds or, at most, hours. If our car doesn't start because of a dead battery, we might blame the battery's demise on the cold weather or our failure to turn off the headlights. It makes no sense to think back to the way we drove the car two weeks ago. Our body is a different story. If we come down with a cold, it probably has nothing to do with last night's weather or what we had for breakfast. It could be that our immune system was compromised by the breakup of a significant relationship a week earlier.

Another reason for our myopia concerning the causal links between psychological issues and illness concerns denial. Virtually all of us have actively avoided thinking about unpleasant experiences. Some issues are so painful that we deceive ourselves into thinking that they don't exist. Sigmund Freud persuasively argued that we employ an arsenal of defense mechanisms, such as denial, compulsive behaviors, and even dwelling on physical symptoms, in order to screen out anxiety and psychological pain. Wheezing when around parents or headaches in sexually threatening situations can be safely attributed to purely physical causes (e.g., pollen or caffeine). Admitting to struggles concerning one's autonomy or sexuality will usually be avoided when less threatening alternative explanations exist.

Fortunately, once we become aware of the psychological causes of a recurring health problem such as headaches, back pain, or asthma, the problems often subside to some degree. There are several reasons for this. Once we see the psychological basis for a particular health problem, we can then use the health problem as a signal of distress. By focusing our energy on reducing the cause of the distress, we more quickly resolve the underlying psychological issues that we may not have known were issues in the first place. Another reason that seeing the cause-effect relationship is beneficial is that it makes the health problems more predictable and, hence, controllable. Perceptions of control and predictability over our world are essential to good psychological health.

One of my first experiences in discovering this sometimes invisible link between a psychological event and biological activity was with Warren, an extremely bright student who had been the valedictorian of his high school class. After performing quite well his first year and a half of college, he suddenly developed test anxiety. Midway in his fourth semester of college, he began to fail every test he took. He was soon placed on academic probation and later forced to withdraw from school. Over the next year, Warren saw a therapist who specialized in behavioral treatments. Several weeks of relaxation training and behavior modification failed to produce significant improvement.

A year later, Warren visited me and explained his predicament. He agreed to be interviewed about his life while I measured his heart rate. Not until years later did I learn that heart rate was not the most reliable psychological indicator for most people. Warren, fortunately, was an exception. During the first hour-long interview, it became clear that Warren's body was telling a different story from Warren's words.

As is shown in the table, Warren's heart rate increased dramatically whenever the topic of his parents' divorce was discussed. No other issues influenced heart rate to a comparable degree. Despite the fact that Warren claimed to be unaffected by his parents' divorce, it was a significant event. Indeed, he first learned that they had separated about a week before his developing test anxiety. In the two intervening years, he never saw the relationship between the divorce and his poor performance during exams. When confronted with his heart-rate data, Warren was flabbergasted. Over the next few days, he discussed his feelings of anger and

TOPIC	HEART RATE	WARREN'S COMMENTS
Girlfriend	77	Some disagreements about sexuality, but we are close.
College courses	71	Most have been interesting . . . tests have been another matter.
Failing exams	76	It's been hard on my ego. I can't explain it.
Parents	84	We were a close family until the divorce.
Parents' divorce	103	It was no big deal, really. They are a lot happier now.
The future	79	It scares me. I can't bear the thought of failing again.

despair over the divorce with me and, later, with his parents. Although he still harbors some of these feelings, his test anxiety disappeared.

We are often blind to the psychological causes and correlates of our health problems. Many illnesses and recurring health problems have a psychosomatic component. Awareness or insight into the psychological bases of illness can help in the healing process. If we are aware of the conflicts influencing our bodies, we can act to overcome those conflicts.

These were the beginning pieces of the puzzle. When we talk a great deal in a group, we claim that we enjoy it and learn from it. After confessing a crime, our minds and bodies appear to be relaxed. Once we understand the link between a psychological event and a recurring health problem, our health improves.

Each of these phenomena deals with the psychological state of holding back versus opening up. As my students and I began systematically to examine the holding back-opening up continuum, an organizing framework began to emerge. Although it is still evolving, it can be summarized as follows:

Inhibition is physical work. To actively inhibit one's thoughts, feelings, or behaviors requires physiological work. Active inhibition means that people must consciously restrain, hold back, or in some way exert effort to *not* think, feel, or behave.

Inhibition affects short-term biological changes and long-term health. In the short run, inhibition is reflected by immediate biological changes, such as increased perspiration as that measured on lie-detector tests. Over time, the work of inhibition serves as a cumulative stressor on the body, increasing the probability of illness and other stress-related physical and psychological problems. Active inhibition can be viewed as one of many general stressors that affect the mind and body. Obviously, the harder one must work at inhibiting, the greater the stress on the body.

Inhibition influences thinking abilities. Active inhibition is also associated with potentially deleterious changes in the ways we think. In holding back significant thoughts and feelings associated with an event, we typically do not think about the event in a broad and integrative way. By not talking about an inhibited event, for example, we usually do not translate the event into language. This prevents us from understanding and assimilating the event. Consequently, significant experiences that are inhibited are likely to surface in the forms of ruminations, dreams, and associated thought disturbances.

The opposite pole of active inhibition is confrontation. For lack of a better term, confrontation refers to individuals' actively thinking and/or talking about significant experiences as well as acknowledging their emotions. Psychologically confronting traumas overcomes the effects of inhibition both physiologically and cognitively.

Confrontation reduces the effects of inhibition. The act of opening up and confronting a trauma immediately reduces the physiological work of inhibition. During confrontation, the biological stress of inhibition is immediately reduced. Over time, if individuals continue to confront and thereby resolve the trauma, there will be a lowering of the overall stress level on the body.

Confrontation forces a rethinking of events. Confronting a trauma helps people understand and, ultimately, assimilate the event. By talking or writing about previously inhibited experiences, individuals translate the event into language. Once it is language based, people can better understand the experience and ultimately put it behind them.

When first playing with these ideas, my students and I were exuberant. A number of potential experiments that could test and extend the framework popped into our minds. Despite similar theorizing by Aristotle, Freud, and several contemporary psychologists, many of my colleagues viewed the inhibition/confrontation approach as a bit extreme and even radical. Others viewed it with excitement. Given the polarized reception of the early work, I knew I was on to something.

After a boisterous meeting with colleagues where we debated the pros and cons of inhibition, I came home in a wonderful mood. I waltzed in the front door just as the phone began to ring. My brother, who is a graphic designer, called to ask what was new in my life. I excitedly told him about this new approach that I was playing with and its possible links to health, psychotherapy, religion, and, well, just about everything. Not swayed by my grandiosity, my brother asked about the specifics of the inhibition/confrontation framework. When I was finished, the phone was silent. "That's it?" my brother finally said. "What's the big deal? Everyone knows *that*."

He is right on a certain level. We do know that talking about our problems can be good for us. But we also know that we should put on a happy face and look at everything in a positive light. We also know that whining and complaining about our problems will get us nowhere. In other words, in these days of self-help popular psychology, there are often contradictory common sense views that explain everything. As our research journey into the inhibition/confrontation world began, my colleagues and I quickly learned that some common sense ideas were truer than others—indeed, some were completely false. In the remainder of this book, I would like to share with you some of the insights of this journey.

2
Inhibition as a Health Threat

We are living in the age of inhibition. The 1960s and early 1970s were the years of letting go, doing your own thing in your own time, rolling with the flow, and being cool. Now, it's no smoking, no alcohol, no drugs, no casual sex, no fattening foods, no fun. We have learned to feel good by jogging, eating brown and taste-less foods, and going to bed early. One of the few remaining thrills available to us is looking down our noses at people who can't inhibit their urges as well as we can. The new self-righteousness has arrived.

Inhibiting thoughts, feelings, and behaviors has always been a part of life. Two-year-olds learn to inhibit their bowels and bladders the same way adolescents usually control their urges to rape and pillage. Many of our truly natural behaviors, such as sex and aggression, according to Freud, must be controlled for the good of society. Inhibition, then, is the Scotch tape of civilization.

Animal and human researchers have suggested that there are two types of inhibition: active and passive. Active inhibition is effortful and requires our mental attention not to do something. When we first go on a diet, we must actively inhibit our impulses to eat or even to think about eating rich food. Passive inhibition occurs automatically, without conscious effort. After successfully restricting our eating for several months, we may be able to see someone eat a large bowl of ice cream without even thinking about wanting some ourselves. Through practice, then, the initially dif-ficult job of active inhibition evolves into a more passive form of inhibition.

A fascinating real-world example of the distinction between active and passive inhibition has been suggested by Stanley Schachter, a particularly clever researcher at Columbia University. Schachter was perplexed by a paradox concerning people who attempted to stop smoking or lose weight. It is well established that only about 10–30 percent of people in smoking-cessation or weight-loss programs are still "cured" one year after participating in their respective programs. Consequently, some therapists and researchers claim that smoking and overeating are almost impossible to control permanently. However, in interviewing his friends and colleagues, Schachter learned that the majority who had ever tried to stop smoking or lose weight had successfully done so.

Drawing on interviews and over two decades of research that he conducted in this area, Schachter suggested that the key to controlling unwanted behaviors might be practice. Indeed, the average person who has successfully quit smoking for several years reports having tried to stop a number of times. Stopping smoking is initially a form of active inhibition. It is often painful and associated with various withdrawal symptoms. With time and practice, it becomes progressively easier to stop smoking or lose weight without thinking about it or exerting much effort.

It is no wonder, then, why single smoking cessation or weight-loss programs appear to be only marginally successful. Schachter's work indicates that the more times a person goes through programs such as these, the more likely that they will eventually succeed. Extending this work to your own life, if you have tried and failed to stop smoking, drinking, overeating, or indulging in some other unwanted behavior, simply try to stop again. The more times you stop, the easier it becomes. With practice, you move from the hard work of active inhibition to the minimal effort involved in passive inhibition.

For anyone interested in studying problems associated with active inhibition, the logical place to start is among people concerned with dieting and weight loss. The majority of adults worry about their weight and often go to extreme measures to inhibit their eating. In the late 1970s, I intended to begin to study inhibition by surveying people to get an idea of the ways they dieted and the relative effectiveness of their weight-loss techniques. Before the project started, however, my plans changed after some discussions with my students.

It was 1979 and one of my students was complaining about her roommate, who was eating tremendous quantities of food each night and then vomiting what she had eaten. I told this story to a group of my researchers with the air of you'll-never-believe-this. Over the next week, at least half of my research team spoke privately with me and admitted that they, too, binged and purged food on a regular basis. Here was a phenomenon that I had never heard of that was apparently affecting a respectable number of college students. Who were these people and why were they doing it?

Fortunately, Billy Barrios, a clinical psychologist with an interest in behavior disorders, had an office across the hall. Barrios and I, along with a group of students, decided to examine this eating disorder. The first step was designing a massive questionnaire that asked people about their childhood, eating history, friends, stressors, body image, and general health. Because our preliminary surveys indicated that the disorder was overwhelmingly reported by women, we elected to gear the massive questionnaire to women only.

The questionnaire was completed by over seven hundred college women in psychology courses at the University of Virginia and the University of Mississippi. Overall, about 10 percent of the respondents purged their food as a dieting method, whereas another 40 percent were classified as normal dieters in that they simply counted calories and restricted what they ate. Our findings about the eating disorder—which soon became known as bulimia—were interesting in ways that we had not expected. Basically, people who are bulimics are similar to dieters who are not bulimics. Bulimics and normal dieters have similar childhoods, body images, food preferences, and just about everything else. The main difference is that bulimics have tried several different diets, all of them unsuccessful. Bulimia, in our view, was an extreme form of dieting.

Oddly, the bulimics' major problems were not dieting per se. Instead, their cycle of eating and purging food was forcing these women to adopt secret lives. Indeed, in individual interviews with over two dozen bulimics, virtually every one spontaneously noted the inordinate amount of time and effort required to conceal her eating habits from her close friends and family. They all were living a lie and hated it. In fact, one of the first women I interviewed tearfully explained how she had stopped spending time with her friends. Her eating and purging were important issues that she couldn't explain to them. Now, because she was lonely, all she did was eat.

At the time, Barrios and I were also puzzled that almost all of our bulimics were sick a great deal of the time. In fact, they went to physicians for a variety of illnesses almost twice as often as the average student. At the time, we idly speculated that repeated vomiting increased health problems by causing dehydration, which in turn resulted in problems with the cardiovascular and immune systems. In retrospect, this may have accounted for some of the women's health problems. Another contributing factor, however, appears to have been the forces of active inhibition.

Most of the women we had been studying felt they could not tell anyone about their eating habits. They were actively holding back a major secret from everyone they knew. The forces of inhibition were contributing to the women's stressful lives.

TRAUMATIC SEXUAL EXPERIENCES IN CHILDHOOD

My research career investigating eating disorders was short-lived. Although I had seen the processes of inhibition, I didn't know it. Ironically, the importance of the bulimia project had very little to do with eating. Late one night while designing the bulimia questionnaire, Pam Grace, one of the research-team members, suggested that we include an item on traumatic sexual experiences in childhood. There was no particular reason for the question—it just sounded interesting. So toward the end of the twelve-page questionnaire, we threw in a question that very few researchers ever ask:

Prior to the age of 17, did you have a traumatic sexual experience (e.g., rape, being molested)?
        Yes_____ No_____

Much to our surprise, about 10 percent of the college women answered in the affirmative. As a rule, the women who reported traumatic sexual experiences in childhood did not differ from others in terms of age, social class, race, or even number of close friends. Indeed, bulimics were no more likely to have had a sexual trauma than women who were not bulimics. The most striking finding from the survey, however, was that those who reported a sexual trauma evidenced more health problems than any other group we had ever seen.

The very day that I was pondering the results of the sexual trauma question, I received a phone call from Carin Rubenstein, then an editor of *Psychology Today* magazine. She was in the process of writing a general health questionnaire to be completed by *Psychology Today* readers. Did I have any ideas for questions to be put on her survey? Funny that she should ask.

The health questionnaire appeared in the May 1982 issue of the magazine. Over 24,000 people returned the completed survey, which, of course, included a question about sexual trauma. Although the respondents mirrored the readership of the magazine (mean age 35; 68 percent females; median income $25,000), we had to be very careful in interpreting the results, since it is unclear what kind of people elected to voluntarily complete and mail in the survey. Even with these caveats in mind, the results were riveting.

Overall, 22 percent of the women and 10 percent of the men reported having experienced a sexual trauma prior to the age of seventeen. These rates correspond with those found in recent national polls on the topic. Although the sexual-trauma respondents were similar to the others in terms of age, close friends, social class, and related factors, they were much more unhealthy. Even though the reported sexual trauma had occurred almost twenty years earlier, it was associated with large increases in ulcers, infections, heart problems, and virtually every other health category. In fact, those who had had a traumatic sexual experience as a child had been hospitalized 1.7 days in the previous year—almost twice the rate reported by others.

On the original questionnaire, respondents were asked to include their name and telephone number for possible future telephone interviews. Rubenstein called fifteen people who had claimed to have had a sexual trauma. In her article, she writes:

One woman was raped at 16; another was a victim of incest at 8; yet another had been fondled at the age of 5 by a man selling ponies. A 51-year-old woman from Los Angeles told me that she had been raped, at 5, by her neighbor, who was a friend of the family . . . "I never told anyone about it. You're the first," she said. Later on, not making the connection, she remarked, "I've always had health problems with organs in that area . . . since I was 5." (p. 34)

Every person with whom Rubenstein talked reported an experience that all of us would agree was traumatic. In addition, the majority had not discussed this traumatic event with anyone when it had occurred. If they eventually did discuss their trauma, it was not until several months or years later.

Reading these accounts and examining the questionnaire results certainly leads to the conclusion that traumatic sexual experiences in childhood are permanently damaging. What makes sexual traumas so devastating?

Almost a century ago, Freud shocked his contemporaries by claiming that conflicts surrounding sexuality were prime determinants of personality development and, depending on the person, mental disorders. When sexual urges were blocked by society, Freud argued, people experienced tremendous anxiety and conflict. Neuroses served as defenses against such conflict. Many of Freud's students, such as Alfred Adler and Karen Horney, were highly critical of Freud's emphasis on sexuality. Other motives, such as the need to be superior or to be loved by others, were more important in their eyes. These and more recent critics of Freud suggest that a variety of traumas can affect psychological state.

Based on the results of surveys, it is clear that childhood sexual traumas influence long-term health. However, changes in health following the traumas may not reflect sexuality per se. Rather, traumas may be insidious because people cannot talk about them. Trauma victims must actively inhibit their wanting to discuss these intensely important personal experiences with others.

Consider the case of Laura, a thirty-five-year-old lawyer. Laura's parents divorced when she was ten. Two years after the divorce, her mother remarried. Six months after the marriage, Laura's stepfather began to drink heavily. Late one night, Laura awoke to find her drunken stepfather fondling her breasts. Although she slapped him and demanded that he leave, he made light of the situation. This continued off and on until Laura was fifteen, at which time she left home to live with her aunt. Not until she developed uterine cancer at age twenty-four did she admit this experience to anyone.

Laura recounted the agony of those two years:

> I had always been close to my mother. The divorce
> had nearly killed her and she was so happy with Jock
> [the stepfather]. If she had known what Jock was doing

to me, it would have broken her heart. I wanted to tell her so much. Do you know what it is like to be in a family like that? I'd get up in the morning and Jock and my mother would come down together. He would smile and be friendly, like nothing had happened. I hated his guts but could never tell anyone why. Every morning, every evening, every time I saw that bastard, I felt sick to my stomach. I guess it's not surprising that I developed an ulcer before my 15th birthday.

Looking back on it all, the very worst thing was that I couldn't talk to my mother anymore. I had to keep a wall between us. If I wasn't careful, the wall might crumble and I'd tell her everything. The same was true of my friends. I'd go out with my girlfriends and we would all giggle about boys and dating. Their giggles were real, mine weren't. If they had known what was happening in my bedroom they would have died.

Laura is an open, honest, and resilient woman who has been happily married for twelve years. In her own mind, the trauma she experienced was not devastating because it was sexual. Rather, her anguish arose from her desperate need to talk to anyone about it—especially her mother—and the impossibility of her ever doing so. This constant holding back undoubtedly contributed to her health problems.

About the same time I interviewed Laura, I talked in detail with a twenty-three-year-old carpenter named Jimmy. His story was similar to Laura's, except that his stepfather had physically abused him starting when he was fourteen and continuing about three years. Like Laura, he refused to tell his mother for fear of tearing the family apart. During the abusive periods, Jimmy experienced intense migraine headaches. At age seventeen, Jimmy attempted suicide and was hospitalized. During treatment, he disclosed the abuse to a counselor, who notified the state authorities. In the months following the disclosure, the entire family entered therapy. Jimmy can now talk openly about his three years of abuse even though he remains extremely ambivalent about his stepfather.

The cases of Laura and Jimmy suggest that any kind of trauma may result in long-term health problems if the victim cannot talk about it. Fortunately, two of my students, Joan Susman and Claudia Hoover, helped me explore this idea in more detail. In 1985, one of Dallas's progressive companies, the Zale Corporation, agreed to let us pass out questionnaires to its employees in the home office. Over two hundred people completed in-depth surveys that assessed childhood traumas, comparable recent adulthood traumas, physical health scales, and other measures.

The primary childhood and adult traumas that we examined were death of family member, sexual trauma, physical abuse, and a general "other trauma" category. For the childhood traumas we included divorce or separation of parents, whereas for the adult traumas we added divorce or separation of the respondents themselves. For each trauma, people rated the degree to which the event was traumatic and the degree to which they had confided in others about it.

Several fascinating effects emerged. First, those with the most health problems had experienced at least one childhood trauma that they had not confided. Of the two hundred respondents, the sixty-five people with an undisclosed childhood trauma were more likely to have been diagnosed with virtually every major and minor health problem that we asked about: cancer, high blood pressure, ulcers, flu, headaches, even earaches. Oddly, it made no difference what the particular trauma had been. The only distinguishing feature was that the trauma had not been talked about to others. A sexual trauma that was not confided was no worse than a death in the family that was not discussed.

There was a catch, however. Some childhood traumas are more likely to be disclosed than others. Across all of our respondents, people are less likely to talk about parental divorce, sexual trauma, and violence than the death of a family member. Death appears to be "socially acceptable" and, thus, something that a child can talk about with others. These findings square with other large-scale projects indicating that a parent's leaving home because of divorce is more emotionally damaging to the children than a parent's death.

Finally, we were able to evaluate the relative impact of different traumas on current health. Overall, childhood traumas influence adults' health to a greater degree than traumatic experiences that have occurred in the last three years. In fact, these effects are true when equating our groups for age, education, number of close friends, and gender. Translation: Early childhood traumas that are not disclosed may be bad for your health as an adult.

I don't mean to be an alarmist. All of us had upsetting experiences as children, some of which we didn't disclose to others. Further, we are all going to get sick and die. To assume that most of the early events in our lives will be the cause of our demise is a gross exaggeration. It is important, though, to keep some perspective in evaluating all of this research. Some people have had horrible events in their lives that they constantly think and dream about. They are living with these traumas or experiences even though their closest friends may not know about them. It is these people, I think, who are at greatest risk for health problems.

RECENT ADULTHOOD TRAUMAS: THE DEATH OF A SPOUSE

One problem in evaluating the health risks of childhood traumas is that we have to rely on people's recollections of events. In looking back at our own childhood, it is easy to see how we may have distorted events in our minds. Also, we must ask why someone would choose to inhibit an upsetting experience rather than confide it to someone. These are legitimate problems in attempting to understand the long-term effects of inhibition. One solution is to study a group of adults who have all recently suffered a comparable trauma.

After completing the first surveys on childhood traumas, I moved from Virginia to Dallas with my family. At an informal reception right after arriving in town, I met Robin O'Heeron, a woman who had returned to college after working in the real world. Although presenting a charming exterior, Robin was still grieving the sudden death of her husband six months earlier. Given her interest in psychology and my curiosity about traumatic experiences, we had the ingredients for a wonderful friendship.

In our discussions, it was clear that the sudden and unexpected death of a spouse was devastating. Not only do the survivors have to deal with the loss of their closest friend, but they are deprived of the very person to whom they would normally confide. During this time, I kept thinking about the childhood-trauma findings. Sometimes children were free to talk about upsetting experiences like the death of a parent because the event was socially acceptable. However, if the discussion of the trauma was somehow threatening to the children or to others, they usually were inhibited. Wouldn't this also be true of adults whose spouses had died in an acceptable versus unacceptable way?

Dying in an automobile accident is socially acceptable; dying by suicide is not. If a person's death was beyond his or her control, we can express our sorrow openly, without any hint of embarrassment. Usually, when someone commits suicide, we speak in hushed tones. Robin and I pondered the meaning of this distinction. Based on my earlier findings, I would predict that spouses of suicide victims would be the least likely to talk about the death and, in the year following the death, should have the most health problems. If a person's spouse died in an "acceptable" way, such as in a car accident, the survivor would be freer to disclose the event to others.

You may be thinking, What a ghoulish series of issues. Not entirely. The broader question that Robin and I were dealing with concerned coping with trauma. Is there a "best way" of coping with an unimaginably horrible trauma? Robin was still trying to cope with her husband's death. What were her survivor peers doing?

With the help of the coroner's office, we sent questionnaires to all of the surviving spouses of suicide and car-accident victims of the previous year, 1982, in Dallas. Because there are so many issues surrounding sudden violent death, we restricted our potential respondents along several dimensions: the spouse who had died must have been between twenty-five and forty-five years of age, a native English speaker, and a married Dallas resident. In addition, the victim had to have died within twenty-four hours of the suicide attempt or car accident and, in the case of an accident, no other family member was injured or killed. Overall, nineteen of the thirty-one people who received our mailing returned their questionnaire. For surveys such as this, a 61 percent response rate is considered quite good.

One of the basic assumptions behind this project was that spouses of suicide victims would exhibit more health problems in the year following the death than spouses of accidental deaths. After all, we reasoned, spouses of suicides would be inhibited from talking about the death compared to spouses of automobile accidents.

We were wrong. Spouses of suicides were slightly healthier than spouses of accidental deaths. As Aldous Huxley noted, this appeared to be a case of the slaying of a beautiful hypothesis by an ugly fact.

Actually, as we inspected the surveys more closely, we had been both wrong and right at the same time. In the grand scheme of things, it didn't matter how people's spouses died. The most important dimension was whether they talked about the death. Overall, then, the more that people talked to others about the death of their spouse, the fewer health problems they reported having. Not talking with others about their spouse's death was clearly a health risk.

Ironically, the number of close friends that our respondents had was only weakly related to reported illnesses. In fact, some of those who were the sickest in the year after the death never talked about the death even though they had several very close friends. To get a better idea of the respondents' experiences, we asked them what they would recommend to others who had faced the sudden death of their spouse. By and large, those who were the healthiest emphasized the value of talking and acknowledging the pain. A thirty-seven-year old woman whose husband had committed suicide wrote:

> I attended a grief-recovery program that helped. Being able to realize that all of the emotions you are feeling are real and it's OK to hurt and feel the pain helped a lot. The support of true friends and being able to have someone listen and hurt with you was a great outlet for the pain.

An exceptionally healthy forty-one-year-old female sales manager whose husband was killed when a teenager ran a red light:

> Let family and friends support you. Seek counseling. Stay close to God. Look forward to life and the opportunities that it may bring.

A thirty-year-old account executive reported talking with others a great deal about the suicide of his wife:

> It helps to try and look for a complete understanding of what happened and why. Also, move on to new things. Do not stagnate.

In contrast with these healthy responses, those people who reported the most illnesses in the year following their spouse's death had adopted one of two strategies. The first was to move forward and try not to think about the spouse or the death.

A thirty-four-year-old woman in advertising developed migraine headaches, insomnia, and recurring stomach problems following her husband's death. She tried to deal with it by avoiding the topic altogether:

> Find something to keep occupied with, but not just the usual everyday humdrum life. Be with people and don't bring them down.

Similarly, a forty-seven-year-old computer programmer who now has an ulcer and weight difficulties:

> Strenuous exercise. Stay mentally occupied. Stay socially active. Develop new interests. Don't allow yourself to cry. Accept the fact that your life is not the same.

In addition to these obsessive pretend-it-didn't-happen approaches, three people admitted that they have not been able to deal with their spouses' deaths. They were desperate and lonely. As one widower with several major and minor health problems noted, "I don't know what to recommend, as I am having a hard time of it. The loss of my wife, having to take care of my boys, the pressure at work . . . I cannot say."

Some other findings emerged from this project that surprised us. First, those who didn't talk about the death often obsessed or ruminated about it. That is, people who talked about their spouse's death tended not to think about the death as much as those who inhibited talking. Second, ruminating about the death was correlated with poor physical health. In other words, three factors were closely linked:

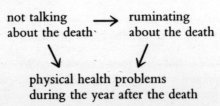

A related finding concerned prayer. The more people prayed about their deceased spouse, the healthier they were. Prayer, in fact, worked the same way as talking to friends about the death. It is easy to see why this is true: Prayer is a form of disclosure or confiding.

Within a year of their spouses' death, three of the seven men were married. Only one of the twelve women had remarried and she had since separated. These statistics square with national trends: Following the death of a spouse, men usually remarry within two years, compared to almost five years for women. Nevertheless, we and others find that men are significantly less happy and healthy than are women after a spouse's death.

There are several reasons for the disparity in marital status and happiness among men. Active inhibition is undoubtedly a culprit. As one recently remarried widower explained to me:

> I'm in a terrible bind. I'm still torn up about my first wife's death. I can't really talk to Clara [new wife] about it. She tries to be understanding, but I know she doesn't want to hear about another woman that I loved. So I pretend and Clara pretends that my first wife and her accident didn't really happen.

A final note. It is interesting to speculate why spouses of suicide fared slightly better than those of accidental deaths. One reason is that a suicide is more predictable and, in a sense, understandable than a random accidental death. In most cases, the husbands and wives of the suicide knew their spouse was depressed and could find some meaning in the action. Not so the accident victims' spouses. After an unexpected car accident, the surviving spouses were faced with the realization that the world was more unpredictable and dangerous than they ever imagined. Faced with a powerful feeling of no control over life's events, many of the surviving spouses' fundamental beliefs about justice and predictability in the world were shaken.

Ironically, every major city in the country has support groups or some form of institutionalized aid for families of suicides. If your spouse commits suicide, you will receive at least one letter and phone call by a state agency or private foundation to help you cope with the tragedy. If your spouse dies in an accident or from most diseases, though, you are on your own. Virtually no official groups exist for people whose spouses die in a socially acceptable manner.

I have tried to convey some of the evidence that suggests active inhibition is associated with health problems. Rather than list the major findings from dozens of experiments, I simply want you to be aware that there is good reason to believe that not talking about childhood and adulthood traumas can be risky.

The interpretation of questionnaire results, by the way, is not a hundred percent reliable. One issue that worries survey researchers—myself included—concerns cause-effect relationships. The problem is that questionnaire studies can rarely pin down whether inhibition causes illness or if illness causes inhibition, or if illness and inhibition are jointly caused by something else. We can be certain, however, that illness and not talking about upsetting experiences often go together.

An example of the interpretation problem is that people who are sickly may not be able to talk with others about their problems, fearing that no one wants to be around a sick person. Or maybe the sick person doesn't have the strength to talk. In any case, our questionnaire results would indicate that not talking and illness go together—but they don't indicate what caused what. Clearly, another approach is necessary to prove the potential health damage of inhibition.

3

Becoming Healthier Through Writing

Barbara, a friend of the family, called me at 7:00 A.M. on a Sunday morning distraught about the previous evening. After a late dinner with friends, she got into her car and, after locking the doors, heard the voice of a strange man from the backseat. Holding a knife, he ordered her to drive to a particular city park where, he said, he intended to rape her. As Barbara drove to the park, she started to accelerate. Between sobs, she lied that she had cancer and would soon be dying. Speeding up to 70 MPH on the deserted city streets, she noted that she might as well kill them both. As she approached a busy intersection, Barbara warned the man that if he wanted to live, he had better jump out while he could. He jumped from the car as she slowed to make a turn.

The story doesn't end there. Barbara was understandably upset by the event and, because of her anxiety, wanted the name of a therapist. Because medication might have been warranted, I suggested she call a psychiatrist we both knew. When she met with him, he recommended that she tell her story to everyone she met. The more she told the story, he claimed, the quicker her anxiety symptoms would disappear.

Why, I asked myself, did talking about a trauma help cure the trauma? Every therapist I talked with at the time knew intuitively that it was sound advice. But no one could say exactly why.

Apparently, talking about a trauma is a natural human response. When this response is blocked or inhibited, stress and illness result. Beyond the potential dangers of long-term inhibition, there is something positive about confronting upsetting experiences. Barbara needed more than the release of inhibition. She needed to come to terms with her terrifying experience. Talking, according to the therapists, was a good way to do this.

The benefits of talking about a trauma, then, go beyond overcoming inhibition. What is it about talking that is so helpful? Usually, when someone talks about a trauma, another person listens. In the case of Barbara, her listeners told her that she was fast thinking, competent, and brave. When she explained that she was still upset, we assured her that her feelings were normal and that we were available to help her in any way. In other cases, talking about a trauma can result in other benefits such as advice, attention, sympathy, financial assistance, and a way of excusing the individuals from carrying out their normal responsibilities.

Although these social benefits can be valuable, there is much more to be gained from talking about upsetting experiences. Specifically, the act of talking can change the ways we think and feel about traumatic events and about ourselves.

WHAT TALKING ACHIEVES: CATHARSIS OR INSIGHT

Most therapists agree that talking about an upsetting experience is psychologically beneficial. The agreement ends there. Some think that talking about a trauma is primarily valuable in achieving catharsis by getting the person to express pent-up emotions. Others believe that talking helps the client attain insight into the causes and cures of the difficulties with the trauma.

In the late 1800s, the young Austrian physician Sigmund Freud began to piece together an overarching theory of personality that pointed to the reasons why confronting a trauma was beneficial. Many of Freud's early ideas stemmed from a technique pioneered by another physician, Joseph Breuer, called the talking cure.

In his medical practice, Breuer found that hypnosis was effective in treating people suffering from symptoms such as paralysis, blindness, or deafness that had no apparent physical basis. His most important patient was a twenty-one-year-old woman, referred to as Anna O., who suffered from a variety of problems ranging from a refusal to drink liquids to partial paralysis on the right side of her body. During his sessions with Anna O., Breuer required her to talk, while hypnotized, about her early experiences with each of her symptoms. For example, one day she talked about her feelings of anger and disgust in seeing a dog drink water from a glass. Immediately after venting her feelings about this episode, Anna O. overcame her refusal to drink liquids. According to Breuer, talking about the causes of symptoms in some way cured them.

Freud was fascinated by Breuer's reports. Although he, too, experimented with hypnosis, Freud learned that he could get comparable results without hypnosis by having his own patients merely talk about their deepest feelings and thoughts while in a relaxed state. Working together, Freud and Breuer believed that the value of the talking cure lay in its ability to release pent-up feelings that the person was holding back. The two men reasoned that the release of these pent-up feelings, or catharsis, discharged psychic tension in the same way that removing the lid from a pot of boiling water slows the boiling.

Although Freud eventually downplayed the importance of the cathartic method, many of his followers continue to extol its benefits. Unfortunately, the definition of catharsis has evolved to mean the mere venting of emotion rather than the linking of thoughts and feelings. Today, many of the more "fringy" schools of thought argue that the venting of emotion by screaming, crying, laughing, or other means can permanently improve psychological and physical health.

Other, more moderate approaches suggest that it is important that individuals freely express their emotions. Actively holding back feelings can be stressful. In addition, admitting our emotions to ourselves and others serves an important communicative function. If I am angry because of an underhanded comment by a friend, for example, it is important that I recognize my feelings so that I can direct my actions in an acceptable way. I can also let my friend know how I feel so that he or she can gauge the intended impact of the comment on me.

Most current therapists believe that it is valuable for individuals to achieve some understanding of the causes and consequences of the traumatic experiences that affect them. By talking about upsetting events, people achieve insight into the events and learn more about themselves. With this knowledge, people can put the traumas behind them. The exact nature of how this process works is explained differently from therapist to therapist.

Can people attain insight through talking per se? Many directive therapists, who have been strongly influenced by Freud and his followers, believe that talking helps achieve insight through the comments of the therapist. You tell me your problems and I'll help you figure out what is really going on. Once the underlying emotionally charged difficulties have been isolated, we will do what we can to clear them up. Other more nondirective therapies, such as Carl Rogers's client-centered therapy, suggest that by your telling me what is bothering you, you will be able to figure out your own problems and solutions. My role as therapist, in this case, will be as a sounding board that is accepting and trustworthy no matter what you say.

I don't want to parody these clinical techniques unfairly because they have been found to be effective in the treatment of most psychological disorders. Attaining insight into our own thoughts and feelings must be valuable. After all, if I know why I feel depressed in one kind of situation or nauseated in another, I can take steps to master or avoid those situations. Further, I can try to change myself so I won't react the way I do or, if I cannot change, my reactions will at least be predictable.

All things being equal, talking about upsetting things to others promotes emotional expression and insight. To what degree, though, do we need other people for catharsis or insight to occur? Is talking to others about our deepest thoughts and feelings necessary for psychological and physical health? In other words, is talking necessary for the talking cure to cure?

My own experiences a few years earlier hinted that talking was not the only way to achieve insight. My wife and I had married right out of college and, three years later, were questioning many of the basic assumptions of our relationship. This dark period of our life was horrible. Until that time, I had never been severely depressed. But now, on awakening every morning, the first thing I felt was an overwhelming pressure on my heart—I had to face one more day of hell.

Like many people who had never faced a major upheaval, I didn't know how to cope with a massive depression. I stopped eating, began drinking more alcohol and smoking. Because I was embarrassed by what I considered an emotional weakness, I avoided friends. Even though I was a graduate student in psychology, I foolishly refused to visit a therapist.

After about a month of emotional isolation, I started writing about my deepest thoughts and feelings. I remember being drawn to the typewriter each afternoon for about a week, where I would spend anywhere from ten minutes to an hour pounding on the keys. I initially wrote about our marriage, but soon turned to my feelings about my parents, sexuality, career, and even death. Each day after writing, I felt fatigued and yet freer. By the end of the week, I noticed my depression lifting. For the first time in years —perhaps ever—I had a sense of meaning and direction. I fundamentally understood my deep love for my wife and the degree to which I needed her.

It wasn't until eight years later that I looked back on that period in an attempt to understand why writing had been so helpful for me. Being a rather private, even inhibited person, writing helped me let go and address a number of personal issues that I was too proud to admit to anyone. Although I hadn't talked with anyone, I had disclosed some of my deepest feelings. If my experience was any indication, writing about upsetting issues must work in ways similar to talking about them.

In late 1983, a number of ideas were coming together. My questionnaire projects indicated that talking about traumas was linked to fewer health problems. My own experiences suggested that writing about upsetting events was psychologically and, perhaps, physically beneficial. These observations demanded that some kind of experiment be run wherein a group of people were required to "confess" so that we could trace any changes in their health.

WRITING AS ILLNESS PREVENTION

In September 1983, Sandra Beall, a beginning graduate student, marched into my office the first day of classes and announced that she was ready to begin work on her master's thesis. Although most students didn't think about a thesis project until their second year of training, she wanted to start immediately. Whereas I was interested in the relation between writing and health, Sandy was curious about the possible psychological benefits of emotional venting.

After much discussion, we agreed on an experiment that addressed our interests: We would get a group of volunteers to write about either traumatic experiences or about superficial topics. In addition, we would have the participants who wrote about traumas write about them from one of three perspectives: 1) just vent their emotions during the writing sessions; 2) just write about the facts surrounding their traumas; or 3) write about the facts and vent their emotions dealing with their traumas. With our volunteers' permission, we would evaluate their health by collecting the number of illness visits each person made to the student health center in the months following the experiment compared with the months preceding the study.

In most college psychology courses around the country, students are given the option of participating in experiments for course credit or money. At Southern Methodist University, where this study was conducted, students were recruited from introductory psychology classes for credit. Since this was the first study of its kind, we warned the participants that they might be asked to write about deeply personal topics. Further, everyone was told on each day of the study that he or she could withdraw anytime and receive full credit. Of the forty-six students who participated, none withdrew. In fact, only two people missed one of the four writing days.

Each person came to the lab separately, where he or she met Sandy. During the initial meeting, Sandy told the volunteers that they would write continuously for fifteen minutes each day on four consecutive days while alone in a small cubicle in the psychology building. Because it was important that everything was anonymous and confidential, the participants were asked to put a code number rather than their name on their questionnaires and essays. In fact, they were told that if they desired, they could keep their essays rather than turn them in to us. After answering any questions, Sandy randomly assigned them to one of the four writing conditions. Random assignment means that each volunteer had an equal chance of writing on each of the four topics. This is an important dimension to an experiment because it helps control many potential biases.

Those assigned to write about their thoughts and feelings about a trauma were told the following:

> Once you are escorted into the writing cubicle and the door is closed, I want you to write continuously about the most upsetting or traumatic experience of your entire life. Don't worry about grammar, spelling, or sentence structure. In your writing, I want you to discuss your

deepest thoughts and feelings about the experience. You can write about anything you want. But whatever you choose, it should be something that has affected you very deeply. Ideally, it should be about something you have not talked with others in detail. It is critical, however, that you let yourself go and touch those deepest emotions and thoughts that you have. In other words, write about what happened and how you felt about it, and how you feel about it now. Finally, you can write on different traumas during each session or the same one over the entire study. Your choice of trauma for each session is entirely up to you.

People who had been assigned to write only about their emotions surrounding the traumas were given the same general instructions except they were specifically instructed not to directly mention the trauma itself. Rather they were to write how they felt at the time and how they felt now. Volunteers who were asked to focus on the facts were simply to describe their traumas in detail without referring to their emotions.

Finally, a comparison or control group of volunteers was asked to write about superficial or irrelevant topics during each session. For example, Sandy had those participants describe in detail such things as their dorm room or the shoes they were wearing. The purpose of the control group was to evaluate what effect writing in an experiment per se had on health changes.

All the students, then, wrote for fifteen minutes a day for four consecutive days. After the writing on the final day of the study, Sandy and I talked to all the participants at great length about their experiences and feelings about the experiment. Finally, four months after the study, the participants all completed questionnaires that measured their long-term feelings about the experiment.

For the students, the immediate impact of the study was far more powerful than we had ever imagined. Several of the students cried while writing about traumas. Many reported dreaming or continually thinking about their writing topics over the four days of the study. Most telling, however, were the writing samples themselves. Essay after essay revealed people's deepest feelings and most intimate sides. Many of the stories depicted profound human tragedies.

One student recounted how his father took him into the back-yard on a hot summer night and coolly announced his plans to divorce and move to another town. Although the student was only nine years old at the time, he vividly remembers his father's voice, "Son, the problem with me and your mother was having kids in the first place. Things haven't been the same since you and your sister's birth."

On all four days of the experiment, one woman detailed how, at age ten, her mother asked her to pick up her toys because her grandmother was visiting that evening. She didn't pick up her toys. That night, her grandmother arrived, slipped on one of the toys, and broke her hip. The grandmother died a week later during hip surgery. Now, eight years later, the woman still blames herself every day.

Another woman described being seduced by her grandfather when she was thirteen. She depicts the terrible conflict she experienced. On one hand she admitted the physical pleasure of his touching her and the love she felt for her grandfather. On the other, she suffered with the knowledge that this was wrong, that he was betraying her trust.

Other essays disclosed the torture of a woman not able to tell her parents about her being gay, a young man's feelings of loss about the death of his dog, or the anger of three different people about their parents' divorces. Family abuse, alcoholism, suicide attempts, and public humiliation were also frequent topics.

Sandy and I were both stunned and depressed by the stories. That our college students had experienced so many horrors and, at the same time, had so readily revealed them to us was remarkable. The grim irony is that by and large, these were eighteen-year-old kids attending an upper-middle-class college with above-average high school grade-point averages and college-board scores. These are the people who are portrayed as growing up in the bubble of financial security and suburban tranquility. What must it portend for those brought up in more hostile environments?

For a researcher, there is nothing as exciting and nerve-racking as collecting data. In a large project such as this one, there were two major types of information to examine. We were primarily interested in changes in physical health over the school year. We also wanted to know how our experiment had influenced our volunteers' moods. Because people had completed checklists after each day's writing, we could evaluate changes in mood as soon as the writing phase of the study was completed.

Sandy believed in the value of venting emotions. In line with current views of catharsis, she thought that writing about negative things should bring about an emotional release that should result in feelings of relief and contentment. I was uncommitted. As it turned out, writing about horrible things made people feel horrible immediately after writing. Our volunteers felt much worse after writing about traumas than after writing about superficial topics. These effects were most pronounced for those who were asked to delve into their emotions while writing about traumas.

You can imagine our anxiety over the next few months. In analyzing the mood findings, it appeared that all we had succeeded in doing was inventing a new way to make people depressed. Almost six months later, the student health center was able to provide the number of illness visits that each student had made in the two and a half months before and five and a half months after the experiment. Within twenty minutes of receiving the health-center information, we had our answer.

People who wrote about their deepest thoughts and feelings surrounding a trauma evidenced an impressive drop in illness visits after the study compared with the other groups. In the months before the experiment, everyone in all the groups went to the health center for illness at the same rate. After the experiment, however, the average person who wrote about his or her deepest thoughts and feelings went less than 0.5 times—a 50 percent drop in the monthly visitation rate. People who wrote just about their emotions surrounding a trauma, just about the facts of a trauma, or about superficial topics averaged visiting the health center almost 1.5 times per person.

Fortunately, our volunteers had completed additional questionnaires four months after the experiment. Virtually everything they said corroborated the health-center findings. Writing about their deepest thoughts and feelings about traumas resulted in improved moods, more positive outlook, and greater physical health.

I'll never forget the initial thrill of finding that writing about traumas affected physical health. But the thrill was tempered with a little anxiety. For every question that the experiment had answered, a dozen more questions appeared. Perhaps the most basic issue that haunted me concerned the trustworthiness of these findings. Were the effects real? Does writing about traumas really affect physical health? Perhaps we had just affected people's decisions to visit the student health center. Or even worse, maybe the findings were simply due to chance. Every now and then, for example, you can toss a coin and come up with heads ten times in a row. In theory, research experiments can work the same way. Being rather impatient, I had to know if I was dealing with something real. And I wanted to know as quickly as possible.

EXPLORING THE IMMUNE SYSTEM: WRITING ABOUT TRAUMAS IS BETTER THAN WE THOUGHT

The medical and science writer for the *Dallas Morning News*, Rita Rubin, had heard a rumor that we had found that writing about upsetting experiences was good for your health. She had recently moved from Ohio, where she had followed an up-and-coming research team that was investigating the links between psychological stress and immune-system function. Rita was the first to suggest that I contact them and, perhaps, join forces.

The research team was Janice K. Kiecolt-Glaser, a clinical psychologist, and her husband Ronald Glaser, an immunologist, both with the Ohio State University College of Medicine. Together, they were blazing a trail by showing that overwhelming experiences such as divorce, major exams in college, and even strong feelings of loneliness adversely affected immune function. Their most recent finding was that relaxation therapy among the elderly could improve the action of the immune system. The work by Jan and Ron was groundbreaking because it relied on precise state-of-the-art techniques to measure the action of t-lymphocytes, natural killer cells, and other immune markers in the blood. Further, unlike most researchers in immunology, Jan and Ron were sophisticated about psychology.

By a wonderful coincidence, Jan and I were invited to a small conference in New Orleans soon after Rita Rubin's introduction. The first night of the conference, before we had finished our first can of Dixie beer, Jan and I had outlined an experiment to see if writing about traumas could directly affect the action of the immune system. Three months later, the study was under way.

The experiment was similar to the first confession study. Fifty students wrote for twenty minutes a day for four consecutive days about one of two topics. Half wrote about their deepest thoughts and feelings concerning a trauma. The remaining twenty-five students were expected to write about superficial topics. Unlike in the first confession study, however, the students consented to have their blood drawn the day before writing, after the last writing session, and again six weeks later.

The week of running the study was frenzied. I had a staff of almost a dozen people helping me with the experiment in Dallas. As before, the experimental volunteers poured out their hearts in their writing. The tragedies they disclosed were comparable to those in the first experiment. Instances of rape, child abuse, suicide attempts, death, and intense family conflict were common. Again, those who wrote about traumas reported feeling sadder and more upset each day relative to those who wrote about superficial topics.

Collecting the blood and measuring immune function was a novel experience that added to the frenzy. As soon as the blood was drawn, we'd pack it and drive like hell to get to the airport so we wouldn't miss the last plane for Columbus, Ohio. Once the blood samples arrived, the people in the immunology lab would work around the clock, in an assembly-line manner. The procedure involved separating the blood cells and placing a predetermined number of white cells in small dishes. Each dish contained differing amounts of various foreign substances, called mitogens. The dishes were then incubated for two days to allow the white blood cells time to divide and proliferate in the presence of the mitogens.

The logic of this procedure is fascinating. In the body, there are a number of different kinds of white cells, or lymphocytes, that control immune function. T-lymphocytes, for example, can stimulate other lymphocytes to make antibodies. Antibodies, along with parts of the body's defense system, can retard and kill bacteria and viruses foreign to the body. The immune measures that we used mimicked this bodily process in the dishes. Just as viruses and bacteria can stimulate the proliferation of t-lymphocytes in the body, the mitogens did the same in the laboratory dishes. If the lymphocytes divide at a fast rate in response to the mitogens, we can infer that at least part of the immune system is working quickly and efficiently.

So what did we find? People who wrote about their deepest thoughts and feelings surrounding traumatic experiences evidenced heightened immune function compared with those who wrote about superficial topics. Although this effect was most pronounced after the last day of writing, it tended to persist six weeks after the study. In addition, health-center visits for illness dropped for the people who wrote about traumas compared to those who wrote on the trivial topics.

There was another important finding as well. Every day, after writing, we asked people who had written about traumas to respond to the questionnaire item "To what degree did you write about something that you have previously held back from telling others?" As you can see, the question was intended to get at people's previous attempts at inhibition. That is, the more they had held back, the more they had inhibited talking about the topic. Overall, we found that those who showed the greatest improvement in immune function were the same ones who had held back in telling others about the things they had written. In other words, those who had been silently living with their upsetting experiences benefited the most from writing.

We had now completed two experiments that showed similar things. Taken together, the studies indicated that writing about traumatic experiences was beneficial depending on how people wrote about them. All indications suggested that the effects were not due to simple catharsis or the venting of pent-up emotions. Indeed, the first confession study demonstrated that writing only about emotions surrounding a trauma did not produce long-term health benefits. Further, both experiments indicated that writing about feelings associated with traumatic experiences was painful. Virtually no one felt excited, on top of the world, or even mildly cheerful immediately after writing about the worst experiences of his or her life.

In the surveys that we sent out several months after the experiments, we asked people to describe in their own words what long-term effects, if any, the writing experiment had on them. Everyone who wrote about traumas described the study in positive terms. More important, approximately 80 percent explained the value of the study in terms of insight. Rather than explaining that it felt good to get negative emotions off their chests, the respondents noted how they understood themselves better. Some examples:

It helped me think about what I felt during those times.
I never realized how it affected me before.

I had to think and resolve past experiences. . . . One result of the experiment is peace of mind, and a method to relieve emotional experiences. To have to write emotions and feelings helped me understand how I felt and why.

Although I have not talked with anyone about what I wrote, I was finally able to deal with it, work through the pain instead of trying to block it out. Now it doesn't hurt to think about it.

The observations of these people, and everyone else who participated in these studies, are almost breathtaking. They are telling us that our thought processes can heal.

These studies were just the beginning of a research project that has been expanding in several directions. Several variations of the writing experiments have now been conducted by us and by researchers in other laboratories. I now trust the effects that we have gotten. In each study that has been conducted, we have discovered some limits to the writing technique as well as methods that boost its effectiveness. I will explore the meaning and applications of many of these findings throughout the book.

In the meantime, I want to share with you some of the main points about the writing method that I have found to be related to health. Keep in mind that I am speaking as a researcher and not a therapist. My recommendations about confronting upsetting events are based on experiments, occasional case studies, and my own experiences. It is very possible that your writing about your own traumas or upsetting feelings may not be helpful. If this happens, you should be your own researcher. Experiment with different topics and approaches. Something may work for you in resolving your own conflicts that may not work for anyone else. With these warnings in mind, here are some questions commonly asked about the writing method.

What should your writing topic be? It is not necessary to write about the most traumatic experience of your life. It is more important to focus on the issues that you are currently living with. If you find yourself thinking or dreaming about an event or experience too much of the time, writing about it can help resolve it in your mind. By the same token, if there has been something you would like to tell others but you can't for fear of embarrassment or punishment, express it on paper.

Whatever your topic, it is critical to explore both the objective experience (i.e., what happened) and your feelings about it. Really let go and write about your very deepest emotions. *What* do you feel about it and *why* do you feel that way.

Write continuously. Don't worry about grammar, spelling, or sentence structure. If you run out of things to say or reach a mental block, just repeat what you have already written.

When and where should you write? Write whenever you want or whenever you feel you need to. I am not convinced that writing about significant experiences needs to be done that frequently. Although many people write every day in diaries, most of the entries do not grapple with fundamental psychological issues. Also be attentive to too much writing. Don't use writing as a substitute for action or as some other type of avoidance strategy. Moderation in all things includes transcribing your thoughts and feelings.

Where you write depends on your circumstances. Our studies suggest that the more unique the setting, the better. Try to find a room where you will not be interrupted or bothered by unwanted sounds, sights, or smells.

What should you do with what you have written? Anonymity is important in our experiments. In many cases, it is wise to keep what you have written to yourself. You might even destroy it when you're finished (although many people find this hard to do). Planning to show your writing to someone can affect your mind-set while writing. For example, if you would secretly like your lover to read your deepest thoughts and feelings, you will orient your writing to your lover rather than to yourself. From a health perspective, you will be better off making yourself the audience. In that way, you don't have to rationalize or justify yourself to suit the perspective of another person.

What if you hate to write—is there a substitute? We have conducted several studies comparing writing with talking into a tape recorder. Among college students, writing appears to be slightly more efficient in getting people to let go and divulge their thoughts and feelings. This probably reflects, in part, the fact that college students are practiced at writing. Some of the people I work with who are not in school find writing to be quite aversive. For these people, I recommend their talking about their deepest thoughts and feelings into a tape recorder. As with writing, I urge them to talk continuously for fifteen minutes a day.

Whether writing or talking is a more comfortable medium for you, remember that letting go and disclosing intimate parts of yourself may take some practice. If you have never written or talked about your thoughts and feelings, you may find doing so particularly awkward at first. If so, just relax and practice. Write or talk continuously for a set amount of time. No one is evaluating you.

What can you expect to feel during and after writing? As we have found in all of our studies, you may feel sad or depressed immediately after writing. These negative feelings usually dissipate within an hour or so. In rare cases, they may last for a day or two. The overwhelming majority of our volunteers, however, report feelings of relief, happiness, and contentment soon after the writing studies are concluded.

Exploring your deepest thoughts and feelings is not a panacea. If you are coping with death, divorce, or other tragedy, you will not feel instantly better after writing. You should, however, have a better understanding of your feelings and emotions as well as the objective situation that you are in. In other words, writing should give you a little distance and perspective on your life.

4

Confession in the Laboratory

A change comes over people when they disclose traumatic experiences for the first time. I became acutely aware of this while conducting a stress interview with Joey, a brawny Vietnam veteran. Joey had been referred to a therapist by a county judge after he had physically threatened his boss. After about a week of intensive therapy, Joey's therapist, Renita Kitchens, called me because she suspected that Joey wasn't leveling with her. Something about his war experience, she reasoned, was weighing on him heavily. Knowing of some of my work, she recommended that I evaluate Joey.

Renita's Texas drawl and good-old-boy humor masked her quick clinical skills. We agreed that when she brought Joey to the lab, she would ask most of the questions and I would monitor his physiological levels. During the first twenty minutes of the interview, Joey talked about his childhood, his current living situation, and several of his experiences in Vietnam. As Renita predicted, Joey's physiological levels changed radically when he briefly remarked about one of the jungle outposts where he had been stationed. She pressed Joey for more details about the outpost. All of a sudden, Joey's entire demeanor changed. His voice dropped and he started to speak in a low, rapid monotone. He began a story about going out on a routine patrol with his buddy. They were about a mile from the base camp when his life changed.

There was a burst of gunfire and my buddy fell to the ground, half of his head blown off. I looked up and a gook was running into a shed carrying a machine gun. I ran to the shed, jumped through the door, and fired, hitting them in both legs. It was a woman who had shot my buddy and who was bleeding on the ground. We stared into each other's eyes. I ripped off her clothes and made love to her. Before I knew it, I could hear choppers overhead—ours. I pulled out my knife and slit her throat. I loved her. I killed her.

It had been fifteen years since this had happened and Joey had never told anyone. Renita and I, who were in a state of shock ourselves, explored Joey's thoughts and feelings about this horror. After about forty minutes of calmly talking about the incident, Joey began to cry. Soon thereafter, the veil lifted and Joey returned to his normal speaking voice. By the end of the session, Joey was fatigued and his physiological levels indicated that he was relatively relaxed. In commenting on his experience in the laboratory, Joey admitted surprise at his revealing what had happened in Vietnam: "It felt like another person was describing my thoughts."

THE LETTING-GO EXPERIENCE

The change that came over Joey is one that I have now seen many times. Often, when people in our experiments either talk or write about deeply personal secrets, certain aspects of their personalities temporarily change. This change is part of a letting-go experience in that the usual inhibitions are no longer in force. During the time that people are letting go, profound changes often occur in their speech and writing styles as well as their physiological levels.

In several experiments, we have asked people to talk about their most traumatic experiences, as well as superficial topics, into tape recorders. Those individuals who have disclosed a particularly intimate side of themselves have shown a variety of changes in their voice and speaking style. When we first started this research, I was convinced that we had somehow mixed up our tape recordings. For example, the very first woman who participated in this type of experiment initially described her plans for the day in a singsong, high-pitched, almost cutesy way. A few minutes later, as she described stealing a hundred dollars from an open cash register, both the volume and pitch of her voice were lower. The voice characteristics were so different that the two recordings sounded as though they were made by different women.

A second reliable effect concerned speaking rate. The more traumatic the topic, the faster people spoke. In fact, those participants who reported never having told anyone about their traumas were the ones who spoke the most rapidly. We had provided the opportunity for many of these people to talk about events that they clearly had thought about for months or even years. The inhibitory flood gates were open and the words poured out.

The letting-go experience is just as obvious when participants write as when they talk about upsetting events. As with talking, for example, people write faster when disclosing traumas than when describing superficial objects or events. More striking, however, are changes in handwriting. Often, handwriting switches from block to cursive and back to block lettering within the same essay as the writers switch from one topic to another. Similar changes can be seen in the slant of the letters, pen pressure, markouts, and general neatness as a function of topic.

Another intriguing phenomenon concerns how people talk and write about upsetting and personal experiences. For example, two conflicting topics often activate one another—apparently without the person's awareness. When one topic is introduced, its opposite soon follows. Here are some fascinating examples from one of the writing studies.

A twenty-year-old college junior writes:

> I love my parents. We have a perfect family life. My parents support me in whatever I do. I wouldn't change anything about my childhood, really. . . . [Later in the same essay] My father has been such a bastard, I know that he has something going with this secretary. My mother takes it out on me. I have to wear the clothes she wants, date the boys she wants.

This pattern is quite common. In fact, whenever an essay begins with something like "we have such a close family" or "my little sister is *so* great," nine times out of ten, the discloser treats me to a vicious attack on his or her family, sister, or whomever. As an aside, a particularly revealing word is *really*—as in, "I respect my roommate, really." Translated, this means, "I don't respect my roommate." Usually, the word appears toward the beginning of an essay when the writer is still holding back. In fact, words like *really* (or *honestly* and *truly*) often indicate inhibition. Once writers move into the letting-go mode, these words rarely appear.

Another example of one topic keying off another can be seen in an eighteen-year-old freshman who, once he remembered that his mother held his spelling in low regard, temporarily lost his spelling skills:

> Today, my mother sent a care package and I was very excited until I opened it. It was all old things that I had left in my room, bills, old letters, etc. I began to realize that my past could follow me anywhere. My mother sent me an old book I used to have on commonly mispelled words. It allmost ofended me. That was such a reminder of all the old habbits and imature actions I felt like a child again.

Finally, the sequence of topics that people disclose is often meaningful. For example, a married woman who was attracted to someone in addition to her spouse showed a similar transition in topics during each day of the experiment:

> I deeply care about Robert, but know that we can never get involved. Sam [her husband] is working on a new project that could mean a lot of money for us . . .
>
> [As a teenager] I looked up to football players like Robert, even though I was afraid to date them. I feel bad that I have criticized Sam and his obsession with tennis.
>
> Robert thinks the reason I quit college was to anger my folks. Sam graduated with honors . . .

As we have found in several similar cases, topic cueing usually goes in only one direction. That is, topic A (in this case, Robert) is always followed by topic B (Sam), never vice versa. Further, topic cueing, changes in writing style, and fewer uses of words like *really* are most apparent when people are no longer inhibiting.

What interests me most about the letting-go experience is its similarity to a trance state. Many people report losing their sense of time and place while disclosing their intimate secrets. Some clinicians, such as Milton Erickson, consider the letting-go experience as a form of hypnotic state. Indeed, Erickson believes that this psychological state is therapeutically valuable both in learning about the client's underlying problems and in influencing the direction of therapy. As we have found, once people are in this hypnotic state, they are no longer self-conscious, worried about pleasing others, or concerned about their normal daily hassles. The letting-go experience signals the temporary stripping away of many of our normal social constraints or inhibitions.

THE PHYSIOLOGY OF INHIBITION: HEAVY HEART, SWEATY HANDS

The letting-go experience sounds magical, even mystical. But that is not why it first interested me. During the time that people were in this letting-go state, a number of remarkable physiological changes occurred. To appreciate them, consider how our bodies react when we are threatened.

Our bodies have evolved to respond almost immediately to an array of stressors. If someone yells "Fire!" or if we see a rabid dog about to pounce on us, we need to be able to think and behave quickly. We usually can do this thanks to the action of the autonomic nervous system. The autonomic nervous system controls our blood pressure, breathing rate, and dozens of other functions needed in times of emergency. In short, the autonomic nervous system controls the fight-or-flight reaction.

Until the late 1970s, many researchers assumed that the autonomic nervous system worked in a very general way. That is, when stressed, a person would show increases in heart rate, blood pressure, reduced digestion, more perspiration on the hands, and so forth. In other words, very different kinds of stressors presumably resulted in the same physiological responses.

This assumption of generalized arousal was challenged, however, by experiments indicating that different autonomic nervous system channels reflected different psychological states. In 1980, Don Fowles of the University of Iowa summarized the results of dozens of studies and suggested that some autonomic nervous system measures worked on completely different principles. Heart rate, blood pressure, and other cardiovascular channels change when individuals prepare for or are engaged in physical movement. Standing, talking, even getting ready to hit someone are all examples of behavioral activation that increases cardiovascular work.

In addition to the behavioral activation measures, Fowles proposed the existence of independent autonomic nervous system measures that reflected behavioral inhibition. Specifically, holding back or inhibiting behaviors results in subtle increases in the perspiration levels on the hands and feet, often referred to as electrodermal activity. The way our autonomic nervous system is wired, perspiration on the palms of our hands and soles of our feet is unrelated to sweating elsewhere on the body. Although most perspiring helps control body temperature through the cooling effect of evaporation, electrodermal activity on the hands and feet is related to stress. Perhaps through evolution, many researchers argue, increased moisture on the hands and feet allowed our ancestors to get a better grasp on tree limbs to aid in a faster escape from predators.

The most common measure of electrodermal activity is skin conductance, or as it is sometimes called, galvanic skin response (GSR). According to Fowles, the more people inhibit their behaviors, the sweatier their hands become and the higher their skin conductance levels. Fowles's paper was important, then, in showing that biological changes in our hearts and hands reflect different psychological states.

You can see why Fowles's observations were so helpful in studying confession and inhibition in the laboratory. By getting independent physiological measures of activation and inhibition, we could learn the degree to which confession was, in fact, a clear release of inhibitions. Further, we now had the basis for evaluating the letting-go experience.

THE BODY'S RESPONSE TO CONFESSION

Why am I telling you all of this? Because of Janie. Soon after I read Fowles's paper, Janie, an old student and good friend of mine, dropped by my office. Since it was almost noon, I suggested that we go across the street for a sandwich. As soon as we sat down, it was clear something was the matter. Janie wasn't hungry, and when I asked her about the weather, she began to cry. It was the first anniversary of the death of both her parents, who had been killed in a private plane accident. Janie was miserable and lunch was ruined. "Let's go back to my office and talk about it," I suggested. As we walked back, we discussed her parents and some of the research I had been conducting. Then it hit me. "How would you feel about going to the lab and talking about your parents while you are hooked up?"

Fortunately, Janie knew my eccentricities and agreed to be "hooked up" to my recently acquired skin conductance apparatus. Over the course of the interview, Janie talked about the details of the accident, including going to the morgue to identify her parents' bodies. I also asked her to discuss some relatively trivial topics, such as her plans for the remainder of the day. At other times, I asked Janie to stop talking and merely to think about the deaths and about more trivial issues. This was an emotionally wrenching experience for both Janie and me. When talking and thinking about her parents' deaths, Janie was clearly in great pain. In addition to crying occasionally, she would sometimes get into a reverie as though she was reliving that horrible day.

Janie's physiological reactions were fascinating. Whenever she talked or thought about the deaths, her skin conductance levels dropped dramatically. Talking and thinking about superficial topics, on the other hand, were associated with increases in skin conductance. Letting go and confronting the deaths, then, represented a reduction in inhibition. In this particular setting, whenever Janie was instructed to think or talk about trivial topics, her skin conductance increased because she was actively blocking out or inhibiting her feelings and thoughts about the deaths.

The case of Janie was important for several reasons. Above all, it appeared as though skin conductance was a potential measure of the letting-go experience. In addition, her data hinted that confronting traumatic experiences was, in fact, indicative of a reduction of inhibition. Unfortunately, case studies are often intoxicating and, therefore, misleading. Just because Janie's body worked in a theoretically meaningful way was no assurance that others' bodies did likewise.

In talking with my research team about Janie, one of my graduate students, Cherie Hughes, kept asking questions about the case. What about Janie's blood pressure? What happened to Janie's physiological levels after the interview? Did it make any difference that Janie and I were friends? Would these effects hold up for everyone? The only way to quell Cherie's curiosity was for us to conduct a full-scale experiment. And that's exactly what we did.

With the help of Robin O'Heeron, Cherie and I conducted two similar experiments using seventy-two college-student volunteers. The gist of the studies was that students were asked to talk about two different topics for about five minutes each: the most traumatic experiences of their lives and their plans for the remainder of the day. While they talked into a tape recorder, we continuously measured their skin conductance, blood pressure, heart rate, muscle tension on the face, and hand temperature. The night before the experiment, each participant was called and told all about the study. It was important that they had thought about what they would say in the experiment.

Consider this study from the volunteer's perspective. You are called by a perfect stranger who identifies herself as a graduate student in psychology. You are told that if you choose to participate, you will talk into a tape recorder about the most traumatic, personal, upsetting event of your life while attached to numerous wires and tubes. During the time you talk, you will be alone in a quiet and dimly lit room in the basement of the psychology department. You are assured, of course, that everything you say will be kept strictly confidential.

We were somewhat skeptical that people would really divulge their deepest secrets in such a short amount of time. We were wrong. In the two experiments, a quarter of the participants cried when disclosing their traumatic experiences. The choice of topics, the self-ratings the volunteers made about their disclosures, and our own evaluations of the tape recordings indicated that this technique was almost as powerful as our earlier studies where people wrote about traumas for four consecutive days. Ironically, we didn't realize the power of the first experiment until it was completed. Although we had assumed that our participants talked about traumas for a full five minutes, our timer was malfunctioning. They actually had talked only about three and a half minutes.

The tape recordings of people talking about traumas indicate that people seemed to fall into two categories: those who disclosed a great deal and those who seemed to be holding back. The high disclosers, who represented about half of the participants, were those who evidenced signs of the letting-go experience, including change in voice, displays of emotion, and their revealing highly personal sides of themselves. Low disclosers, on the other hand, were much less involved in what they said. Although the low disclosers often talked about extremely traumatic events, they seemed to hold back their feelings much more than the high disclosers. In fact, a group of independent judges who listened to each of the tapes had little difficulty in distinguishing high from low disclosers.

In looking at the physiological data, the high disclosers behaved similarly to Janie. As a group, for example, high disclosers had lower skin conductance levels when talking about traumatic experiences than when discussing their plans for the day.

In addition to the skin conductance findings, the high disclosers exhibited an intriguing pattern of blood pressure and heart rate responses. Overall, their blood pressure and heart rate levels were highest during the time they talked about traumas. This makes sense from an activation perspective, since almost half of the high disclosers cried—which tends to involve movement in much of the body. More interestingly, however, these people showed lower blood pressures *after* confessing than before the experiment started.

Compared with the high disclosers, the low disclosers did not seem to get emotionally involved with the study. None cried; most admitted what they talked about was only moderately personal or emotional. Their biological signals reflected this lack of involvement. The only reliable effect across the two studies was that their skin conductance levels were higher when they tried to confront traumas than when they talked about their plans for the day. For the low disclosers, then, broaching personal topics required physiological work. That is, they had to hold back important emotions and thoughts when talking about their traumas.

As I reflected on these results, I remembered some data we had collected in the earlier immune study. In that experiment, we had measured skin conductance and blood pressure levels from all of our subjects before, immediately after, and six weeks after they wrote about either traumas or superficial topics. We had also divided our volunteers who had written about traumas into high and low disclosers (using a somewhat different criterion). Overall, we found that high disclosers showed significant drops in blood pressure from before to six weeks after the experiment compared to low disclosers. A similar trend appeared for skin conductance levels.

Tying it all together, an interesting picture begins to emerge. When (and if) people really let go and disclose their very deepest thoughts and feelings, a number of immediate and long-term bodily changes occur. Skin conductance, which is an indicant of inhibition, drops during the confession. Blood pressure, heart rate, and other cardiovascular changes increase during the confession. After high disclosers confide, however, their blood pressures drop to levels below what they had been when the participants entered the study.

Do these results mean that if you really let go and disclose your most traumatic experiences your blood pressure will permanently drop to low levels and your hands will never sweat again? Yes . . . really. [Translation: Of course not.] First of all, these studies were done with healthy college students, not grizzled, hypertensive, harried adults. Also the blood pressure drops were statistically but not clinically significant (about 6 mm/hg for both systolic and diastolic blood pressure).

Finally, these results were most reliable for the high disclosers. Right now, I can't explain why the other half of our participants didn't exhibit the letting-go experience. One very real possibility is that low disclosers didn't trust us and were not about to reveal their deepest secrets to a group of strangers in the dingy basement of the psychology building. Alternatively, some of the low disclosers might not have the ability to let go.

CONFESSION ON AND IN THE BRAIN

Confronting traumas has some powerful effects on the body. Up until 1987, we had seen how disclosing secrets had beneficially affected immune function, physician visits for illness, blood pressure, heart rate, and skin conductance. All of these bodily changes were merely reflections of something happening in the brain. What was the brain doing when a person let go and disclosed upsetting experiences? Could it be measured? If so, would the findings be meaningful?

In many respects, I didn't allow myself to think about questions such as these. Measuring real-world brain activity is an expensive, exacting, and time-consuming enterprise. Not the sort of thing that a poor and impulsive person with a short attention span should explore. Things changed quickly, however, in October 1986, when I attended a psychophysiology conference in Montreal.

By chance, I spent almost all of the three-day conference talking to experts who measured the action of the brain. On the bus ride from the airport into town, I met a young brain wave researcher named Vicki Pollock, who explained the basic theory and measurement of brain wave activity. At dinner, I was seated next to Tyler Lorig and Gary Schwartz of Yale, who were experimenting with a new and cheap way to measure brain waves. The next evening, I ended up eating dinner with a group of people who studied cerebral blood flow and other techniques that map which parts of the brain are, in essence, working the hardest.

By the end of the conference, I couldn't get the thought of brain waves out of my head. What could an analysis of brain waves tell us about the nature of confession? On my flight back to Dallas, a number of possibilities came to mind.

By way of background, the brain is made up of millions of interconnecting nerve cells. Rather than being randomly distributed throughout the brain, the nerve cells, or neurons, are organized so that different groups of neurons specialize in certain tasks. One group of neurons in the brain, for example, specializes in vision, another in the understanding and production of speech, others in emotional reactions, and so forth. As groups of neurons are activated, they use and discharge minute amounts of electricity, which can be measured on individuals' scalps. This electrical activity is amplified and recorded in the form of electroencephalograms, or EEGs, allowing the researcher to assess the degree to which different brain regions are activated at a particular time.

The most dramatic division in the brain is between the left and right hemispheres. Although there is some variation from person to person, the parts of the brain governing speech and language are usually on the left side of the brain for right-handed people. Indeed, a number of brain researchers have provided evidence that consciousness, or at least our conscious thoughts, is highly dependent on the language capabilities provided in the left brain. The parts of the brain that control negative emotions tend to be localized on the right side of the brain.

That different brain regions exist highlights the fact that our brains process different types of information at the same time. While reading these words, for example, different parts of your brain are converting visual signals into meaningful word and thought units. At the same time, your brain is monitoring head and eye movements, occasional thoughts about the past or future, and a bewildering array of physiological channels.

Let's speculate what must happen in the brain when people are dealing with a trauma that they are either inhibiting or disclosing. A trauma includes major emotions, vivid images, and conscious thoughts. In other words, an overwhelming psychological experience demands that information be compiled and integrated throughout the brain on a very sophisticated level. When inhibition is involved, a new level of complexity and conflict will be added.

Think back to the case of Joey, the Vietnam veteran introduced at the beginning of the chapter. Before participating in the interview, he had recurring images, thoughts, and emotions about his raping and killing the woman in Vietnam. By his own admission, he also had conflicting feelings of respect and even love for the woman, as well as anger about her killing his buddy. On top of all of this, in his own mind he had to be on guard against telling others about this experience. Clearly, these issues were not well integrated. Different parts of this complex experience were probably being processed independently in different parts of his brain. However, because he did not allow himself to bring these different parts of the same experience together, he never resolved the issues.

Following this reasoning, I would think that if we placed brain wave sensors on the left and right sides of Joey's head before versus after his confessing, there would be some major changes in the way his brain processed information. Specifically, before confessing, there should be very little congruence in brain wave activity between the left and right hemispheres if information was being processed independently. However, in the midst of a letting-go experience (and possibly thereafter), emotional and linguistic types of information should be processed together. In short, confession should lead to greater congruence in brain wave activity between the left and right hemispheres.

I desperately wanted to test this idea even though I didn't have the equipment, staff, or training. About this time, I was asked to consider a unique application from a woman who wanted to enter our graduate psychology program. The applicant, Lisa Sharp, was a cross between a punk rocker and a precise scientist. After receiving her undergraduate degree, Lisa moved to New York City to work in a hospital as a registered nurse and, later, in a personnel company as a computer consultant. During her New York period, she had devoted thousands of hours exploring the seamier sides of the city. In short, Lisa had the perfect qualifications for setting up the brain wave laboratory. Indeed, Lisa found the prospect of working with brain waves as, well, cool.

After months of work, we were able to measure brain waves from four locations on a person's scalp. The brain wave signals went directly into a computer that, with some coaxing, could evaluate the degree to which different brain regions were emitting signals that were correlated or congruent. We were ready for our first experiment.

To be safe, we stayed with the same general confession technique that had been used in the skin conductance studies. Twenty-four student volunteers came to the lab and wrote (rather than talked) about the most traumatic experiences of their lives, as well as their plans for the day. Every other minute, they stopped for twenty seconds and closed their eyes while we measured brain wave activity, skin conductance, and heart rate. In the experiment, then, we could compare brain wave activity during periods of confession with periods when people were thinking and writing about superficial issues.

It worked. When people confronted traumas, the brain wave activity on the left and right sides of the head was much more highly correlated than during periods of thinking about trivial topics. Confession brought about brain wave congruence.

The results were even more provocative when we split our volunteers into those who evidenced signs of getting into the letting-go experience and those who did not. Predictably, the high disclosers showed much greater congruence during the trauma topic than did the low disclosers. Further, the more that people achieved brain wave congruence, the more their skin conductance levels dropped.

I should emphasize that the brain wave work is still in its early stages. These preliminary findings, however, are encouraging. Hopefully, they can tell us more about how confession and psychotherapy influence the ways in which people think. Brain wave congruence, then, is merely a working hypothesis. We now need to explore the thought processes themselves.

THE LABORATORY'S ROLE IN CONFESSION

By now, it should be clear that a large percentage of college students readily disclose their deepest secrets once they are in the psychology laboratory. Even when they are tape-recorded, when sensors and cuffs are attached to their arms, hands, and faces, or their blood is drawn, our participants let go and show us the most intimate side of themselves. If you were in one of these studies, would you show signs of the letting-go experience? Would I?

I have asked myself that question many times. I think I would. A laboratory experiment is a unique event. The participant is put in a situation where he or she can divulge anything without repercussion. In many ways, it is safer than talking to a close friend, entering psychotherapy, or, for many people, praying. In the laboratory, we have inadvertently provided people with a safe, nonjudgmental haven for disclosure.

Interestingly, these experiments say a great deal about both the power of the laboratory as well as the nature of confession. The context of the laboratory signals that the participants do not need to inhibit their thoughts and feelings the way they usually do. The underlying message that we try to convey is: Say whatever you want . . . it doesn't matter to us. . . . we are simply a group of researchers interested in what makes you tick.

Although the laboratory provides a safe setting in which to disclose secrets, the degree to which our participants readily do so is also important. People seem to have an underlying urge to confess. Inhibition is not pleasant for most of them. Although many have been holding back their personal secrets for months or years, they are still eager to discuss them. Whether there is a true biological need to confess is certainly debatable. In any case, people are open to disclosing sides of themselves that are potentially humiliating, shameful, or downright illegal.

The physiological results that have been summarized in the last two chapters point to the profound power of confession. Or perhaps, the profound effort involved in inhibition. When people disclose deeply personal experiences, they exhibit immediate changes in brain wave patterns, skin conductance levels, and overt behavioral correlates of the letting-go experience. After their confessions, there are significant drops in their blood pressure and heart rate as well as improvements in their immune function. In the weeks and months afterward, people's physical and psychological health is improved.

Something very important is going on.

5

The Battle to Inhibit Our Thoughts

A distinguished-looking businessman, about forty-five years old, sat down next to me for the flight from Boston to Dallas. While the plane taxied to take off, we chatted about the weather and the traffic in Boston versus Dallas. He was on his way to Dallas to attend a sales meeting related to office furniture. On learning that I was a psychologist, he laughed nervously and assured me that he was as "fit as a fiddle." Except for an occasional headache.

And some problems with insomnia.

Oh, and sometimes, waves of tension or nervousness. It was nothing, really. It had only lasted about six or seven months. About the time that he and his wife had started remodeling their house.

And the carpenter always seemed to be around. And whenever he was on a sales trip—which was quite often—his wife frequently wasn't home when he called at night. Even after he spotted his wife and the carpenter embracing in the backyard, he decided not to say anything. He was certain that his wife was having an affair.

We hadn't been in the air twenty minutes and he had disclosed more about his thoughts and fears than he had to anyone in years. He described his recurring intrusive thoughts and emotions concerning his wife, the carpenter, and himself. Forbidden thoughts of suicide, murder, failure, and humiliation had become more and more frequent. Commuting to and from work, lying in bed at night, even in meetings, vivid images flashed before him.

He explained how he had tried to stop these thoughts. His attempts to keep busy all the time didn't work. He was exercising heavily and consuming more alcohol. However, the images and emotions kept returning. Although distressed, the man on the plane was quite sane. Due, in part, to his reluctance to discuss his marital problems with anyone, he had become a prisoner of his own thoughts. Where do these unwanted thoughts come from? How can we escape from them?

PRISONERS OF UNWANTED THOUGHTS

Most people suffer from intrusive and unwanted thoughts at some point in their lives. Surveys of adults and college students indicate that the majority of unwanted thoughts deal with sex, aggression, illness and death, failure, relationship problems, dirt and contamination, and food. A closer examination of unwanted or obsessive thoughts, however, reveals that people become prisoners of their own thoughts at fairly predictable times in their lives. Most unwanted thoughts begin to surface soon after people experience a trauma or when they are reminded of a trauma that may have occurred earlier in their lives.

The biggest danger of unwanted thoughts is that they can become larger and more threatening the more we dwell on them. A common unwanted thought among new parents, for example, concerns images of hurting their babies. Many individuals think to themselves, What would other people say if they knew I had these murderous thoughts? The thoughts then expand from harming the baby to overarching negative beliefs about themselves: I am a horrible person. Their original thoughts, which were quite normal, soon become out of control. People will often engage in a variety of behaviors to try to block the thoughts from their minds. Numerous case studies document that people can develop a fear of knives based on their thoughts of harming the baby and demand that all sharp instruments be removed from the house. Others, in coping with these unwanted thoughts, insist that another person always be present whenever the baby is around. Some people simply become compulsively organized or throw themselves into a project of some kind—which helps block the thoughts altogether.

Disturbing and intrusive thoughts usually occur when people try to suppress naturally occurring images that pop into their minds. At various times in our lives, all of us have had sexual, murderous, and even suicidal thoughts. Usually, these thoughts are not a problem in and of themselves. However, if the idea of having a particular thought is so repugnant, so threatening, so unacceptable that we immediately try to censor the thought, we often find that it returns to haunt us.

Much of the problem, then, is not our having unique or perverse thoughts. Rather, one clear danger is trying to suppress the thoughts themselves. The more we try to suppress thoughts, the more likely it is that they will resurface in our mind. The white-bear dilemma is a perfect example.

Try not to think about a white bear. No, I'm serious. Try not to think of one for the next minute or so. If you really try this little thought experiment, you will probably fail. At one time or another, some aspect of a white bear will appear in your mind. This example comes from a fascinating line of studies conducted by Dan Wegner at Trinity University in San Antonio and is described in his recent book *White Bears and Other Unwanted Thoughts*. Across several experiments, Wegner finds that people have great difficulty burying their unwanted mental images and thoughts.

Given the difficulty of suppressing thoughts of white bears, imagine the effort involved in trying to control images of unacceptable sexual perversions, the death of your child, or the murder of your spouse. Wegner finds that the problem of suppressing psychologically threatening thoughts is multiplied when we are depressed. When we are happy, it is relatively easy to put a negative thought out of our minds. When we are depressed, on the other hand, negative thoughts build on themselves. Each attempt to suppress them tends to backfire, thereby making us even more depressed.

Is there any way out of the cycle? That is, once we are suffering from recurring unwanted thoughts, is there some psychological trick that allows us to break away? Well, yes and no. Some techniques we now know do not work. Others are effective some of the time.

Wegner's work clearly indicates that attempts to inhibit thoughts actually exacerbates them. The moral of this research, then, may be just what you don't want to hear. If you are suffering from forbidden or unacceptable thoughts, allow yourself to think about them. In Wegner's words, stop stopping.

A twenty-three-year-old woman, Lauren, is a good example of this. Lauren had been happily involved with a man about her age for a year. One day while shopping, she started watching another woman trying on a new dress. Out of nowhere, according to Lauren, a thought appeared: What would it be like to kiss and make love with that woman? The thought so horrified her that she began shaking. For the next several days, Lauren actively tried not to think homosexual thoughts—which, of course, led to her thinking about them all the more.

After talking with Lauren, I suggested she try a series of short experiments, each lasting about an hour. In one session, I asked her to continue not thinking these homosexual thoughts in the way she had been trying. As expected, unacceptable thoughts came into her mind about a dozen times in the next hour. We then changed the rules by discussing homosexual thoughts. In my experience, thoughts such as these are completely normal—everyone has them on occasion. If they pop into your mind, it is no big deal. For Lauren, this meant letting her sexual thoughts enter and leave her mind naturally. With this strategy, she reported having homosexual thoughts only twice in the following hour.

Making an unacceptable thought acceptable is the first step to healthy thinking. After our brief experiments, Lauren decided to enter psychotherapy to explore the thoughts in greater detail. As she later told me, talking about her forbidden thoughts helped her understand her anxieties about sexuality and her relationship with her boyfriend, as well as with other women.

HEALTHY AND UNHEALTHY THINKING STYLES

Lauren's story raises the question whether there really are such things as healthy versus unhealthy ways to think. Such a question presupposes that we know how to measure and define thinking styles in the first place. Nevertheless, if we could measure thinking styles, we could see if they buffered people against the adverse effects of specific traumas or stress in general.

I became interested in thinking styles in a rather roundabout way. Several years ago I was preparing a lecture on thought and memory. The first place I turned was *The Principles of Psychology*, by William James. In his classic 1890 textbook, James was fascinated by the ways that people think. He likened thought processes to a stream—continuously moving from topic to topic. One problem of which James was keenly aware concerned the measurement of stream of thought. During any given day, all of us think about thousands of different topics. How do we capture the richness of streams of thought?

After reading James's chapter, I attempted to convey the difficulty of measuring thought to my class. To illustrate the nature of stream of consciousness, I asked the forty or so students to simply get out a blank piece of paper and begin to write continuously about whatever was on their minds. The students tracked their thoughts for ten minutes and then handed in their stream-of-consciousness writing sample. Fortunately, that same day students had completed a general health survey, which allowed me to link writing samples with health data.

Two striking findings emerged from this exercise. First, there was a tremendous diversity in what people wrote. Some discussed the meaning of life and their relationships with close friends. Others wrote about the weather, their plans for the day, or the clothes they were wearing. No one ran out of things to write about.

The second finding concerned the link between writing style and health. Because I had no way to define thinking styles, I pulled out the writing samples of the eight "sickest" students—those who had been to the health center for illness two or more times in the last two months—and compared them with eight students who had not been to the health center. Virtually all of the "sick" students wrote about superficial topics, whereas the healthy students' writing samples were broader in scope, more emotional, and more self-reflective.

Could thinking style actually influence physical health? If so, it would be imperative to devise a method by which to measure thinking style. By looking over the writing samples, it became possible to arrange the ways that people tracked their thoughts along a continuum, which I called level of thinking. High-level thinking is characterized by a broad perspective, self-reflection, and the awareness of emotion. Low-level thinking is the relative absence of these attributes. In later studies that my research team conducted, we learned that we could quickly identify people's writing samples along the level-of-thinking continuum. To give you an example of different levels of thinking, look how two students wrote in a stream-of-consciousness manner during one of the experiments we conducted:

High-level example: I've been thinking about my parents. We recently had a fight about the car. It's not just the car, though. They won't accept that I'm 18, that I can think on my own. When I talk to them on the phone, I feel these powerful emotions of anger and love overpowering me. Have they forgotten their college years? I AM WORTHY. I AM WORTHY. "Another identity crisis," I can hear the experimenter say when she reads this.

Low-level example: Let's see. The wall is brown. The floor is dirty gray. Hmmmm, matches my shoes. Have to get them cleaned. As soon as this study is over, go to my room, sort the laundry, go to the laundromat. Don't forget the shoes. Where will I get change for the machines? Maybe Jeannie (roomie). Got to get back by 4:30. Go to dinner at 5:00. Wonder what they'll serve for dinner tonight?

From these examples, you can also see that high-level thinking is characterized by more emotion words, self-references such as *I* and *me*, and more complex sentences. Across several studies, we have found that level of thinking is not consistently related to intelligence, age, or sex of the writer.

One of our first tasks was to see if level of thinking is a consistent personality style. That is, if you are a high-level thinker today, will you also be a high-level thinker several months from now. We asked about eighty students to come to the laboratory on four occasions over a four-month period and talk into a microphone and/or write on paper in a stream-of-consciousness manner for five to twenty minutes each time. In general, we found that about half of the participants were remarkably stable in their level of thinking over time. The other half tended to bounce around between high and low thinking levels.

We divided our participants into three groups: chronic low-level thinkers, chronic high-level thinkers, and everyone else. We then compared the groups in terms of physician visits for illness, nonprescription drug use (e.g., aspirin), and alcohol consumption. Interestingly, those people who were chronic low-level thinkers and high-level thinkers had more health problems and consumed more alcohol and aspirin than any other group. In other words, flexible thinking styles were associated with better health and less stress-related behavior than rigid low or high levels of thought.

In some ways it is difficult to define a flexible thinking style. Are there times when it is beneficial to be a high-level thinker and other times to be a low-level thinker? Perhaps.

Russell Culpepper, a graduate student from the swamps of Louisiana, was eager to conduct a study that looked at the ways that midlevel thinkers changed when they were under stress. In telling stories about his Cajun buddies from high school, Russell would remember that when so-and-so was suspected of robbing a liquor store, his thinking level dropped. Or when this other guy left his girlfriend, he moved to a higher level of thinking.

In Russell's and my view, an important factor was control. When people don't have control over a stressor, they move to a lower level of thinking. With potential control, however, people move to a higher level. The reasons are fairly straightforward. Low-level thinking helps people avoid thinking about the stressor as well as their own feelings about lack of control. High-level thinking allows individuals to consider the complexity of the stressor. If people have potential control over the stressor, it will be to their advantage to be aware of the various facets of the stressor and the surrounding situation.

Russell and fellow graduate student Ed Staak set out to test this idea by having people write in a stream-of-consciousness manner for fifteen minutes. During the first five minutes, the participants were in a quiet room. They were then escorted to an adjacent chamber, where they wrote for another five minutes while listening to brief unpredictable bursts of loud noise. The noise, although unpleasant and annoying, was not harmful or dangerous. During the last five minutes of writing, the volunteers sat in an adjacent room free from the noise bursts.

During the five-minute noise period, half of the volunteers believed they could control the noise. These perceptions of control, however, were subtly manipulated. Those volunteers who were randomly assigned to the perceived-control group were told:

> If at any time you find the noise sufficiently unpleasant, simply press this button and it will stop. You are completely free to stop the noise at any time. Many people have, in fact, done so. I want to emphasize

that you have complete control over the noise at all times.

The remaining participants in the no–perceived–control condition were informed:

> Once the noise begins, you must continue to listen to it. Do not try to stop the noise by tampering with the tape recorder. I want to emphasize that you do not have any control over the noise.

This ingenious technique has been shown to manipulate perceptions of control even though all participants listen to the same noise bursts. As with other experiments using the perceived–control paradigm, no one attempted to stop the noise during the study.

Based on the writing samples both before and during the noise, the students who had no control dropped in their thinking levels once the noise began. During the noise period, they were unemotional and focused on superficial topics. The thinking levels of the perceived–control volunteers, on the other hand, were completely unaffected by the noise bursts. Indeed, the perceived–control students freely expressed emotions, feelings about the experiment, and even themselves during the noise.

In talking with the volunteers after the experiment, it was clear why people naturally gravitated to low-level thinking during the uncontrollable noise. During stress, low-level thinking serves as a method by which people distract themselves from the cause and emotional consequences of the stressor. As one woman noted, "At first, the noise drove me nuts until I started thinking about going to the mall—what stores I'd go to, the clothes I would look at . . ." Low-level thinking, then, made it easier not to think about the noise. High-level thinking, on the other hand, was associated with the awareness of feelings of irritation, anger, or anxiety that the noise caused.

There was an interesting cost to low-level thinking, however. No–perceived–control students were less perceptive and thoughtful about the experiment. They didn't attempt to figure out the purpose of the study, the nature of the noise, or the motivations of the experimenter. Perceived–control students, on the other hand, were actively problem solving during the noise period. "I kept asking myself, 'Is there a pattern to the tones?' and 'Does everyone else hear the same tones that I do?' and 'Is the experimenter going to see if the noise changes my mood?' "

If the laboratory experiments are to be trusted, we should see similar changes in levels of thinking among people under stress in the real world. Further, these changes in thinking level could signal potential health problems as well as changes in creative problem solving.

GETTING STUPID AND AVOIDING PAIN

We had just finished analyzing the data from the noise study when Peter, a friend who teaches in the English department, dropped by my office. He explained in a flat voice that his wife of twenty-two years had recently moved out "to try something new." Although he claimed not to be too distressed, consider what he was doing to avoid thinking about his wife. Usually a little sloppy, Peter confessed that he was vacuuming his entire house two or three times a day. He had stopped writing a book that was important to him. Rather than writing, he had devoted the last several days to checking his bank statements to be sure that the bank hadn't made an error.

Most shocking was the change in his general thinking style. One reason Peter and I have been friends is that we enjoy talking about books and articles. Peter, being a voracious reader and broad thinker, has an uncanny ability to tie together ideas from literature, anthropology, and related fields. As we talked, Peter maneuvered the topic of conversation away from his wife to a book he had read by Bret Easton Ellis, *Less Than Zero*. His analysis of the book caused my jaw to drop. In Peter's view, Ellis's book had some major problems: several instances of dangling participles, a few questionable spellings, and some incomplete sentences. But, I pressed, what about the general tone, the book's reflection of a generation influenced by drugs, television, and anomie? Peter wasn't interested in these issues. Rather, the dangling-participle problem was far more urgent.

Peter was thinking like a participant in the no-perceived-control condition of the noise experiment. By narrowing his focus to specks of dust on rugs, bank statements, and sentences rather than books, Peter was able to deny much of the pain that he was undoubtedly experiencing. The work of inhibiting unpleasant thoughts and emotions had taken its toll, however. The quality of his work suffered, as did his relationships with other people. Peter's low-level thinking had alleviated the pain at the cost of his becoming temporarily stupid.

Peter's behavior is typical of many people facing massive uncontrollable stressors. In one study, for example, researchers examined the behavior of Israeli women whose husbands were listed as missing in action during the 1973 Arab-Israeli war. A common response among the women was a compulsive preoccupation with trivial problems such as paying bills, choosing a carpet, and the like. By moving to extremely low levels of thought, the women were actively avoiding thinking about a potentially devastating event.

Historically, several investigators have studied how thinking patterns change when people are under stress. Freud, for example, discussed a number of defense mechanisms that individuals employ to protect themselves from overwhelming feelings of anxiety. Many defense mechanisms, such as denial, suppression, and obsessions, are akin to low-level thinking strategies.

More recently, scientists have attempted to identify how thinking patterns affect problem solving in general. In the mid-1970s, Harvard psychologist Ellen Langer began a compelling project that sought to understand when people became "mindless" versus "mindful" in their everyday thinking. When people are mindless, they are rigid in their thinking and cannot appreciate novel approaches to problems. When mindful, people are active problem solvers, looking at the world from a variety of perspectives. According to Langer, all of us can be mindful at one time and mindless at others. Being mindless, a state similar to low-level thinking, has some major drawbacks.

All of us can be lulled into mindless thinking in a variety of ways: living completely predictable lives, letting others do our thinking for us, watching television, and being in completely uncontrollable settings where we think that nothing we do can make a difference. When we are mindless or thinking on a low level, we don't feel much pain, nor do we feel much happiness. We don't feel much at all. As Langer has found, people in retirement homes are often encouraged to live boring, routine lives. When this happens, they are likely to become and remain mindless during most of their day. In a mindless state, people are not motivated to talk with others, develop new interests, or learn new things.

Across several studies, we know that when people are mind-less, they perform more poorly on tests of creativity and complex thinking. Mindless people are also far more likely to be persuaded by con artists, television advertisements, and political speeches. In a very real sense, mindlessness makes us stupid. Mindfulness makes us smarter.

Low-level thinking and mindlessness reflect thinking styles that can protect us from feeling and thinking. If our lives are miserable, any escape can sometimes be welcome. Most of the examples I have mentioned suggest that low-level thinking reflects an automatic way of dealing with upsetting experiences. Usually, people move to lower thinking levels without any conscious awareness. As in the case of Peter, the English professor, as soon as he was separated from his wife, he automatically moved to a low level. Indeed, he wasn't even aware of his mindless behavior.

Low-level thinking in the service of avoiding stress or unwanted thoughts requires work. Ellen, whose husband of forty years died suddenly, allowed me to read her diary several years later. In an entry written ten days after his death, Ellen points to the psychological struggle of dealing with the pain:

> I went back to work today . . . it was good therapy—I cleaned that desk and organized the papers like a mad-woman, but when I got home I fell apart. There's so much to tell and share, and no one to share it with. [two days later] The hardest times at the office are when I do automatic work, when I can think while I'm doing. Given a task that needs thinking through, I get involved and absorbed. Given a pack of cards to alphabetize, I cry. I remember how he used to call me during the day, cheery and loving and full of plans.

Whereas Ellen was tremendously insightful about her behavior and could structure her day to minimize her grief, many people turn to specific hobbies or habits that force a sustained lower thinking level.

I have long been interested in exercising. In recent years, Americans have turned to jogging, racquet sports, weight lifting, and exercise groups like no other people in the world. Part of the exercise craze reflects a general concern with physical health. I suspect it also provides an efficient way to get stupid; i.e., move to a lower level of thinking.

I speak from experience. During the most stressful periods of my life, I have derived great enjoyment from long-distance jogging. Problems at work or at home disappear as soon as I hit the track. Indeed, all difficulties cease because I am unable to concentrate for more than a few seconds on anything. Even if I wanted to, I could not contemplate the meaning of life, my deepest thoughts and feelings about love and death, or even how to rearrange my desk. While running, I might be in physical pain, but I am happier and stupider.

As an aside, in most of our trauma-writing experiments we ask students to estimate the number of hours they exercise each week. Across three studies, we have consistently found a weak trend indicating that writing about traumas makes people healthier *and* results in their exercising less in the months following the study. Writing about traumas may undermine some participants' exercise obsessions by reducing their need to avoid facing unpleasant thoughts or feelings.

As much as I like to taunt exercise fanatics, jogging and other forms of physical self-abuse—when done in moderation—provide a healthy form of escape from the stressors of daily life. Indeed, exercise is a far healthier way to delve into low thinking levels than most of the alternatives. Alcohol and many psychoactive drugs are abused because they are quick and efficient in transporting the consumer to a lower level of thinking. Under the influence of alcohol, most people are incapable of being too self-reflective, aware of their own emotions, or grappling with complex psychological problems.

Finally, there is a host of psychological addictions that are, in effect, low-level-thinking inducers. People completely immersed in their jobs (workaholics), in their eating and dieting patterns (foodaholics), sexual conquests (sexaholics), or even relationships with others (relationshipaholics?) often use their jobs, eating, sex, or whatever to avoid thinking about relevant psychological issues in their lives. In fact, the recent popularization of the codependency movement and various twelve-step programs (e.g., Alcoholics Anonymous) reflects a growing awareness of the personal, social, and societal dangers of the low-level thinking associated with addictive behaviors.

★   ★   ★

Unwanted thoughts can dominate our lives. The white-bear research vividly demonstrates the difficulty of directly suppressing thoughts and images. The low-level-thinking work points to inherent problems of distracting ourselves from unpleasant thoughts and emotions. Mindlessness, compulsive and addictive behaviors, and other forms of low-level thinking dull our pain by making us less thoughtful and aware. In short, low-level thinking usually serves as a mental Band-Aid to chronic psychological anxieties.

Fortunately, if we can see a drop in our thinking level, we can usually take steps to address the underlying problem. As our writing and talking studies indicate, psychologically confronting upsetting experiences produces long-term benefits in psychological and physical health. Among people whose spouses have died suddenly, the more they report having talked about the death, the less they thought about the death. Among Vietnam veterans, one of the most successful treatments to cure the unwanted flashbacks of battle is to encourage the veterans to talk about and relive their wartime experiences.

Study after study points to the value of confronting unwanted thoughts directly. Writing or talking about the unwanted thoughts is clearly helpful. Recall from previous chapters, however, that confronting our unwanted thoughts can be painful and anxiety producing. Fortunately, the pain is usually temporary. Confronting the source of our problems undermines the need for low-level thinking. In short, acknowledging and disclosing our thoughts and feelings can make us smart again.

WHEN NIGHT FALLS: INSOMNIA AND ITS TREATMENT

Traumatic and other stressful experiences alter the ways we normally think. During most days, we can escape unwanted thoughts by engaging in low-level thinking. Although low-level thinking may make us unhealthy and even slightly dim-witted, it allows us to screen out feelings of anxiety and pain. As we have seen, it is fairly easy to adopt low-level-thinking strategies in the daytime—jogging, drinking, or immersing ourselves in mindless tasks.

When it's bedtime, however, the rules change.

A hallmark of anxiety and depression is insomnia—the inability to sleep. You lie in bed partially exhausted, partially tense. You may briefly think about a relationship problem and then what you need to do tomorrow and why the room temperature isn't right and what you should have done yesterday and back to the relationship problem and, my God, if you don't fall asleep within ten minutes you will be exhausted tomorrow. Your thoughts change direction at a furious pace. In the darkness of your room, there are no distractions, just you and your thoughts gone wild.

If there could just be some way to suck out all of these thoughts from my brain, I pondered in the middle of a sleepless night a few years ago, some kind of thought extractor that serves as a psychic vacuum cleaner. Perhaps it was the vacuum-cleaner analogy, but it occurred to me that having people talk into a microphone about their thoughts and feelings could somehow clean out their minds. Their unwanted thoughts would be sucked from their brains into the tape recorder.

Since I couldn't sleep, I decided to try it. I quietly got up, found a tape recorder, and lay down on the couch in the living room. With my eyes shut and the tape recorder going, I quietly talked about my thoughts and feelings in a stream-of-consciousness manner as they occurred to me. Within ten minutes, I was sound asleep.

Holly Williams, a second-year graduate student, listened to my story of the thought-extraction technique the next day. Although dubious about the effectiveness of it, she agreed to try it out. About two weeks later, she returned to my office and suggested a way to see if thought vocalization (as she preferred to call it) really worked. The study we eventually conducted involved thirty students who reported having problems with insomnia. Each student spent the night in a vacant dormitory room, completing a questionnaire before going to bed and another on awaking the next morning. On going to bed, all students wore a modified oxygen mask with a microphone attached to its base.

The students were randomly assigned to one of three sleep groups. The no-talk students simply went to bed and tried to fall asleep. The experimental group of students were instructed to track their thoughts and feelings out loud in a stream-of-consciousness way. The final third of students, who were assigned to the count group, were told to count sheep (or other creatures) out loud until they fell asleep. The recordings from the microphone allowed us to estimate when the students fell asleep, since breathing patterns change markedly with the onset of sleep.

The thought-vocalization strategy was highly effective in improving both the quality and immediacy of sleep. The experimental students reported sleeping better, having less difficulty falling asleep, and having fewer sleep disruptions during the night than people in the other groups. Interestingly, participants who counted sheep (or men—in the case of one female subject) took the longest time to fall asleep. Another old wives' tale bites the dust.

Since Holly's experiment, I have recommended the thought-extraction technique to several people suffering from occasional bouts of insomnia. Among individuals whose insomnia appears to have a probable psychological basis, the technique is highly effective. Examples of psychologically linked insomnia include a forty-year-old lawyer about to marry for the first time or a twenty-four-year-old student whose apartment roof was lifted off by a tornado a week earlier. In cases where the insomnia may reflect injury or other underlying biological problems, the technique has not worked.

We are often surprisingly ignorant of our needs, motivations, and conflicts. When out of control, anxious, or upset, we naturally change our thinking style. Although low-level thinking can reduce our pain, it can also narrow our thinking to such an extent that we fail to see that something is the matter. We can then become the central feature of our self-constructed paradox: If we naturally escape from the knowledge that something is wrong, how can we ever know about it? How can we ever hope to control our problem or change our lives?

The answer to the paradox can be deduced from our own behaviors. We must be sensitive to changes in our health, sleep patterns, and dreams. If we become sick, our illness may reflect some random virus. But it could also signal a significant stressor that we may be actively not thinking about. Similarly, sleep problems and major changes in the content or vividness of dreams can serve as important bellwethers of our psychological health. Once aware of the warning signs, we can adjust our thinking levels accordingly.

By now, it should be clear that there are several facets to

understanding and coping with unwanted thoughts. Having recurring thoughts about traumas or other upsetting images is a
stressful burden. All of us have had thoughts such as these on
occasion. We can deal with unpleasant thoughts in a variety of
ways, many of which are successful in the short run. Fewer strategies, however, neutralize unwanted thoughts over the long run.

If you are plagued with unwanted thoughts, remember first
that they are only thoughts. Accept them as your thoughts rather
than try to fight them. One way to cope with thoughts such as
these is to write about them in a self-reflective and emotional
manner. What are those unpleasant thoughts? How do they make
you feel? Why? Remember that self-reflection will work far better
than wishful thinking in your writing. If you are obsessed with
someone's death, for example, wishing he or she were alive will
probably upset you all the more. If you are angry at someone,
writing about getting even with that person or wishing his or her
demise will exacerbate rather than diminish your ire.

Finally, be attentive to the ways you deal with unwanted
thoughts. Low-level thinking, compulsive behaviors, and other
distraction strategies can be effective in the short run. Indeed, many
stressors we face—such as uncontrollable or unpredictable
noises—will go away no matter what we do and will bother us
less in a low-level thinking mode. However, if you find that you
are now living in a low-level mode in order to avoid threatening
thoughts, it might be time to stand back and reevaluate your
coping style.

6
On Speeding Up Coping

I have always had a perverse desire to make late-night television commercials. This one would have a fast-talking actor sporting a gray polyester suit with a fake look of concern on his face:

> Hi, folks. Are you out of sorts because your best friend died? Gloomy because your spouse left you for the next-door neighbor? Or just plain down in the dumps because you were fired from your job and face bankruptcy? No problem, folks. For only $49.95, you can get the Power Grieving Solution. In just seven days, you can come to terms with death, separation, or other disasters and start living again. Forget about that old friend, spouse, or job. Get the hassle of grieving over with in one week or your money back.

In our culture, we are obsessed with speed and power. We become impatient with the natural pace of things. We can send our two-year-olds to schools to get them to read, swim, or play the piano. Our cars can pull much more weight and go much faster than we really need. Our modern kitchens are equipped with appliances that allow us to prepare and clean up after a meal in record time. We have speed reading, power talking, mind power, and power leadership seminars. We need to suck in our guts and power through lunch, business meetings, and hardships.

Are we ready for power grieving?

There is something both horrifying and fascinating about this idea. As in teaching a two-year-old to read, accelerating the grieving process is toying with the natural order of things. On the other hand, the prolonged pain associated with losing a loved one or dealing with numerous other traumas is often overwhelming. Any techniques that could temper the magnitude or duration of the pain would be welcome by most of us.

Before we contemplate tampering with the coping process, however, it is important to consider how coping normally progresses in the real world.

THE NATURAL SEQUENCE OF GRIEF AND COPING

In 1986, a freshman committed suicide by hanging himself in his dormitory room. Although somewhat quiet, Darryl was well liked by the other people in his dormitory. Several, in fact, considered him to be their primary confidant. Because of the suicide's profound impact on the students, John Tiebout and I were called in to talk with Darryl's friends. John, a former graduate student of mine, had served as a leading Dallas counselor for family survivors of suicide. Through his warmth and gentle humor, John was excellent at getting the students to talk about Darryl's death.

Perhaps the most striking aspect of this event was the different ways in which people coped with the death. Darryl's next-door neighbor, Newt, for example, was genuinely sorry to learn about the suicide. He talked about it openly and nondefensively. The death, however, didn't appear to affect his behavior in any tangible way. Indeed, he was remarkably well adjusted and happy despite the death. Two months after the death, Newt discussed his reactions:

> It just didn't affect me. Darryl was a great guy and I'm happy that I got to know him. I wish he hadn't killed himself, but he did. Life goes on and sometimes there's no value in looking back.

Contrast Newt's response with that of another hallmate, Ewart, who had only spoken to Darryl a few times during the entire school year. The day after the suicide, Ewart talked nonstop to John Tiebout for an hour and a half. At that point, his emotions vacillated between despair and anger. His anger was alternately aimed at himself for not seeing signs that Darryl was suicidal and at Darryl himself. Two months later, Ewart was still grieving about Darryl's death:

> At first, I kept thinking, If only I had known. If only I had said something to him or gone by his room that day. Maybe it wouldn't have mattered. It has been hard for me to accept that he died in this building. He did, though. It has been hard in general, but I am slowly coming around. This is the closest I have ever been to death, and it scares me. Darryl has caused me to rethink what I want out of life. I hardly even knew Darryl, but he has changed me more than anyone since I came to college.

Ewart's reactions, unlike Newt's, evolved over time. Whereas Newt appeared to have come to terms with the death almost immediately, Ewart was just beginning to move past Darryl's suicide. Whereas Ewart's grieving progressed in stages, Newt's seemed to reflect his natural orientation toward life and death. Do most people typically go through a series of stages in coping with traumas or do they usually have a set grieving style similar to Newt's? Is one approach better or healthier than another?

One of the most sensitive and controversial books on death, entitled *On Death and Dying,* was published in 1969 by Elisabeth Kübler-Ross. In her book, Kübler-Ross suggested that once people learned that they were dying from a terminal disease, they progressed through a series of well-defined stages. Based on hundreds of interviews with terminally ill patients, Kübler-Ross isolated five distinct coping stages: denial, anger, bargaining, depression, and acceptance. Since her original book, others have applied these same stages to people who have had to deal with the death of others, divorce, rape, and other traumas.

The original conception of stages in coping was quite insightful. It helped explained why people, on learning that they had a disease such as AIDS, behaved in such different ways. Workers in AIDS clinics, for example, report that more than half of AIDS patients do, in fact, exhibit one or more of the stages suggested by Kübler-Ross at various points during the course of their disease. Some deny either the diagnosis or its fatal implications. Others fly into a rage, threatening to sue the clinic or old lovers. A number of forms of bargaining can also be seen. One man of my acquaintance has become deeply religious, implicitly hoping that now that his soul has been saved, his body will be spared. Depression, not surprisingly, can be an intermittent problem for many AIDS victims throughout the course of their illness. Acceptance, according to AIDS workers, refers to the fundamental understanding that death will occur. Once patients accept the fact of their own impending death, they often exhibit a sense of peace and contentment.

The major difficulties with Kübler-Ross's stage models is that not everyone goes through all or even most of the stages that were originally posited. In fact, it is common for a person to bounce from one stage, such as anger, to another, such as acceptance, and then back to anger again. Researchers often find Kübler-Ross's model supremely frustrating since it doesn't predict or explain who will progress through which stages. Many counselors and therapists have also become disillusioned because it fails to specify how to get patients to the acceptance phase. For example, if an AIDS patient is angry about his or her diagnosis, should the therapist encourage the patient to start bargaining or get depressed?

More recent stage models have overcome many of the criticisms of Kübler-Ross's model. In studying individuals who have faced major traumas such as rape, psychoanalyst Mardi Horowitz reports that people typically progress through three general stages: denial, working through, and completion. The goal of therapy, in Horowitz's view, is to aid in the working-through phase so that completion or assimilation is attained.

Horowitz, like many current cognitive therapists, assumes that traumas disrupt people's basic beliefs about the world. Before the occurrence of a trauma, individuals might think that the world is basically predictable, fair, and benevolent. After the trauma, according to Horowitz, these beliefs may be shattered or turned upside down. When beliefs about the world are threatened, traumatized individuals experience intense anxiety, depression, or denial because their world doesn't make sense. With time, individuals may reorient their lives in order to force new experiences into their existing belief systems. Alternatively, people's original belief systems may gradually return by their having positive experiences.

A revealing example of a cognitive stage model is a former student of mine, Barbara, who at age fifty-five almost drowned in a flash flood. Having moved to Dallas from Seattle, Barbara viewed rain as a fairly predictable and benevolent event. Her world view changed when she took a shortcut home during a brief but intense rainstorm. As she started to drive through what appeared to be a puddle, her Oldsmobile stalled as flood waters quickly began washing over the hood of her car. Luckily, a group of construction workers saw Barbara's car and were able to pull her to safety.

In the months afterward, Barbara became a nervous wreck. She constantly made excuses for not leaving her house. Whenever rain was forecast or the sky looked at all threatening, she demanded that her husband leave work and stay with her. Her new belief system was based on the premise that the world was random, that she could be killed by natural forces at any time. Fortunately, Barbara's beliefs about a random world gradually disappeared over the next two years. With each rainstorm, Barbara came to realize that flash floods are rare events that occur in predictable locations. She now freely admits that she dislikes thunderstorms but is no longer terrified by them.

Stage models assume that individuals naturally progress from one coping strategy to another. If this normal progression is disrupted, psychotherapy can help guide people back to appropriate coping levels. Implicit in stage models, then, is that coping cannot be accelerated beyond certain limits. Most proponents of stage models, including Kübler-Ross, acknowledge the large differences among people in the ways they cope with traumatic experience. Some people become demonstrably upset about virtually any unwanted event, ranging from the death of a friend to the demise of a sparrow eaten by the neighbor's cat. Other people take all sorts of traumas in stride—a roll-with-the-punches mentality.

In stark contrast to the stage model of coping is one that emphasizes basic personality differences in coping. The personality-based approaches to coping assume that we all have our own unique coping styles that we usually use for most traumas and that these styles tend to be permanent and unmodifiable.

Probably the most impressive research supportive of the personality-based approach has been conducted by Camille Wortman, of the State University of New York at Stony Brook, and Roxane Silver, of the University of California at Irvine. Over the last decade, Wortman, Silver, and their colleagues have interviewed hundreds of people who have suffered one of several types of major traumas: people who have suddenly become paralyzed due to accidents; widows and widowers whose spouses died in automobile accidents; parents who lost a child to sudden infant death syndrome, or SIDS; people victimized by incest.

From their work, Wortman and Silver conclude that there are four primary coping styles that follow irrevocable loss. Counter to common sense, the researchers find that almost half of the people who have suffered major traumas do not experience intense anxiety, depression, or grief after the loss. Rather, in the weeks, months, and years after the event, these roll-with-the-punches people are psychologically well adjusted. Another 18 percent would be classified as chronic grievers. That is, their distress and depression immediately following the loss continue unabated for months or years.

Interestingly, about 30 percent of the participants in the Wortman and Silver projects evolve in their feelings about the loss in ways consistent with many stage approaches to coping. That is, immediately after a trauma, they report feeling depressed and distressed. After varying lengths of time, however, they eventually return to normal levels of well-being. A final group of delayed grievers—those who appear to be well adjusted immediately after the loss but who are distressed at least a year later—represent only about 2 percent of the people surveyed.

The Wortman and Silver work exposes several myths of coping. Not all people feel or express overwhelming grief when faced with terrible traumas. Further, many people who do not get particularly upset or depressed following major loss may actually be psychologically well adjusted. These roll-with-the-punches individuals would not demonstrate major shifts in coping strategies as suggested by stage models. The stage-model approaches, however, are not irrelevant. For the 50 percent of the people who do, in fact, experience significant anxiety and depression following loss, it may be possible to accelerate the coping process.

POWER COPING WITH LIFE CHANGES

By mid-1987, our experiments indicated that writing about traumatic experiences that had occurred years earlier produced improvements in immune function and physical health. It was also clear that some people benefited from writing more than others. From all indications, those who demonstrated the greatest improvements in health were people who did not feel free to confide their deepest thoughts and feelings to others. The Wortman and Silver work further hinted that many people were naturally good copers and would not benefit from our writing intervention.

It was about this time that I received a letter from a woman in New England. She had read about my research in the popular press and needed advice. Within the last year, her oldest son had died. In an attempt to keep her mind off the death, she decided to get involved in the family business. She writes:

> The 2nd day at work found a letter from a woman about whom I had had suspicions. This letter indicated something had been going on for awhile. Later I discovered there were gifts, flowers and for 3 years some relationship [with my husband] was going on . . . At 47, I was numb and shocked and my world had fallen apart. Two weeks ago I took the two children and moved out to start a new life. I am in a new town with no friends, a new church, and single for the 1st time. I know I can do it but am depressed off and on. If I write about all of this now, will things get better sooner?

Here was a woman in the middle of a crisis. In essence, she was asking if the writing technique accelerated adjustment to fundamental life transitions. My response to her was that I couldn't answer her question. Her best bet, I recommended, was to talk to a therapist and to continue writing. (She eventually did both —which she found quite helpful—and decided to return to her husband after his suffering a major heart attack.)

The more I pondered her question, however, the more important it became to me to find an answer. Where could I get a large number of people whose lives were in upheaval and who would agree to participate in a laboratory study? I made some tentative calls to the courthouse about the possibility of using people recently divorced and to the chamber of commerce about companies that were laying off hundreds of workers. Nothing was working out. There had to be a place where I could find distressed but willing volunteers for a study on accelerating the coping process.

And then the obvious hit me. I teach at a university.

There is a supreme irony here. Psychology researchers are

often criticized for conducting most of their studies on college students. Although much of this criticism may be justified, we often forget the stress involved in attending college away from home.

Leaving home and moving into a college dormitory at around age eighteen is a major upheaval for most students. The transition to college involves leaving family and friendship networks. In addition to coping with new living arrangements, most entering freshmen are changing roles within their families and within society in general. Further, most face more difficult courses and greater levels of social and academic competition than ever before. Several studies in Great Britain and the United States indicate that the transition to college is associated with high levels of loneliness, depression, and increased physical and other psychological health problems. Further, new social pressures often make it difficult for the new students to be open and honest with their peers.

An illustration of the conflicts felt by many beginning students can be seen in the following writing sample. The author, a woman who had come to college only a month earlier, wrote this passage as a participant in one of our studies:

> I believed college was going to be a fun, exciting experience. Now that I'm here though, I find it's not all that way. This is the first time I've been away from home, and although I've met a lot of new friends, sometimes I feel like I am all alone, that I am living with a bunch of strangers and no one really knows who I am or what I am about. Living in my dorm is fun, but I feel like I always have to act like someone I'm really not just so people will like me. At home, I would get in bad moods and be bitchy to my family, but I feel I can not do that here because then everyone always says you're a bitch and talks behind your back.

In many respects, the transition to college was ideal for studying the coping process. Large groups of people enter a novel psychological, social, and physical world. Although there is greater day-to-day freedom in the college community compared with their high schools, the students must actively cope with the changes in their lives in order to perform well academically. On top of it all, the university is a wonderful bureaucracy where health and academic records are scrupulously maintained. From my perspective, the perfect laboratory for studying power coping.

In the fall of 1987, about 130 entering freshmen agreed to participate in an experiment that dealt with "writing and the college experience." Much as in previous studies that we had run, students came to the laboratory and wrote for twenty minutes each day for three consecutive days. By a flip of a coin, students were asked to write either about superficial topics or about their deepest thoughts and feelings about coming to college. Volunteers asked to write about college were told:

> For each of the writing sessions, I want you to let go and write about your very deepest thoughts and feelings about coming to college. . . . In your writing, you might want to write about your emotions and thoughts about leaving your friends or parents, about issues of adjusting to the various aspects of college . . . or even about your feelings of who you are or what you want to become.

Critical to this study, which was conducted with the help of Michelle Colder and Lisa Sharp, was that students were run in one of four waves. The first wave of thirty-three students participated during the first week of classes in early September. The next wave wrote during the first week of October; wave three, close to the beginning of November; wave four, during the first of December. The purpose of running people in waves was to see if we could, in fact, accelerate coping. If the power coping concept was true, we would have expected to see equivalent health and psychological benefits for wave-one and wave-four participants.

The results were intriguing. Until this experiment, every study I had conducted had had people write about the most traumatic experiences of their lives. On the surface, this project sounded rather benign. After all, we only wanted people to write about coming to college. In fact, many participants told about suicide attempts, family violence, rape . . . basically the same things that I had read when people had been asked to write about traumas.

More important, however, power coping works. Whenever people wrote about coming to college—whether in the first week of classes or three months later—visits to the doctor for illnesses dropped afterward. People who wrote about superficial topics, as with college students not in psychology experiments, demonstrated a gradual increase in physician visits over the course of the first semester.

A second phenomenon of interest concerned the nature of the long-term health benefits of writing. Because the study had enough participants, we were able to examine how long the positive effects of writing persisted. In general, writing about coming to college promoted health for a little over four months. By the fifth month after writing, however, students who had written about their thoughts and feelings were getting as sick as everyone else. Writing about upsetting experiences for three days, then, does not bring about permanent health improvements.

As with our other studies, confronting painful issues temporarily made our participants less happy—or at least, they were more willing to admit they were unhappy. In the month or two after writing about the transition to college, students admitted being more anxious about school and missing their friends and family more than did the students who wrote about superficial topics. Their questionnaire responses suggested that we had temporarily stripped away their defense mechanisms and forced them to deal with college at a higher level of thinking. This period of self-reflection and negative moods, however, was short-lived. Within three months after writing, students who had written about coming to college reported being as happy as or happier than those who wrote about superficial topics.

In trying to understand our results, I was reminded of my own first year of college. In retrospect, my first semester aroused tremendously mixed feelings. Although exhilarated by my freedom, I also had periods of feeling overwhelmingly lonely, depressed, and incompetent. However, whenever people asked me how I was liking college, I would immediately paint a forced grin on my face and assure them that college was wonderful, great, really terrific. Perhaps, had I been a subject in my own experiment back then, I would have been a little more honest with myself and with others about my complicated feelings surrounding college.

A final interesting trend concerned how the students in our study performed during their first year. In terms of their grade-point averages, both groups did equally well their first semester, with their average grade being a C+. During their second semester, the people who wrote about coming to college evidenced a very small improvement. People who had written about superficial topics dropped to an average grade of a mid-level C.

Caveat emptor. Confronting ongoing crises appears to promote long-term health and adjustment. In this experiment, we were able to accelerate the coping process for many of the participants. Keep in mind, however, that we are dealing with statistics here. Not everyone was helped. In terms of illness measures, for example, most people did not change in their physician visits from before to after writing. Overall, about 11 percent of the participants who wrote about college got sicker after participating in the study, compared with 39 percent of the students who wrote about trivial topics. Extrapolating across our various measures, the experiment probably resulted in a real improvement in physical and psychological health for 20–30 percent of the participants. Put more cynically, the experiment did not affect the majority of students one way or the other. As Camille Wortman and Roxane Silver concluded from their projects, as many as half of all people naturally cope well with major traumas. These roll-with-the-punches individuals are probably not helped significantly by writing about crises.

All people do not roll with the punches, however. Although writing about ongoing crises is clearly helpful for many, the effect is neither instantaneous nor permanent. After writing about coming to college, many participants felt less happy, more homesick, and more anxious about college in general. Although we found health improvements soon after writing, the effects lasted only about four months.

The major point I want to emphasize is that writing about or confronting upsetting experiences is not a panacea. Across hundreds of people in different experiments, there is clearly a net positive effect. If you are currently facing a major crisis in your life, don't expect writing will make your life wonderful. The magical idea of power coping is a misnomer in that most crises take a long time to overcome. All these experiments promise is that, for many people, writing can reduce the grieving time.

Finally, remember that this project has focused on one particular type of crisis: the transition to college. In the grand scheme of traumas, going to college is significant but not catastrophic. Can coping be accelerated for people who have faced overwhelming and, for most of us, unimaginable horrors? We soon were able to find out.

COPING WITH THE HOLOCAUST

In 1984, Sue Kollinger and Carol Levy were appointed to head the newly established Dallas Memorial Center for Holocaust Studies, or DMCHS. Sue and Carol were intent on creating a top-flight exhibit, library, and archive dedicated to those who suffered and died in the Holocaust. One of their most ambitious projects was to oversee the creation of a video archive of Holocaust survivors' personal recollections of their experiences. Using a format pioneered at Yale University, the Dallas project sought to interview survivors living in the region, using a staff of volunteer therapists. Carol and Sue were interested in me as a potential interviewer. I was drawn to the project because I wanted to know how such an intensive and personal interview affected the survivors' health.

Life in the Nazi concentration camps during World War Two surely was one of the most overwhelming traumas suffered by a group of people in all of history. Most Holocaust survivors have been permanently scarred by enduring starvation, disease, torture, and subhuman existences that lasted up to six years, ending in 1945. Following their years of imprisonment, their torment was not over. At the war's completion, most survivors were detained in displaced person camps for up to three years until they could obtain a visa to move to a host country. On arriving in the new country, most had to learn a new language, gain employment as unskilled laborers, and try to forget or bury their pasts.

As I soon learned, Holocaust survivors living in the United States are quite remarkable. Most are Jewish and are from countries where up to 95 percent of the Jews were killed. Typically, their extended families and native communities were eliminated. In the small group that survived concentration camps, the death rates due to cancer and heart disease since World War Two have been far above average. The stressful life of survivors has continued long after their leaving Europe.

Dallas has a surprisingly high number of Holocaust survivors—perhaps as many as two hundred. In several American communities, such as Dallas, the survivors are not a cohesive or identifiable group. After immigrating in the late 1940s, most moved to Dallas either individually or with their immediate families. Once here, they attempted to assimilate to American culture as best they could. Of those we have studied, virtually all of their children learned only English. Rarely were Holocaust experiences discussed with anyone—either within or outside the family. Indeed, only 30 percent of the people we have studied report ever having talked with anyone about their Holocaust experiences in detail since coming to the United States. The most common reasons for not talking about the Holocaust were such things as "I have tried to forget about it," "no one would understand," or "I didn't want to upset our children."

Despite not talking about their experiences, the survivors continue to think about and live with painful memories. Before one of our first interviews, one woman confided that she relived war scenes in her mind dozens of times per day. She didn't talk about them, but they were always with her. One that kept recurring:

> They were throwing babies from the second floor window of the orphanage. I can still see the pools of blood, the screams, and the thuds of their bodies. I just stood there afraid to move. The Nazi soldiers faced us with their grins.

Transfixed by stories such as this, John Tiebout, who had been involved in the dormitory-suicide study, and I immersed ourselves in the project. The survivors we were seeing were still living with their experiences forty years after the war. Could talking about what had happened to them as adolescents or young adults affect their health now? Was it possible to accelerate the coping process with such a unique group of hardy survivors?

Each interview lasted about two hours and was highly emotional. After each one, I would have nightmares. Hearing so many tragedies and seeing the unbearable pain on the people's faces were brutal on all of the DMCHS volunteers. Had I not been able to talk with John about each of these interviews, I'm not sure how long I could have continued. As I heard story after story, however, I came to appreciate the durability of people. These survivors had been to the edge of human existence and most had returned with a sense of triumph. Most had some psychological scars, but virtually all had raised families, had succeeded professionally, and reported being happy with their lives.

Over the next two years, over sixty survivors were interviewed. In addition to the videotapes, we were also able to measure each survivor's heart rate and skin conductance during the session. About one year after each interview, we called the survivors in order to get an indication of any changes in their health. About this time, a new graduate student, Steve Barger, joined the Holocaust team. On the surface, Steve gave the impression of being a mellow California surfer. Once on the project, however, Steve zeroed in on the physiological and health data as though he had been involved in the project for years.

Using the skin conductance data as well as ratings of the content of each survivor's testimony, Steve, John, and I could define each survivor as a high discloser, a mid-level discloser, or a low discloser. High disclosers were people who, when they told of the personal traumas that they had suffered, remained physiologically relaxed. Low disclosers, on the other hand, exhibited biological signs of increased inhibition and tension when disclosing traumatic events. Overall, we found that high and mid-level disclosers were significantly healthier in the year after the interview than before it. Low disclosers, on the other hand, were more likely to have been to a physician for illness in the year after the interview than before. Given that the average age of the participants was sixty-five, the findings are quite encouraging.

These results parallel a number of experiments that had been conducted with college students. Particularly important, however, is that the testimony was a psychologically beneficial experience for most survivors. Indeed, almost all of the survivors reported that the interview had a profound effect on them and their families. Because participants were given a copy of the videotape of their testimony, we could ask them how often they had watched it and/or shown it to others. Remember that 70 percent of the survivors had not talked to others about their experiences since coming to the United States. After the interview, the survivors viewed their own videotapes, on average, at least twice and shared the taped interviews with three other people.

WHEN COPING CAN AND CANNOT BE ACCELERATED

The Holocaust project and the study examining the transition to college bring me back to the question posed at the beginning of this chapter: Can the coping process be accelerated? The answer is yes—but a qualified yes. Some of the qualifications that we currently know about include the following:

Many people cope naturally well with traumas. Not everyone progresses through stages in grieving or coping. In fact, as many as half of all adults may face torture, divorce, the loss of a loved one, or other catastrophe and not exhibit any major signs of depression or anxiety. By definition, then, a substantial number of people may not benefit from attempts to influence their coping strategies.

It is critical to appreciate the large differences among people in coping with trauma. For example, if you see someone who, after suffering a major trauma, appears to be relatively normal, happy, and nondefensive, it is entirely possible that the person really is normal, happy, and nondefensive. Never discount that many people do, in fact, roll with the punches.

Conversely, at least half of the population *does* experience major depression, anxiety, or other signs of grief following a trauma. Among these people, coping strategies will also vary tremendously—often in unpredictable ways. Denial, anger, low-level thinking, and other defense mechanisms may occur at random intervals or even in sequence. Among those who do exhibit signs of grief, writing or talking about the experience is likely to help.

The degree to which coping can be accelerated is limited. Coming to terms with any major upheaval takes time. No known procedure can help you overcome a significant personal loss overnight. If your lover left you yesterday, for example, writing about it may shorten the time that you suffer from, say, five months to three months. But, then, no one knows. For some people, writing or talking about a trauma can make a dramatic difference, for others it may have no effect whatsoever.

By the same token, the benefits of writing or talking about a trauma may be temporary. The coming-to-college study indicated that the health benefits lasted about four months. The results from the Holocaust project suggest that the health improvements may last longer if people are confronting an event that occurred several years earlier.

Potential problems if you are still in the midst of a crisis. If you are currently in the middle of a divorce, someone close to you has just died, or you have suffered some other major trauma quite recently, writing or talking about your experience will tend to improve your health and, over time, your psychological adjustment. However, confronting the ongoing crisis may very likely make you more distressed temporarily. Don't expect that writing or talking about your thoughts and feelings will automatically make you buoyant.

A related issue about ongoing crises is that, by their very nature, new upsetting events may still be in store for you. If, for example, you are in the middle of a divorce, writing about it may help you come to terms with being alone. It may not prepare you for a future ugly trial, vicious rumors, or receiving the final divorce papers in the mail. Continuing to write throughout the entire ordeal, however, may buffer the impact of each subsequent event.

The trauma has long since passed and you are still living with it. The Holocaust project offers a particularly promising message. Even after forty years, the Holocaust survivors benefited physically and psychologically from talking about their wartime experiences. Other studies in addition to the Holocaust project point to the same conclusion. If you are currently living with a trauma from years gone by, writing or talking about your thoughts and feelings associated with it can help you get past it. You know you are living with an experience if you still think and dream about it frequently.

While we are on the topic, you may have resolved not to talk or write about a personal upheaval right now on the assumption that things will improve with time. You may be right. The intense pain associated with most traumas often goes away in stages. Usually, the most intense intrusive thoughts surrounding major traumas diminish significantly by about a year and a half. Gauge yourself accordingly. If something horrible happened to you five years ago and you are still living with it, writing about it will likely help.

And the usual admonitions. The ways you write or talk about upsetting experiences are important. In your writing, explore your deepest thoughts and feelings in a self-reflective way. Set aside a specific time and location to write continuously. If you talk to someone else, it helps if the person is objective and not personally involved. Don't be surprised if you feel somewhat sad or depressed immediately after writing. The work of self-reflection can sometimes be painful even if the benefits are clear.

7
Understanding the Value of Writing

Even now, I am amazed that writing or talking about basic thoughts and feelings produces such profound physical and psychological changes. Across studies using people whose spouses have recently died, Holocaust survivors, and college students at several universities, the phenomenon has endured. Although the findings are real, the explanations for them are less clear-cut.

Why does writing produce such beneficial effects? When I began this research, I thought that the primary value of writing was in its reducing the work of inhibition. From my own experiences, however, it was clear that writing accomplished much more. In writing about upsetting events, for example, I often came to a new understanding of the events. Problems that had seemed overwhelming became more circumscribed and manageable after I saw them on paper. In some way, writing about my haunting experiences helped resolve them. Once the issues were resolved, I no longer thought about them.

THE NEED FOR COMPLETION AND THE SEARCH FOR MEANING

That we remember, think about, and dream of unresolved issues has been a central feature of psychological study for several decades. In 1927, Bluma Zeigarnik and her mentor, Kurt Lewin, found that people had a far better memory for interrupted tasks than completed ones. For example, if you are interrupted just before the end of an exciting movie, you will remember the movie more vividly and for a longer time than if you saw the movie's resolution. People have a basic need for completing and resolving tasks. The tasks may be as trivial as buttoning all of our buttons in the morning or as profound as resolving the major conflicts we have with our parents or children.

We all tend to think and dream about things that are unresolved in our minds or about tasks that are not quite completed. In the last hour, for example, I have had fleeting thoughts about my mother's health, what I will cook for dinner, the broken copying machine, what the purpose of this paragraph should be, and dozens of other minor and major issues. Once each of these issues is resolved, I will cease thinking about it. I never think about my mother's health if she is healthy or the copying machine if it is working. When our family gets together over the soon-to-be-decided dinner, we will each talk about what happened to us today. Many, perhaps most, of the issues that will be brought up will be those that are not yet fully resolved or understood. Finally, the dreams I will have tonight will probably reflect certain unresolved fears, urges, or thoughts that I am currently living with.

Major tasks or goals in our lives are difficult to resolve or complete. Consider what researchers find to be some of the more common life tasks that we set for ourselves: to love and to be loved; to make the world a better place; to raise healthy and happy children; to succeed professionally and financially; to be honest with ourselves and others. As if these tasks weren't difficult enough to accomplish, imagine the problems we face when confronted with an overwhelming trauma. Divorce, death of a loved one, financial ruin, public humiliation, or other upheaval by definition disrupts an entire series of life tasks. If our marriage is falling apart, for example, we have to deal with our life goals of being permanently married, being loved, raising happy children, succeeding financially, and so forth. Traumas, according to this approach, represent interruptions of life tasks.

If people naturally seek completion of disrupted tasks, the changes that occur following an unexpected trauma become far more understandable. Among people in the midst of a divorce, it makes good sense that they would ruminate, talk, and dream about the many aspects of their lives touched by the breakup of their relationship. Indeed, thoughts and dreams have long been considered symbolic ways of completing unresolved life tasks. One function of dreams, Freud claimed, was wish fulfillment. More recent thinkers have suggested that dreams can help us work through uncompleted life tasks.

But thoughts and dreams do more than attain completion of a disrupted task. If our closest friend is killed by a drunk driver, we also have to accept that the event happened and that our lives will inexorably be different from what we had planned. Our thoughts wander from if only I had done this or if my friend had done that to asking why this happened. In other words, we seek to understand why the event occurred. More broadly, we try to find meaning to the event and, perhaps, life itself.

A motivation closely akin to the need for completion is the basic need to understand the world around us. This need for understanding and meaning is probably central to most vertebrates. A mouse that narrowly escapes the jaws of the neighborhood cat needs to know what factors predict the presence of the cat and how to avoid the cat in the future. A toddler who is yelled at for sticking her finger in the direction of an electrical outlet seeks to understand the meaning of the yell. As our mental apparatus becomes more sophisticated, our search for the meaning of events becomes more intensive. We go to great lengths to understand such things as why we got that parking ticket or why our boss turned down our reasonable request for a raise.

In our culture—perhaps in all cultures—the major key to understanding is learning what causes what. Usually, if I can isolate the cause of something that, up to then, I couldn't figure out, I am satisfied. I have attained a form of psychic completion. For example, if my newspaper isn't on my doorstep in the morning, I have to ask myself why. What could explain this relatively minor event? Possible explanations that might go through my mind include: It is in the bushes; some passerby stole it; it wasn't delivered due to the delivery person's negligence; I haven't paid my bill; this isn't my house. Once I can isolate any of these possibilities as the cause, I can take corrective action. Once I understand the problem and have received my paper, I can put the entire episode behind me without giving it another thought.

We are driven to complete tasks and to understand our world. These motives serve us well until we are faced with massive, overwhelming traumatic experiences. This is especially true for unpredictable events that can never be truly explained. Think back to the example of a close friend killed by a drunk driver. By definition, you can never complete your relationship with your friend by saying goodbye. Further, it is difficult if not impossible to find any meaning in the event. Nevertheless our brains are constructed, and/or our minds are trained, to move toward completion and to find meaning.

Some religions offer answers to meaningless tragedies: God has a plan, or I will see my friend when I eventually die. Others take a more detached perspective by noting that death is merely an evolution of the life force. Several researchers have found that people who can turn to their personal religious beliefs—no matter what the actual religion may be—fare better in the face of certain traumas than those who are not religious.

The issue goes far beyond religion, however. We are often so intent on finding meaning to an event that we become irrational. Several intriguing experiments have demonstrated that if we see someone who is physically abused for no reason, for example, we tend to come up with a reason. A ready explanation is to blame the victim.

Read the letters-to-the-editor section of your local newspaper for evidence of this. Recently, I have seen letters in *The New York Times* that have blamed the brutal attack by a gang of youths on a woman in Central Park on the woman rather than the youths. She should have known better than to go out jogging by herself at that time, was the gist of some letters. Another letter writer accused AIDS victims of being the cause of AIDS due to their "disgraceful" life-styles. The logic of these letters is that if something bad happens to someone and there is no clear rationale for it, the person must have deserved what happened to him. Such reasoning is able to maintain people's belief that we live in a just world.

Among those who can easily explain all bad things, whether through strongly held religious beliefs or more paranoid blame-the-victim belief systems, feelings of anxiety are not a problem. The majority of people in Western society, however, have drifted away from simple cause-effect explanations for tragedies and traumas. With the awareness that the world is ambiguous and unpredictable comes the anxiety of not attaining completion and not understanding many events.

And therein lies the problem. We naturally search for meaning and completion to events that we know at some level don't have meaning and can never be resolved. We are too smart for our own good but can't admit it. In fact, studies among women who were incest victims as children reveal that the search for meaning can be both futile and unhealthy. Roxane Silver, for example, cites evidence to suggest that 50 percent of former incest victims who continue to search for meaning report never making any sense of it. As two incest victims wrote:

> I always ask myself why, over and over, but there is no answer.

> It is useful to have the past in mind, but not always. It can stimulate thought but can also keep one from really listening and learning in the present.

Recent work with incest, rape, and other traumas by Ronnie Janoff-Bulman of the University of Massachusetts at Amherst suggests that it is usually easy to answer a question like Why did the sexual trauma occur? It is much harder to answer Why did it happen to me? According to Janoff-Bulman, victims of traumas often answer these questions by blaming themselves, saying, in essence, I deserved it. Again, you can see how this happens. People have a desperate need to understand an event that may not have any real meaning. After thinking about various causal explanations, people may opt for the simple explanation that they brought it on themselves. Although a self-blaming explanation may be inaccurate and personally devastating, it meets the need for an understanding of the event.

The mind torments itself by thinking about unresolved issues. One reason that writing about traumas can be so beneficial is that it is a powerful tool to discover meaning. Writing promotes self-understanding.

The strongest evidence about the role of writing in helping individuals resolve upsetting experiences comes from the participants in our experiments. Months after people have written about traumas, over 70 percent report that writing helped them understand both the event and themselves better. A typical volunteer in the first writing experiment, for example, responded to a questionnaire we mailed to her five months after the study:

> I had to think and resolve past experiences. . . . One result of the experiment is peace of mind, and a

method to relieve emotional experiences. To have to
write emotions and feelings helped me understand how
I felt and why.

Words such as *realize, understand, resolve,* and *work through*
appear in approximately half of the open-ended responses we receive to questions about the general value of the writing experiments. Intuitively, people see writing as a method by which to
understand and resolve personal upheavals. Their intuitions, I
think, are accurate. What they don't tell us is how writing accomplishes these cognitive changes.

The secret may lie in how we naturally think about things.
If we analyze our day on a minute-by-minute basis, we are able
to resolve, understand, or perhaps ignore most everything that
confronts us: why there is a squeak in the chair; why the coffee
is especially bitter; why the electricity bill is so high. Our minds
are ideally suited to simple and even moderately complex problems. But traumas are a different matter. The events themselves
may be so intricate that attaining any understanding may be impossible, yet their effects cannot be ignored.

A striking example of the confusion faced by people when
they suddenly are thrust into a psychic maelstrom can be seen in
the case of a man laid off from an oil company for which he had
worked for twenty-one years. On my recommendation, Brian, a
forty-three-year-old geologist, wrote about his predicament:

> I have always loved my job, this company, and the
> people I work with. All our friends are with the com-
> pany. Now, after two decades I receive a notice that
> falling oil prices forces them to do away with my entire
> office. We will have to move into a cheaper house, maybe
> to a new town. I even have to think about switching
> occupations. I am angry at the company, at Ronald Rea-
> gan, even at Saudi Arabia for putting me in this situation.
> It is so demeaning. Other people think I am a loser. I
> feel like it sometimes, too.
>
> In the last month, my world has turned upside
> down. My identity, my friends, my moods, my time.
> As soon as I start thinking about one change in my life,
> some other aspect occurs to me. It is impossible to keep
> my attention on much of anything for more than a few

minutes. Anger, depression, bitterness . . . Sometimes
brief bursts of optimism. I have never had so many
moods in one day. Why did this happen?

The enormity of losing his job touched virtually every aspect
of Brian's life. No matter how intelligent Brian may have been,
it is unlikely that he could have sorted out all of the issues while
moping around his house or during the many hours he spent
watching television.

In Brian's case, writing helped because it forced some degree
of structure and organization of his thoughts. When writing, he
was forced to slow down his thinking process. Before writing, he
would have one thought followed by another and another. No
thought or emotion was ever resolved. When he began writing,
however, he was able to follow an idea to its logical conclusion.
Indeed, as his writing progressed day by day, he began to focus
on specific topics in an orderly manner. By the third day of his
writing, he disclosed his anxieties about being unemployed and
not making money; his sixth writing period was devoted to the
added tension that he was experiencing with his wife; within two
and half weeks, he was focusing on his social and professional
skills in order to assess his possibilities in alternative careers.

Another common phenomenon that occurs when people
write about the same trauma repeatedly is a gradual change in
perspective. Over time, individuals who are writing about a specific event tend to become more and more detached. They are able
to stand back and consider the complex causes of the event and
their own mixed emotions. Perhaps because they address the
trauma multiple times, people's emotional responses become less
extreme. In other words, repeatedly confronting an upsetting experience allows for a less emotionally laden assessment of its meaning and impact.

THE ROLE OF LANGUAGE

When I first began teaching, I became aware how little I really
knew. The public unveiling of my ignorance in my role as teacher
occurred during my second lecture, where I planned to talk about
how psychologists measure relationships between two variables

using a statistic called a correlation coefficient. I had used, computed, and interpreted correlations for years and assumed that I would simply explain how these statistics worked. The next lecture, I stood in front of the class and began to describe what a correlation was. Within a minute or two, I realized my explanation made absolutely no sense. I tried another tack—again, what I was saying was absurd. By my third attempt, students began asking very reasonable questions that I could only answer with mumbles. I remember looking out at the students as I stammered incoherently and thinking to myself, My God, I honestly don't understand correlations.

Virtually every beginning teacher has experienced this phenomenon. If you can't explain something to someone else, you probably don't understand it yourself. I know it is true for correlation coefficients and suspect it to be so for personal traumas. Translating a phenomenon into language alters the way it is represented and understood in our minds.

Unfortunately, very little research has examined how translating an image into language alters the image itself. We know, for example, that talking about an image involves different parts of the brain than focusing on the image alone. There is also converging evidence to suggest that the parts of the brain involved in language are closely linked to all conscious experience. Particularly upsetting traumas that are not discussed may well be stored in a nonlanguage form.

The evidence for the detachment between language and traumatic emotional experiences is quite new and exciting. A number of well-known psychological disorders, such as multiple personalities and posttraumatic stress disorders, have been linked to massive psychic traumas that have never been discussed with anyone. Whereas posttraumatic stress disorders are usually linked with identifiable instances of violence or victimization, most instances of multiple personalities have been tied to childhood sexual traumas. Both posttraumatic stress disorders and multiple personalities appear to be problems related to the separation of traumatic emotional experience from language. Indeed, the ability to detach language-based conscious experience from emotional experience appears to be closely linked to hypnotic abilities. Recent work at Stanford University Medical School by David Spiegel and his colleagues indicates that people suffering from posttraumatic stress disorder are especially hypnosis prone. That is, they can easily disengage their language system, probably due to the traumas they have faced.

Whereas the failure to translate powerful emotions into language appears to be psychologically unhealthy, linking the two systems is beneficial. In fact, recent studies indicate that one of the very best treatments for individuals suffering from both post-traumatic stress disorders and multiple personalities is active talk therapy, wherein sufferers are forced to relive and talk about their wartime or other traumatic events.

Another way to think about one of the functions of language is to consider it a tool by which to simplify our experiences. Think of a time that you have told the same story to different people over and over again. Right after we had our first baby, my wife, Ruth, and I excitedly talked about the birth in detail with our relatives and friends. It was such an emotional and unique event in our lives that we relished telling about our childbirth adventure. One thing we both noticed independently was that the account of the event subtly changed over time. Initially, it was a jumble of sights, sounds, emotions, and thoughts—both in our minds and in the way we talked about it. Later, the experience became more of a story, with a clear beginning and end. Even the story itself changed by becoming shorter and more concise. The act of repeatedly telling about our experience resulted in both an organization to the event and a summarizing of it.

A similar phenomenon occurs in our experiments when people write about the same trauma several days in a row. The description of the event is gradually shortened and summarized. Irrelevant issues and tangential impressions are dropped; central features of the traumas are highlighted and analyzed. The experimental volunteers have created a mental summary of their experience which, often, is psychologically less daunting to deal with. One woman, after writing about being raped by a casual acquaintance, explained:

> I haven't been able to talk about the rape in detail to anyone. In the last three months, it has dominated my being. I've had fears and problems with other people that I've never had before. Being in this [writing experiment] has made a difference. Somehow, just writing about what happened has made it all less overwhelming. I won't ever

forget what happened but I see more clearly that it was an isolated event in my life.

Note that any type of an event is less overwhelming and easier to think about once it is summarized in some way. Psychologists have long known that it requires much less work to remember something by organizing it. For example, if I ask you to memorize the following numbers in sequence:—1,2,2,5,0,7,0,4—it will be harder to do so if you consider them as eight separate numbers than as the single eight-digit number 12,250,704. If you structure the digits as two numbers, 1225 and 0704, the task becomes slightly simpler. Summarizing the numbers and giving them meaning as Christmas Day (12–25) and the Fourth of July (07–04) makes memorizing the numbers extremely simple, requiring virtually no thinking ability. Summarizing information in any form—whether eight-digit numbers or traumatic experiences—reduces cognitive work.

Translating events into language and writing them down can reduce cognitive work in another way. Many times, when we write something down, we don't have to think about it any longer. I've noticed this in myself when I'm preparing to go on a vacation. There's packing, stopping the mail and newspapers, getting the car checked, and on and on. In the middle of meetings or talking to someone on the phone, overlooked chores come to mind: Oh, I can't forget to pack the fishing rod, or Get someone to water the plants. As much as I try to avoid it, I usually break down and start making lengthy lists of last-minute tasks to perform. Before list making, I actively juggle the tasks in my mind. Once I start the lists, however, my mind becomes freer and I feel less distressed. I have, in essence, transferred my mental notes from my head onto a piece of paper.

Several researchers have discussed how memory and thought processes can be viewed as external to our brains. Dan Wegner of Trinity University has provided fascinating examples of how partners in a marriage gradually become repositories of each other's thoughts and memories. One spouse may remember restaurants, the other may keep track of movies. I never have to think about finances, for example, because all financial thoughts are housed in my wife's brain. (Extending Wegner's idea of transactive memory, you can see how divorce can make people stupid.)

As with list making or marriage, we can also construe the act of writing about a trauma as a method of externalizing a traumatic experience. Once it has been written down or told to another, the memory and value of it have been preserved. There is now less reason to rehearse the event actively. In the computer world, this is analogous to downloading—where information previously stored in the chips or hard disks of the computer is transferred to diskettes or computer tapes, where it can be saved elsewhere. In every one of our writing studies, at least one participant has asked to keep his or her essay. These people report that what they have written is a part of themselves and they want to be able to refer back to their thoughts and feelings in the future. They have downloaded their traumas but don't want their memories destroyed.

THE DRIVE TOWARD SELF-EXPRESSION

When under great conflict, individuals have been known to produce major literary works. Eugene O'Neill's *Long Day's Journey into Night,* Sylvia Plath's *The Bell Jar,* Alexander Solzhenitsyn's *Cancer Ward,* and many other masterpieces express the fundamental psychological fears and traumas of the authors. A parallel phenomenon occurs within the visual arts, music composition, and dance. The stark photography of Diane Arbus, the twisted visions of Van Gogh, the conflicted musical themes of Gustav Mahler or Hank Williams, Jr., or the haunting choreography of Alvin Ailey or Bob Fosse attest to the expression of conflicts across a variety of media.

Is there a basic human need to express ourselves? One highly respected scholar, Abraham Maslow, has suggested that if their most basic needs are satisfied—such as food, sex, and security— people exhibit a strong drive toward self-expression. When this drive is blocked, tension results. One reason that writing about traumas may be physically healthy is that writing itself is a fundamental form of self-expression.

Writing, of course, is only one of many forms of self-expression. Looking back to our previous experiments, would people have shown similar improvements in physical health if they had been asked to draw, sing, or dance about their most upsetting experiences? This is a tough question to answer, because there is no solid experimental evidence one way or another. I have, how-

ever, explored the idea of confessional singing and disclosive drawing with several individuals.

Over the last few years, I have asked people to sing about
their very deepest thoughts and feelings associated with personal
traumas while, at the same time, I monitored their heart rate and
skin conductance levels. The first person to do this, a graduate
student in the music department, sang a moving version of "Sum-
mertime." While singing, her physiological levels behaved in ways
identical to the levels of people who are asked to write or talk
about their most traumatic experiences. In other words, she appeared to be in a similar type of disinhibited psychological state.
Afterward, she described feeling in touch with the pain of her
recent breakup with her boyfriend. For her, the experience was
purely emotional rather than cognitive. While immersed in her
singing, she had no vivid images or thoughts. A week later when
I talked with her, she reiterated the emotions associated with the
singing but said that it had not affected her thoughts or feelings
about her boyfriend or the relationship at all.

Other singing experiences in the laboratory have not been
as interesting or successful. Nonsingers feel extremely inhibited
and have difficulty imagining what I mean by having them sing
about their most traumatic experience. As one woman put it,
"My singing repertoire is 'Happy Birthday' and 'It's a Grand
Old Flag'—which of those is more related to the death of my
grandmother?"

Disclosive drawing has been about as successful as confessional singing. Among people who feel at ease drawing, all have
demonstrated reductions in physiological levels while expressing
emotional topics. Some have further noted that they paint or draw
when they are depressed. Again, for most, the experience seems
to be more emotional than cognitive. As I was told by an artist
friend of mine:

> If I am bummed out, I'll pick up my pad and start
> to sketch. When I do it, I stop thinking and just draw.
> Sometimes I'm not even aware of what I am drawing
> until I have been going for a few minutes. Yes, it can be
> really cathartic and emotionally draining. It can also be
> kind of a distraction as well. Maybe it's more of a med-
> itative state.

It is not coincidental that there are a variety of therapies that use self-expressive techniques unrelated to writing. Art therapy, dance therapy, and music therapy have gained widespread popularity and are used with children and adults. In my interviews with clients and therapists, I am convinced that these alternative approaches are beneficial. Their effectiveness, however, is not merely in fulfilling self-expressive needs.

Art and music therapies can be powerful in getting individuals to experience emotions related to relevant upheavals in their lives. As I have found in the laboratory, expressive drawing or singing can quickly strip away inhibitions and other defenses. In this state, people are more emotionally aware but not necessarily closer to an understanding of their thoughts and feelings. Indeed, most art and music therapists go far beyond encouraging self-expression. During or after drawing, singing, or dancing, clients are strongly encouraged to talk about their emotional experiences. In other words, non-language-based therapies rely heavily on language once the clients' inhibitions are lifted.

One broad question keeps returning: Why does writing or talking about upsetting experiences produce improvements in physical and psychological health? One important answer is cognitive: People think differently after writing about traumas. In translating experiences into language, people begin to organize and structure the seemingly infinite facets of overwhelming events. Once organized, the events are often smaller and easier to deal with. Particularly important is that writing moves us to a resolution. Even if there is no meaning to an event, it becomes psychologically complete. In short, there is no more reason to continue to ruminate about it.

Not talking or writing about upsetting experiences, then, can be unhealthy for several reasons. Holding back and not talking about an upsetting experience is bad in and of itself because of the physiological work of inhibition. A deeper problem is that when individuals inhibit, they fail to translate their thoughts and feelings into language. Without resolving their traumas, they continue to live with them. The health benefits of writing or talking about the traumas, then, are twofold. People reach an understanding of the events and, once this is accomplished, they no longer need to inhibit their talking any further.

8

The Social Price of Disclosure: Whom to Tell and How to Listen

Most individual traumas have social components. Even if they are not caused by other people, we turn to others to cope with them. Although we may relish reading about fires, murders, or messy divorces in the newspaper, when these same events happen to people we care about, they are extremely distressing. Indeed, it is usually painful to hear someone we know recount a personal tragedy that he or she has experienced.

The death of a child violates every conception of meaning that we hold about the world. For parents, the mere thought of their children's death inspires nothing short of terror. Last year, I was invited to speak to a support group of bereaved parents who had recently faced that ultimate horror. One by one, the parents recounted their experiences of learning of the death of their children by murder, suicide, car accidents, and disease. Racial, social class, and religious differences were completely irrelevant. Their bond was a common tragedy.

Because I had devoted my research efforts to the cognitive changes that accompanied tragedies, I had planned to discuss ways to come to terms with death. Writing and talking to others about their tragedies, I explained when I arrived, would undoubtedly be helpful. I understood what they must be going through, I assured them. The group sat respectfully listening to me, the "expert," talk about something I couldn't even fathom. It was immediately clear to all of us that I wasn't getting through.

Finally, a man in the back row raised his hand and said in a gentle voice, "You don't know what we feel—no one can ever know until it happens." Everyone nodded in agreement. "Please, never say that you understand what we are going through, because you can't. Some of our friends say the same thing and they don't know what they're talking about."

An honest discussion emerged. Their children's death was beyond description in terms of its impact. What they were least prepared for, however, was their social isolation. Yes, the two or three weeks after the death, their friends had been wonderful—bringing food to the house, offering to help do the shopping, taking care of their other children. But then, the phone calls stopped. Their friends and coworkers began to avoid them. Casual conversations became stilted because no one wanted to broach the topic of the death.

One couple tearfully recounted what had happened to them in the three months since the death of their two-year-old son. They were deeply religious, and their entire social life revolved around their small, tightly knit church. In fact, the church had organized several services to pray for their son when he was diagnosed as having a terminal liver disease. About a month after their son's death, the couple began to feel ostracized by the minister and other church members. Former close friends no longer sat by them during regular church services. They were no longer invited to informal social gatherings. Whenever they tried to talk about their son's death, people quickly changed the topic of conversation. In the span of three months, they had lost their son and their entire social support group. Finally, when they hinted to their minister that they might join another church in a neighboring town, he agreed that it "would probably be best for everyone."

The social problems faced by bereaved parents are readily apparent. The parents desperately want to talk about their loss with others. Their friends, however, find the topic too horrifying and psychologically threatening to even think about. Friends of the grieving parents often deal with the problem by simply avoiding the parents altogether.

Interestingly, the problem is exacerbated by the lack of any clear norms on how to behave. In interviews, friends of people who have faced a trauma fear that by their broaching the topic, the traumatized person will become upset. On numerous occasions, I have heard individuals say, "I didn't want to remind them about it," or "I thought it would be best to try to keep their minds off it," or even, "If they wanted to talk about it, they would have said so." These rationalizations that most of us have used at one time or another may occasionally be true. However, my own experience tells me that we usually employ these beliefs so that we won't have to hear about the traumas ourselves.

If a friend of yours has suffered the death of a child or relative or faced some other significant trauma, your friend is probably thinking about it a great deal. Don't be hesitant to ask if he or she would like to talk about it. Platitudes such as "You will get over it," "I know just how you feel," or "At least you had some good times together," are usually not helpful. Unless you have dealt with a similar trauma, you probably don't know how your friend feels. For your friend's own good, let him or her talk freely about the loss. Finally, if you have fond memories of your friend's child or relative, mention them. Even if the death occurred several years earlier, your friend will be glad that the memory of his or her loved one lives on.

If you have suffered a loss, many of your friends will not know what to say or how to deal with your feelings. It is easy to interpret your friends' behaviors as being cruel or insensitive when it probably is not the case. Very often, they would like to talk about the tragedy but don't know how to bring up the subject. In casual conversations, both you and your friend may be thinking about your loss, but neither person says anything. As one person told me, "It is as if there is a giant elephant in the living room and both of us pretend nothing is there." Bereaved parents who have coped well tell me that they have learned to say something like, "Please feel free to talk about it." In other words, the burden of introducing the topic will be on you.

Finally, I strongly recommend support groups. In most cities, there are groups of people who have suffered traumas similar to yours. For the loss of a child, groups such as Compassionate Friends or Bereaved Parents can be invaluable. Similar groups are available for people who have lost a lover, spouse, or family member due to suicide, AIDS, or other tragedy. Other organizations that focus on specific problems—such as drug and alcohol problems, eating disorders, compulsive gambling, smoking, victimization from rape or violence, and spouse or child abuse—can be found in most areas of the country. If you are unable to locate a relevant group, contact a United Way office or crisis center in your area. Note that groups such as these encourage talking among people who have faced similar problems rather than provide therapy or counseling per se.

MARITAL PROBLEMS RESULTING FROM SHARED TRAUMAS

In normal social situations where one person has experienced a trauma and the other hasn't, the two people are in fundamentally different psychological states. A very different problem occurs when two people have both suffered the same loss. Among parents who have lost a child, divorce rates are far above national averages. Similarly, couples who share other types of traumas, such as financial ruin, the arrest of a child, or even moving to a new community, are at higher risk for marital problems.

A shared trauma is particularly difficult because neither person is able to provide strong support for the other since both are grieving. This problem is compounded by the fact that people tend to grieve at their own pace, in their own way. I saw a tragic example of this in a recent interview with Dolores, a woman who had just separated from her husband of eighteen years following the accidental shooting death of their fourteen-year-old son seven months earlier:

> Bob [her husband] withdrew the minute he heard about the shooting. He would sit at the supper table and not say a word. I always was crying, wanting to talk about Mikey [the son]. Bob sometimes just got mad at me for talking so much. The more I wanted him to listen, the quieter he got. . . . He didn't touch me. He didn't want anything to do with me. . . . Bob's brother told me that they'd go fishing together and sometimes he would cry like a baby. After Mikey's death, I never saw one tear from him.

Dolores's case raises the issue of the different grieving styles of men and women. In general, women in our society are more likely to openly express their emotions for longer periods of time than are men. Perhaps because of our cultural beliefs that men should be tough, men are far less likely to cry or, following a major loss, to talk about their feelings of sadness. This, of course, is not always true. In about a third of the couples I have interviewed, the men are more openly expressive than their spouses. When grieving styles are markedly different between the spouses, problems often occur because one spouse may think that the other is not sufficiently sensitive. By the same token, a spouse who is more quiet or withdrawn can feel as though the other is not understanding of his or her intense emotions. Marital therapists attempt to remedy these problems by getting both spouses to openly talk about their feelings. Communication, whether by openly expressing emotions or simply by talking, is the key to the survival of a relationship following a shared trauma.

TALKING TO OTHERS: BENEFITS AND DANGERS OF SOCIAL SUPPORT

In 1976, Stanley Cobb, a researcher from the University of Michigan, published a groundbreaking article that demonstrated the health benefits of having a friendship network during times of stress. In summarizing several large-scale studies, Cobb found that a friendship or social-support network protected people from illness and death following a wide range of tragedies. Since then, hundreds of studies have supported his conclusions. Health problems following rape, miscarriages, death of a family member, job loss, divorce, and other traumas are greatly reduced if people can turn to close friends.

In recent years, our understanding of social support has expanded considerably. A friendship network can buffer the effects of stress in a variety of ways. One of the most obvious is that friends can provide money, food, housing, or other tangible benefits if needed. They also can offer advice and an objective perspective to help people deal with problems in their lives. Hardly earth-shattering psychological news.

More interesting is that having a strong friendship network can help people maintain a stable view of their world and of themselves. One of the frightening aspects of traumas is that they cause us to question who we are. When a person unexpectedly loses her job due to layoffs, for example, she may try to understand it by saying to herself, I deserved it; I am a bad person. As discussed in the last chapter, self-blame is a relatively common result of upheavals. Without friends, people are much more likely to blame themselves, since they have no other concrete information available to them. William Swann of the University of Texas at Austin has shown that in times of crisis, friends maintain people's self-esteem. After a layoff, then, friends subtly bolster the person's world view by assuring her that she is, in fact, a good person.

Ironically, friends can also maintain some people's low self-esteem. In a series of interesting experiments, Jonathon Brown of the University of Washington has found that people with low self-esteem have major difficulties dealing with success. Hence, if you basically hate yourself, you may become distressed if you receive a large raise or learn that others think you are a fascinating person. Interestingly, people with a poor view of themselves who do not have a friendship circle have particularly severe health problems with success. When they have a friendship network, however, low-self-esteem people have fewer health problems following success because their "friends" assure them that they probably didn't deserve the success. In other words, a social network can keep us healthy by maintaining our self-view no matter what happens to us.

I recently witnessed an amazing example of this with a student who had written a brilliant paper for one of my classes. The student had always had a very low opinion of himself and was genuinely surprised by my enthusiastic comments. A week later, he mentioned a letter from his father that said, in essence, Anyone can write a psychology paper. Why did you make B− in your accounting course? The student's low self-esteem remained intact. He is now an accounting major.

Fortunately, most people have reasonably good feelings about themselves and also have access to social support. My own belief is that the most interesting and perhaps potent benefit of social support is in providing an outlet for people to talk about their thoughts and feelings. In large surveys with corporate employees as well as college students, for example, we find the same thing that other social-support researchers have shown: The more friends you have, the healthier you are. However, this effect is due, almost exclusively, to the degree to which you have talked with your friends about any traumas that you have suffered.

But here is the kicker. If you have had a trauma that you have not talked about with anyone, the number of friends you have is unrelated to your health. Social support only protects your health if you use it wisely. That is, if you have suffered a major upheaval in your life, talk to your friends about it. Merely having friends is not enough.

CHOOSING A CONFIDANT

One reason I recommend writing about upsetting experiences is that it is safe. If you use a journal to explore your deepest thoughts and feelings, you can be completely honest with yourself. No one else will judge you, criticize you, or distort your perceptions of the world. Writing, however, has its drawbacks. It can be a slow and painful process. Many people find it difficult to express themselves on paper. Sometimes, people's perceptions of their own world can be distorted.

Ideally, we should be able to express all our most intimate thoughts to someone. But we can't. Even with our closest friends, there are usually some topics that we avoid because what we say might deeply hurt their feelings or make us look bad in their eyes. Is it possible to be totally honest with another person? Yes, sometimes. But there are several issues that must be considered before disclosing ourselves. In addition, there are important implications for a relationship when we let our guard down and honestly talk.

Trust. Central to true self-disclosure is an overriding sense of trust. In 1987, Cheryl Hughes, Robin O'Heeron, and I examined the importance of trust in a project that we dubbed the father-confessor study. Forty-eight college students were asked to talk about their most traumatic experience for a few minutes while we continuously monitored their physiological levels. Half of the students sat alone in a room and talked into a tape recorder. The other half spoke aloud to a psychology professor they did not know who sat on the other side of a curtain. That psychology professor was me. They never saw me and I never saw them. They were told that I would just sit there and never respond to anything they said—all of which was true.

When alone, students let go and disclosed highly intimate parts of themselves. Indeed, their physiological measures, such as skin conductance levels, indicated that the highly disclosing students were not inhibiting what they said. Among the students talking to the anonymous father confessor, however, their physiological levels were constantly elevated. They remained on guard the entire time. Afterward, they admitted that they didn't trust the person sitting on the other side of the curtain. One student, for example, noted that it was impossible that the father confessor was really a psychology professor because his shoes (which they could see) were shabby and cheap(!).

There is a certain irony in these findings. People readily opened up when talking into a tape recorder even though they didn't know who would ever listen to the tape. When there was an anonymous person present, however, they became reticent in expressing their feelings and experiences.

Nonjudgmental responses from the listener. People are far more likely to disclose their feelings if they feel safe that others won't criticize what they say. Carl Rogers, the influential founder of client-centered therapy, maintained that the effectiveness of therapy hinged on a therapist who held the client in high regard no matter what was said. Even if a client had murdered his parents and robbed churches for a living, Rogers believed that it was critical to accept the individual.

The logic of Rogers's approach is sound. If individuals honestly disclose their feelings about something, their feelings are real. To deny their feelings and perceptions is to deny the person. Several studies have found that when people are punished for disclosing their traumatic experiences, their psychological and physical health suffers. Nowhere has this been more striking than among people who have been victimized by incest.

Molly, a twenty-year-old undergraduate, came to my office on learning that I was interested in eating disorders and psychosomatics. In addition to being about fifty pounds overweight, she suffered from a variety of health problems including ulcers, migraine headaches, and high blood pressure. Both her natural parents were normal weight and healthy. Molly, too, had been in good health until age fifteen. Her parents divorced when she was around age four, and her mother remarried when she was twelve. In my experience, when people become overweight and sickly within a short period of time during adolescence, there is a better than average chance that a sexual trauma occurred.

After talking with Molly for about an hour, I broached the issue of sex. Specifically, was she a victim of incest or rape shortly before her weight and health change? Her face flushed and she was silent for almost a minute. Yes, she finally admitted, about that time her mother had gone out of town on business and her stepfather had molested her. The trauma did not end there. On her mother's return, she told her what had happened. According to Molly, her mother denied that any molestation had taken place, saying that the stepfather was undoubtedly just being affectionate. In that instant, Molly lost her only confidant and friend—her mother. Although the molestation stopped, Molly could never be honest with her mother again.

Because I have studied so many college students who are still grappling with the last stages of identity crises, our studies reveal that at least a third of our participants complain about their relationships with their parents. Of these complaints, the majority deal with the perceptions of parents as judgmental. Especially in late adolescence, individuals want both autonomy and some degree of security. Parents, who usually have the best interest of their children at heart, seek to provide moral and intelligent guidance to help shape their children's lives. Guidance, unfortunately, usually entails judgment. With the prospect of their attitudes or behaviors being judged critically, many adolescents opt to shut out their parents, ceasing to use them as confidants at all. According to Roy Baumeister of Case Western University, the attainment of identity in our culture virtually guarantees that teenagers not confide many central aspects of their lives to their parents.

The safe but anonymous listener.   Several of the psychologists I know travel frequently. On planes, many avoid identifying themselves as psychologists because their fellow passengers often want to tell them everything about their lives. In my own case, I have heard innumerable shocking, heartbreaking and, professionally speaking (of course), fascinating stories. On one recent trip, a woman quietly confided her marital infidelity and unhappy marriage as her husband slept soundly next to her. Airline passengers are not the only ones to hear stories such as these. Studies suggest that bartenders, taxi drivers, prostitutes, and hairdressers serve as listeners to people's confessions.

Why do people tell their deepest thoughts and feelings to strangers but not to their spouses or friends? It's not that they trust the listeners or even that the listeners are nonjudgmental. Rather, according to the classic sociologist Georg Simmel, it is freedom from recrimination. If I want to talk to my airplane seatmate about my darkest secrets, I am safe with the knowledge that I will never see the person again. That knowledge is liberating. By definition, whatever I say will never affect any long-term relationship. Further, if the person *is* judgmental, it will have no ramifications.

One of the most fascinating developments attesting to the urge to confess to others who are safe and anonymous is the confession hotline. Starting in Los Angeles in 1988, confession hotlines are telephone numbers that people call to disclose their deepest secrets. Tandem phone numbers are often available to allow callers to listen to others' confessions. According to Jeanne McDowell in a recent *Time* magazine article, the Los Angeles confession hotline receives two hundred confessions a day and up to ten thousand calls to the tandem numbers for people to listen to the confessions.

The professional listener. Before the growth of psychotherapy, people often disclosed their deepest secrets to their religious leaders, private physicians, or alternative healers such as palm or tea-leaf readers. In most cases, these professional listeners offered trust and confidentiality. Beginning in the 1950s, America and Europe witnessed a rapid expansion in the professionalization of listening. Graduate programs in clinical and various forms of counseling psychology, for example, produced about 370 therapists in 1960, compared with almost 2,000 in 1980.

At the same time that therapy was growing, other professions that had informally provided therapy declined in numbers or phased out the therapy role. In medicine, for example, there has been a drop in the number of general practitioners. Church attendance has dropped. Even within many religions, the role of the minister or rabbi has changed. Many large congregations now employ a therapist to provide counseling. A fascinating symptom of this change can be seen in the Roman Catholic Church. Before the early 1970s, weekly private confessions were strongly encouraged. After Vatican II, however, the confession procedure became much more informal. The confession booth, or confessional, is fast becoming obsolete, with face-to-face meetings with the priest replacing it on an as-needed basis.

Psychotherapy offers a powerful setting for the disclosure of secrets, thoughts, and emotions. Therapists usually provide the essential ingredients of honest self-disclosure: trust, nonjudgmental feedback, and safety from recrimination. Distressed individuals also receive specific information on ways to cope with the source and symptoms of their stress. Therapy can also help people feel better about themselves more quickly than writing. A recent study by Edward Murray, Alicia Lamnin, and Charles Carver of the University of Miami compared two sessions of confessional writing with two sessions of brief psychotherapy. Although both methods were equally good at reducing subsequent health problems, people in psychotherapy reported feeling happier and less distressed after each session.

Professional listeners play a central role in our society. Large-scale studies indicate that psychotherapy of any form is effective in reducing physical-health problems, depression, and an array of major and minor thought and behavior disorders. If you or a friend suffers from an intractable psychological problem, I *strongly* recommend psychotherapy. Writing about your deepest thoughts and feelings should not be used as a substitute for therapy. Much as talking to a friend, writing is best viewed as a form of preventive maintenance.

Is transference necessary? In developing psychoanalysis, Freud emphasized that therapy could only be effective if patients transferred their deepest or repressed emotions to the therapist. These basic emotions, which had usually been associated with a parent, were now the basis of a powerful attachment between the patient and the therapist. Often, when the transference of emotion occurs, the patient expresses deep love and/or hate toward the therapist. More recent views of therapy continue to hold that the patient must develop some type of emotional attachment with the therapist if therapy is to succeed.

In a sense, some degree of transference is necessary within a therapeutic relationship. However, therapeutic gains can follow from writing or even talking to a stranger on a plane—situations where transference is irrelevant. Freud and his followers, I think, confused therapy with a therapeutic relationship. When people begin therapy, for example, they know that they will be maintaining a close bond with the therapist for an extended period of time. They must implicitly trust the therapist before they feel safe divulging their secrets. Hence, the therapeutic dance must take place.

The therapeutic dance occurs during the first few sessions of therapy, wherein the patients gauge their therapists' reactions, trustworthiness, and competence. In any kind of ongoing relationship, the building of trust takes time. At first, patients divulge a little about themselves and carefully monitor the reaction of the therapist. As in the mating dances of birds or lovers, the patient and therapist go through a period of posturing before basic disclosure can occur. With writing or talking to strangers, the elements of disclosure are immediately present.

Final considerations in choosing a confidant. In our lives, we face a number of upsetting events that we want to discuss with someone. Divulging our deepest feelings can forge a powerful and lasting bond with others. Several experiments, for example, suggest that when one person discloses a secret to another, the other person often reciprocates. The interpersonal cycle of self-disclosure, according to social psychologists Irwin Altman and Dalmas Taylor, works much like the therapeutic dance between therapist and client. If neither person is rebuffed during the dance, the nature of disclosures becomes more intimate over time. Once the cycle is in place, the two people will have established a stable and trusting relationship that will provide an outlet for disclosure in case of future traumas.

But the dance can also pose psychological and social risks. People who unburden themselves and then are rejected by the listener can become depressed, hostile, and withdrawn. If you are currently living with a trauma and need to talk with someone, there are several safeguards that you should consider.

1. Self-disclosure will change the nature of your friendship. Usually, revealing a deep secret will bring you and your friend closer. However, your friend may be threatened or hurt by what you say. If this happens, your relationship may be at risk. Telling your spouse about your desires for an extramarital affair, for example, may result in recriminations rather than understanding.

2. Hearing your traumas can be a trauma for the listener. Oftentimes, the listener will need to discuss what you said with someone else. Your urge to confess may become contagious. How many times have you heard and later passed on someone else's secret? Gossip, although sometimes motivated by malice, can reflect people's needs to discuss unsettling information with others.

3. Social blackmail exists. Telling your dark secret can put the listener in a powerful position. The biblical story of Samson and Delilah serves as a nice illustration. Under God's orders, Samson was supposed to keep his secret that the source of his strength was his hair. In a weak moment, he confided his secret to his lover, Delilah, who then sold the information to the Philistines. The upshot of Samson's poor judgment was that he lost his secret, his hair, and his strength.

4. The expectations of the listener can affect the content of the disclosure. People can consciously or unconsciously change the ways they explain and interpret their deepest thoughts and feelings depending on their audience. The description of your feelings about a sexual trauma may variously emphasize guilt, powerlessness, or anger if your listener is a religious leader, psychologist, or the perpetrator. Ideally, your listener should allow you to explore all of your conflicting feelings about the event.

5. People's motivations for disclosing their secrets are not always pure. Before disclosing an intimate secret to someone, ask yourself why you are choosing this particular person. In my research, I have been struck by the times that people have truly hurt others by confiding. Although they claim to be acting in an honest and open way, their disclosures are clearly motivated by revenge. The tenor of the confession is often You hurt me, so I am going to hurt you.

6. Telling and holding secrets can be a maladaptive substitute for taking action. Many times, an upsetting experience can be corrected directly. As a manager of a research team, I have witnessed many cases where one person unintentionally hurt the feelings of another. The aggrieved individual either stewed about the event or complained to others. In most of these cases, the entire incident could have been resolved if the aggrieved person simply expressed his or her feelings to the person who caused the problem in the first place.

THE BURDEN OF LISTENING TO OTHERS' TRAUMAS

A central theme of this chapter has centered on the distinction between confronting and being confronted by traumas. Psychologically confronting your own trauma by talking about it can be healthy. Being confronted by someone else's trauma can be an emotional burden. Indeed, listening to accounts of traumatic experiences may pose a health risk.

In 1985 when I began the Holocaust project, I was not ready for the horrors that I would soon hear. About a week after interviewing my first two Holocaust survivors, I was devastated by a case of influenza. At the time, of course, I was certain that my illness had nothing to do with stress—I had just been exposed to a flu virus, that's all. In looking back, I have no doubts that my interviews probably compromised my immune system, thereby making me more vulnerable to illness.

In talking about this experience with one of my graduate students, Joann Wu Shortt, it occurred to us that we could examine the biological changes of people who watched the videotapes of the Holocaust survivors. And that is exactly what we did. About sixty students watched one of thirty videotapes in groups of two while we monitored their skin conductance and heart rate. We then compared their physiological records on a minute-by-minute basis with those of the survivors during the time that the survivors were talking. Overall, the more the survivors' skin conductance levels dropped while they talked about traumatic experience, the more the viewers' skin conductance levels increased. Whereas talking about horrors reduced inhibition (as measured by skin conductance), hearing accounts of the horrors brought about increases. In other words, simply watching and listening to people talk about traumatic experiences on a television monitor brought about pronounced physiological activity.

Even in the laboratory, hearing an upsetting story can be unsettling and physiologically arousing. Imagine what happens to people who are confronted with hearing dozens of stories about traumas. I know from my own experience with the Holocaust project that the more interviews I conducted, the less I wanted to participate. After about a dozen interviews over the course of a year, I found myself coming up with excuses not to conduct an interview. Indeed, after two years, virtually none of the original fifteen interviewers for the Holocaust project was still participating. Our ability to empathize with the survivors' lives was severely undermined. We had become victims of burnout.

Burnout was first examined in the late 1970s by Berkeley psychologist Christina Maslach. Individuals in many "people-work" occupations often report that over time, they become emotionally exhausted and callous and derive less satisfaction from their job. Professions with the highest rates of burnout include nursing, social work, and even sales and personnel positions. Each of these professions has traditionally had a high turnover rate, greater than average absenteeism due to illness, and reports of job dissatisfaction.

Burnout, in many respects, is a problem of inhibition. One of the dangers of repeatedly being confronted by other people's traumas is that there is very little opportunity to talk about them. Particularly damaging, according to Maslach, is that burnout victims feel as though they have very little control over the lives of the people they talk with. This explains why physicians and therapists are less prone to burnout than similar groups such as nurses, who have far less control. The more control the listener has in affecting the talker's life, the healthier the listener will be.

The symptoms of burnout are not limited to individuals in the helping professions. They can occur among friends of traumatized individuals. One of my research assistants, in telling me about her best friend, who was being psychologically abused by her husband, explained to me one afternoon:

> When Sally and Rick first started having problems, Sally came by my apartment every day after work. She would tell me everything that Rick was doing to her. Taunting her, telling her about other women, physically threatening her. It killed me to see her so upset. I kept saying, "Get out of the relationship, kick him out of the house." She ignored me and kept on complaining about what a horrible person Rick was. I tried to be as supportive as I could. After a couple of weeks, the minute I saw her I would feel exhausted and depressed. I started studying in the library after school just so I would miss her if she came by. Now I'm thinking that it is her own fault that she is still with Rick. I don't have it in me to care about her anymore.

Not only was Sally in a terrible marriage, but in her attempt to cope with it, she had destroyed her relationship with her long-time friend. Could there have been some way for my research assistant to avoid burnout without compromising her friendship with Sally? Second-guessing a relationship is always difficult. However, had my assistant been more attentive to her own feelings about Sally's effect on her, she might have been able to take corrective actions sooner.

Listening to others' problems is an art for which we have very little training. One of the very first cases I worked on involved a young man who had an intense phobia associated with dogs licking their genitals. Whenever he witnessed a dog behaving in this way, he experienced an uncontrollable wave of anxiety so severe that he had to go home immediately and drink several beers. The problem apparently stemmed from his childhood when, around age eight, he witnessed his older brother engaging in oral sex with his uncle.

Because it was my first case, I was overwhelmed by the man's suffering and the incident itself. Professionally, I knew that I should not talk about this case with anyone. But the images kept recurring in my mind. I remember visiting my girlfriend, now my wife, and trying not to talk about the case. After half an hour of small talk, I couldn't control myself any longer. I blurted out the entire story. Ruth admonished me sternly, noting that I should talk to another psychologist about my cases and never to her. Ever.

That experience has been a vivid reminder that listening to others' traumatic stories is stressful. It is also a learned art. When psychologists and other people in the helping professions undergo training, they usually spend one or more years working under the close supervision of an experienced clinician. Every case they work on is discussed in detail with the supervisor. This period of supervision serves as a training ground for keeping other people's secrets. Now, several years later, I can listen to any kind of trauma at work and not think about it a single time when I get home.

Unfortunately, learning to suppress thoughts of other people's secret lives can take months or years. Assuming you don't want to spend the next few years in graduate school, how can you be a trustworthy listener when someone wants to tell you something intensely personal and upsetting? In posing this question to clinical psychologists, I usually get two overlapping answers. The first is to write about it. (This may be a biased response, since the clinicians I have asked know about my research.) The second recommendation is to talk about it in veiled form to someone who doesn't know the person from whom you have heard the secret.

You might consider calling a long-distance friend, for example. Remember, however, that talking it over with anyone always poses a risk, because your behavior could be interpreted as a betrayal of trust.

The final strategy in listening to another's problems is knowing when to quit. When another person's trauma starts to become your trauma, your relationship with that person—as well as your own psychological and physical health—is at risk. You must honestly be able to admit to yourself and to the other person that you can no longer cope with the problem. Never be embarrassed to recommend a therapist or a support group. What may appear to be callous may also be far more helpful for your friend and yourself.

9

Love, Passion, and Thrills

Falling passionately in love. Having a baby. Delivering my first well-received talk to a professional audience. These have been some of the experiences in my life that have been absolutely, totally thrilling. With each one, I walked on air—everything was right with the world. Each experience dominated my thoughts and conversations for days afterward.

Ironically, there are remarkable parallels between our reactions to exhilarating and to devastating events. In addition to producing similar levels of emotional intensity, both classes of events trigger recurring thoughts and the urge to talk about them. Is it possible that both positive and negative experiences result in comparable physiological responses and unwanted health outcomes? To the degree that inhibition plays a key role, I think the answer may be yes.

Feeling good is different from feeling bad. Hardly a profound insight. More interesting, however, is that our bodies react similarly to disclosing diverse positive and negative experiences. Jeanne Czajka, one of my graduate students, and I discovered this peculiarity a few years ago in a simple laboratory experiment. In the study, we asked twenty-four students to write about the most traumatic and the most wonderful experiences of their entire lives for four minutes each. We also asked them to write on a trivial topic such as describing the shoes they were wearing. The entire time that the participants wrote, we measured their skin conductance, heart rate, and blood pressure levels.

Not surprisingly, writing about traumas made the volunteers feel miserable and writing about wonderful ones made them happy. Although the writing assignments produced different moods, they yielded identical physiological patterns. Compared with their biological states before the experiment, their skin conductance levels dropped and their blood pressure levels temporarily increased. Writing about trivial topics resulted in totally different patterns.

What particularly fascinated us were the topics about which people chose to write. The traumatic experiences were similar to those in our other studies: death of loved ones, breakup of relationships, sexual or violent traumas. About a third of the exhilarating topics dealt with love and passion; another third, on winning awards or the praise from others. The remaining positive experiences were quite diverse: getting a pet, having a child, viewing the terrain from a mountainside. For several people, there was an odd symmetry between their best and worst experiences. For example, one person's best experience, falling in love, resulted in his worst when the relationship ended. Another's best was getting accepted to college with a scholarship, which soon brought about her worst memories of saying goodbye to her friends. One woman poignantly described the horror of learning that she was pregnant in high school. Later, she wrote that the most wonderful experience of her life was getting married and having the baby.

Wonderful and traumatic experiences are often intertwined. Not discussing or understanding one may make the other even more difficult to grasp. The disclosure of both positive and negative events brings about comparable physiological changes that reflect the letting-go process. All biological changes between expressing good and bad events are not identical, of course. In writing about traumas, people often cry. Disclosing positive events can lead to the expression of smiles and laughter. The central physiological similarity, then, between the disclosure of positive and negative thoughts and feelings is in the reduction of inhibition.

Are positive experiences a health risk? Consider findings from previous studies. We know that horrible traumas are associated with a variety of diseases. Writing about them, however, reduces physiological activity and improves health. But writing about positive experiences also lowers physiological levels in the same ways. Several large-scale studies find that presumably positive life experiences, such as marriage, childbirth, job promotion, and sudden wealth, are correlated with increased incidence of heart disease, hospitalizations, and minor health problems. Even less dramatic positive events are linked to illnesses. A recent study that my students and I conducted found that women who succeeded in getting into the sorority of their choice went to the health center almost three times more frequently in the month after they were selected than did women who failed to be selected.

Why do positive life events correlate with health problems? At least three overlapping factors contribute to this peculiar phenomenon. First, many positive events, such as marriage or childbirth, greatly disrupt people's lives and self-images. The transitions from single to married or from free and easygoing to parent require that individuals understand and assimilate new views of themselves and adapt to new roles in society. Similarly, with the change in roles, people often face a host of new tasks that they may not be prepared for. A second phenomenon that occurs following a positive life transition is psychological letdown. Accountants get sick after April 15; law students, after final exams; people are more likely to die right after important anniversaries. When people work toward an important goal, their physiological and psychological defenses are up. Further, their lives have a sense of meaning and purpose. As soon as the goal is reached, however, their bodies undergo a number of biological changes that often accompany a state of helplessness such as lowered immune function.

Finally, many supremely positive events are linked to inhibition. That is, people may feel wonderful but are unable to express their thoughts and feelings to anyone. A person who has just won an important competition can have difficulties talking about the event if all of his friends were his competitors. Indeed, in our sorority study, women who got into top sororities whose roommates failed to do so had the highest illness rates. As one woman noted:

> At first, getting into [a top-rated sorority] was the best thing that ever happened. But since I am the only one on my hall that got into the one they wanted, I can't talk about it with anyone . . . Last night, I went to the 7-11 to call [a friend from high school] to tell her about getting into [the sorority]. I couldn't stand to have my roommate hear me boast.

From what I have said, don't get the impression that wonderful events are inherently unhealthy. It is far healthier to face a positive life change than a horrible trauma. Similarly, feelings of euphoria, joy, pride, and happiness are fun and usually associated with good health. The basic issue is what we do with positive experiences and the good moods that follow. As with traumas, positive events should be talked about and openly expressed. Actively holding them back is yet another form of inhibition—with all the attendant health risks.

In the last few years, a surge of studies have demonstrated that openly expressing positive feelings is extremely healthy. Much of this work was spurred by Norman Cousins who, in 1976, published an article in the *New England Journal of Medicine* detailing how he recovered from a form of cancer by laughing and taking large doses of vitamin C. Following his diagnosis, Cousins watched humorous movies and induced himself to laugh heartily throughout the day. He found that ten minutes of belly laughter greatly reduced his pain as well as various physiological markers of inflammation. More recently, Herbert Lefcourt and Rod Martin of the University of Waterloo in Canada report that they and others have found links between laughter and improved immune function, cardiovascular tone, and pain endurance.

Positive emotions, then, are most healthy when they are openly expressed. If you are in the unhappy position of not being able to express your euphoria after a wonderful event, write and laugh about it while you are alone.

FORBIDDEN PLEASURES: SEX, LOVE, AND PASSION

Modern-day psychologists tend to dismiss many of Freud's contributions by claiming that he overemphasized sexuality. Indeed, he studied people who grew up in Victorian society, where the mere mention of sex was taboo. Now, the reasoning goes, the pleasures of sexuality are open topics and no longer drive psychological problems as they did in Freud's time.

Oh, really?

At both Southern Methodist University and Stanford University, I have asked several hundred students to write down their most secret or forbidden thought. For both men and women college students, sexual thoughts are expressed by over two thirds of the people. The most common include: sex with multiple partners; sex with someone they love; sex on a desert island with a friend or acquaintance; or just plain old sex. Sure, some forbidden thoughts include suicide, murder (as in "kill the professor"), getting a straight-A average, and making the world a better place. But sex, at least among college students, appears to be a common obsession.

And not just college students. Adults in communities across the country are dealing with graphic sexual and aggressive movies, books, and magazines that exploit children and adults. Peep shows, strip joints, and prostitution cater to adults of all ages. On top of all of this, rates of rape, incest, sexual killings, and teenage pregnancies have increased markedly over the last two decades.

What is driving America's obsession with sex? Is it that we are now completely free to talk about it in an open way, as some antipornography proponents claim? I doubt it. We obsess about sex because we are not able to openly discuss our deepest thoughts and feelings about our sexuality. This is not a legal issue. Rather, in most families, frank and open discussions about sexuality are discouraged. For most, the few discussions about sex are usually limited to father-son and mother-daughter lectures about the birds and the bees, birth control, and perhaps AIDS. How many dinnertable conversations in your childhood focused on deep and self-reflective feelings related to masturbation, homosexuality, or passionate love?

In a recent survey of almost a hundred college undergraduates, 83 percent reported that they had never discussed masturbation in an open way with their families. Almost 70 percent had never had a discussion about passionate sexual love with family members. The median number of frank talks about homosexuality was only two. Contrast these numbers with their current concerns about sexuality. Within the last twenty-four hours, the average student thought about sex three times but did not talk about it with anyone. Most important in all of this was that the more that the students openly talked about sexuality in their families, the less they currently obsess about sex.

The more people openly talk about an issue, the less they obsess about it. Whether the topic of concern is a recent trauma such as the death of a spouse or it surrounds a broad issue such as sexuality, talking neutralizes unwanted or recurring thoughts.

Pornography as a symptom of family dynamics. It is little wonder, then, that our society faces major upheavals concerning pornography. We are dealing with a fundamental conflict between sexual issues in the home and the broader legal trends concerning free speech in society. Important topics that are actively excluded from open discussion—especially those driven by biological drives—will become the source of recurring thoughts and fantasies. Without talking to others about strong sexual drives, individuals can never gauge if their urges are normal or healthy. Ironically, access to erotic material, whether from the pages of *National Geographic* or *Slash* magazine, can serve as the only education that many adolescents will receive about their sexual feelings.

It strikes me that our society must make a choice in dealing with sexuality. One alternative is to return to the repressive standards of Freud's era, when sexuality was never openly discussed and pornography was, by and large, unavailable. Because people will always masturbate and have sexual urges, this strategy will assure a variety of neuroses but statistically fewer sex crimes. The second approach is to encourage a more open and accepting view of sexuality in the family and other social institutions such as schools, churches, and the like. Note that such a strategy goes far beyond the current teaching of sex education that emphasizes cold biological facts. People, especially adolescents, need to talk and think about their own deep feelings surrounding sexuality, love, and passion. Although talking and writing about sexuality may make it less mysterious, it would also come to be viewed as a normal and less emotionally charged biological urge.

Homosexuality and AIDS. Anthropological and cross-cultural research indicates that homosexuality exists in virtually all cultures. Indeed, a 1951 study of remote cultures found that the majority openly accepted it as a normal sexual practice. In the United States, the Kinsey surveys indicate that 37 percent of men and 13 percent of women have had at least one orgasm with a person of their own sex by the age of forty-five. Current estimates of exclusively homosexual individuals are 4 percent of men and 1 percent of women. Despite widespread homosexual behavior, homosexuality remains frowned upon in our society.

Gay women and men in our society face a terrible dilemma. The open admission of homosexuality brings with it potential social censure. In many states, homosexuals can be barred from jobs in education, religion, and, of course, the military. Indeed, recent Supreme Court decisions have upheld laws that make many homosexual behaviors criminal offenses. Unfortunately, society's concern with regulating sexual preferences forces a large percentage of gays to remain in the closet. In effect, hundreds of thousands of Americans are opting to live secret lives.

Living a lie is living a life of inhibition. People who are unable to talk about significant personal experiences are at increased risk for a variety of diseases. Although there is very little good data, our surveys at Southern Methodist University indicate that gay men and women go to the health center for illness far more frequently than heterosexuals.

The health problems of gay men are compounded by the current epidemic of AIDS. Even among gay men not infected with the HIV virus, the fear of AIDS, together with the inhibition of daily life, results in their scrutinizing their bodies far more closely for signs of illness. Among HIV-positive individuals, the problems are far more severe. It would follow, for example, that to the degree to which a person's friendship network disapproves of homosexuality, the faster the person will die once he is diagnosed with AIDS.

It is too early to tell if psychotherapy or expressive writing can prolong the lives of AIDS patients. We and others are currently testing this idea. Nevertheless, I am optimistic. AIDS is an immunological disorder with symptoms that wax and wane with stress. Adults with AIDS are stigmatized for having the disease and, in cases of homosexuality or intravenous drug use, for their life-styles as well. Any techniques that can reduce the stress of inhibition among AIDS sufferers will surely provide some physical and psychological relief.

Extramarital affairs.   Tens of thousands of computer users currently use electronic bulletin boards. Different bulletin boards are used to discuss dozens of topics, including politics, childrearing, scientific discoveries, restaurants, and sex. Lots of sex. Because users can be anonymous, many discussions are quite frank. A few months ago, this one caught my eye:

She is Venus.	The moment we first spoke there were sparks.
I love her.	We touch and steal glances at one another.
Her eyes.	Time stops as I fall into her brown gaze.
Warmth.	Our love making is so tender and pure.

And I am tortured.
I go home and my wife asks
What happened at work today?
I cannot look her in the eye.
What if she finds out?
I cannot hurt her. I love her.
And I am tortured.
At work.   I am in heaven, in a cloud, in a trance.
At home I act innocent and pretend.
At work.   We send notes. When will we meet again?
At home I am tearing myself apart.
And I am tortured.

    This man's torture is not unique to him. Roughly half of all married men and women have had an extramarital affair. From an inhibition perspective, marital infidelity places great stress on individuals. Whereas homosexuality requires that gay men and women inhibit their behavior in public settings, extramarital affairs demand inhibition at home. According to a well-known Spanish proverb, gold and love affairs are difficult to hide.

    James Lynch, a researcher at the Johns Hopkins Medical School, points out that affairs are particularly insidious because they undermine trust between marriage partners. In his view, trust is critical in protecting people from heart disease. Indeed, exciting new work by Redford Williams and his colleagues at Duke University Medical School suggests that people whose sense of trust is severely undermined are at greater risk for heart disease and other major health problems. One of the only studies to examine the health dangers of marital infidelity was undertaken by a Japanese pathologist, who studied 5,559 cases of sudden death due to heart attacks. Of the thirty-four cases involving heart attacks during sexual intercourse, 80 percent occurred during extramarital affairs. These findings do not speak directly to the issues of trust and inhibition. They suggest, however, that sex and deceit can be a risky combination.

    Homosexuality, extramarital affairs, and other forbidden sexual practices are further complicated by the intense emotions behind them. Sex and passion are exhilarating. When the experiences are new, people desperately want to talk about them. The social and marital costs of discussing these intensely pleasurable experiences are potentially devastating. There is an irony that subjectively positive events have such a close parallel with overwhelmingly negative traumas. Effective coping techniques may be the same.

In several interviews with gay men and women as well as with people engaged in affairs, I have found that writing has been effective in reducing their interpersonal stress levels. Although the majority of them have talked in detail with their lovers, most have found it necessary to reflect on their feelings and actions outside of their relationships. In our large-scale writing experiments, for example, every person who has disclosed alternative sexual practices has evidenced improvements in immune function and/or reductions in health-center illness visits.

COPING WITH PASSIONATE LOVE

Whether or not love is forbidden, let's not lose sight of the fact that love is grand. Not just love, but passionate love. The kind of love that drives us wild. That euphoric, thrilling, out-of-control, wonderful passion when we are unable to shake our lover from our minds. I can't help grinning as I think about it. It is almost sacrilegious to compare it with traumas.

But the links are inescapable.

Passionate love and horrible traumas are both characterized by all-consuming obsessions. They follow similar time courses. We have an overpowering need to talk about them. Consider, for example, the dominant themes in song lyrics, poetry, novels, and other art forms. People are driven to express life's most wonderful and most devastating experiences.

Feelings of passion are intense and unique emotions. As with any strong emotions and new experiences, we seek to understand them. Love letters and poetry may help to accomplish this goal. Among the classic poets, for example, the expression of love is usually accompanied by a desire to understand it:

> Love bade me welcome: yet my soul drew back,
>   Guilty of dust and sin.
> But quick-eyed Love, observing me grow slack
>   From my first entrance in,

Drew nearer to me, sweetly questioning
If I lacked anything.
George Herbert, *Love (III)*

Scholars, for example, emphasize poets' use of verse to integrate emotional expression with self-understanding of the emotions themselves. William Wordsworth, in his preface to *Lyrical Ballads*, explains poetry as:

the breath and finer spirit of all knowledge; it is the impassioned expression which is in the countenance of all Science. . . . I have said that poetry is the spontaneous overflow of powerful feelings: it takes its origin from emotion recollected in tranquillity.

Anaïs Nin, in the fifth volume of her diaries, expands this theme. In her view, the purpose of poetry is to express the subtle shades of emotional and psychological experience. During a time that she was undergoing psychoanalysis, she wrote:

I chose poetry and the metaphor not for the love of mystery or elusiveness but because that comes closer to the way we experience things deep down. Explicitness and directness cannot be applied to our psychic life. They are not subtle enough.

What we cannot see within ourselves, what we cannot seize within ourselves we project outside. A great part of our life is an invention to avoid confrontation with our deepest self. (p. 83)

If poetry and other art forms truly bring about a "confrontation with our deepest self," an unanticipated consequence emerges: the neutralizing of passion. In writing about love, as in the writing about grief, overpowering obsessions and emotions are most quickly understood and assimilated. Once we understand them, we are less driven to ponder them. Love letters, then, may be an antidote to love.

The Grinch who stole love.   "You are a cruel man," I remember my student Jeanne Czajka slyly remarking as we discussed the downside of love letters. She was one step ahead of me in knowing that we needed to perform an experiment to rob students of their current passions. The study we planned together was deviously simple.

With the help of Hema Patel and Kathleen Ferrara, we tested twenty-four college student volunteers who reported feeling infatuated with someone. Much to my surprise, almost everyone we contacted was in love or in a state of infatuation. Half of the students were asked to write for twenty minutes about their deepest thoughts and feelings about their infatuation. The remaining students wrote about a superficial topic such as their plans for the day. Before, immediately after, and about three months following the writing period, the students completed a brief questionnaire assessing their moods and degree of infatuation.

Immediately after writing, those who had written about their infatuation reported being happier and more upbeat than those who had written about trivial topics. Unfortunately, we received follow-up questionnaires from only about 60 percent of the participants, which poses a problem in interpreting our results. Nevertheless, there was a strong trend to suggest that self-reflective love writing tempered the infatuation that our volunteers were feeling about those of whom they originally wrote. But, alas, love was not dead. Even though the love writers were less infatuated about whom they had written, they had found new loves to replace them.

Although not a perfect study, I think the experiment illustrates the value, or perhaps danger, of writing about intense, positive experiences. Immediately after writing, our euphoria may briefly intensify. Over time, however, self-reflectively writing about the sources of our strong affections brings about an understanding and eventual diminishing of passion.

LOVE AND GRIEF: A TEMPORAL THEORY

I have yet to have a distraught person come into my office and say, "I am madly in love. When can I expect these feelings to go away?" As anyone who has been in love knows, the quality of love changes over time. Love can be passionate, delicate, or deep and abiding. Grief, too, changes in its intensity and tenor. In talking with people, I have been struck by a recurring pattern in the evolution of powerful emotions. Rather than gradually diminishing over time, intense feelings seem to transform themselves in stages. Although there are differences from person to person, most overpowering feeling states exhibit three distinct stages over a year and a half: intensity, plateau, and assimilation.

For both love and grief, people first enter a stage of intense emotional activation that lasts between four and six months. During the intensity stage, individuals constantly think about their new or departed lover. At about six months, people move to a relatively constant plateau of getting on with life. The plateau period, which lasts about a year, is characterized by a generally pleasant (in the case of love) or unpleasant (grief) mood state. Although people think about their new or departed love many times each day, the thoughts are more reflective and less emotionally charged. Around a year and a half after the entire process began, most people have assimilated or come to terms with the love or death. In the assimilation stage, passionate love is replaced by an enduring, loving friendship. In the place of intense grief come fond memories and new experiences.

Over the years, several people have generously allowed me to read and study their personal diaries. I have been particularly interested in the diaries of people whom I consider to be exceptionally healthy and well adjusted. Two diaries stand out. The first was written by a twenty-six-year-old woman named Julie, who had kept a diary since she was only ten. When she was twenty-two, she fell deeply in love with Charles—a man she married three years later. The second diary was written by Ellen who, at the age of sixty, unexpectedly lost John, her husband of forty years, to a heart attack. Five years after John's death she remarried and, by recent indications, is flourishing.

The intensity stage is easiest to identify. During the first four to six months, lovers and grievers are consumed with new emotions and recurring thoughts. The following diary entries were written two weeks after Julie's first date with Charles and, for Ellen, the death of John.

JULIE: I think I am in love! I honestly have never felt this way before about anyone—I *love* being with Charles, and my God he occupies my every thought. This weekend we were together the whole time. . . . I feel like I'm walking on clouds. It's the best!

ELLEN: Two weeks today. It's like yesterday and like forever.

I stroked his dear dead face and said, "Good night, sweet prince." And my beautiful life ended.

Three months later, both women were still in a stage of emotional intensity. Both diaries, however, indicate that the women were also beginning to think of other things. Their respective feelings of joy and grief, however, were dominant.

JULIE: The trip to California with Charles! It was the best trip ever. Since then we have talked so much and written many a letter back and forth. I've never felt like this before—it's a new one for me, that's for sure.

ELLEN: Three months and where am I? I play foolish games. His shaving glasses are still on the shaving mirror. I cry when I see dust on them, but I can't throw them away. . . . I still have aching memories of his death and of sad days in Spain. I wish he hadn't suffered.

Soon after these entries, the tenor of the emotions changed, suggesting that both women had entered the plateau phase. Julie, although she frequently refers to Charles, devotes much of her writing to problems at work or telephone conversations with her parents. Charles's presence, however, is always felt. Four months after the death of Bob, Ellen stopped writing in her diary for almost eight months. The reason, she later told me, was that she was trying to get on with life. Interestingly, it was during this period that Ellen volunteered to help a bereavement counselor write manuals on coping with death.

The following entry for Julie was written seven months after her first date with Charles. The entries for the previous week had been devoted to topics other than Charles.

JULIE: Last night Charles and I had another talk. I am convinced that we will end up together later in life. I am in love with him and he knows I am. It's very special. Sometimes I really do get scared about the future. I think we will be fine—it's just that I have never been in love before and here we are talking about the future. I'm learning a lot from this relationship—both about him and myself.

A little after one year, both Julie and Ellen exhibit signs of standing back and analyzing their situation. In Julie's situation, the mad passion is no longer ever-present. For Ellen, there has been a sharp drop in the intense grief she had been feeling in the four months after John's death.

JULIE: What is he thinking? It's like I want to jump inside his mind and know each thing that goes through his head. When we aren't hand in hand or not smiling I think that something's wrong. TRY REALITY, Julie. Couples aren't constantly smiling—starry eyed. . . . Oh, I do feel good about being with him. I feel that we are very close. Closer than I've ever been with anyone. But I do make it difficult for people to get to know me.

ELLEN: It's been a year of selfishness. I've mainly thought of my own comfort, my own needs. I suppose it's time now to broaden my outlook and I hope this will come, in time, but I still have hangups that put obstacles in my way. The longing is gone, I guess. He's gone, and he'll never come back to me. Oh, but I miss him so. . . . It's better and I think it will continue to get even better. I really rejoice to see how the children and I have moved on . . . and that's as it should be.

Signs of the assimilation stage were apparent a few months later. Almost exactly a year and a half after their first date, Julie and Charles moved in together. Julie's journal entries became much more sporadic. When Charles was mentioned, it was usually in the context of a disagreement or noting the differences in their personalities. Otherwise, her writing reflected a union between them. Many of her experiences were now expressed in the first person plural, "we," as their shared experiences: "We went camping and we felt so thrilled by the fresh air."

A year and a half after John's death, Ellen took on a new job, sold her house, and moved into an apartment. She stopped her diary writing altogether. In talking with her about her diary, Ellen noted that she "just got stronger" and didn't need to write any longer. She knew that John would have wanted it as much as she needed it.

I have found the temporal model to be quite useful in evaluating people's reactions to both positive and negative events. The transition points at six and eighteen months vary considerably, depending on several factors. For completely new, unique, and overpowering life events, the six- and eighteen-month time periods serve as useful guideposts for about half of the people I see. They can fluctuate one way or another by several months, depending on other events that may occur in the interim. The time periods are usually much shorter for people who have been passionately in love before (in the case of understanding love) or for those who have suffered another major loss (in the case of grief).

The six- and eighteen-month transition points make a certain amount of sense for several reasons. Perhaps most important is that by definition, they fall in the season directly opposite of the first love or grief. If your passion or grief begins in January, for example, the six- and eighteen-month transition points will be in July. Reminders such as the weather, holidays, and the anniversary of the emotionally charged event are furthest removed. In addition, the assimilation of any powerful event can be a slow process. It takes time to establish a new understanding of the world.

I think the greatest use of a temporal theory of passion and grief is as a gauge of your own emotions. In the case of passion and love, what may maintain a relationship during the first six months will probably be quite different a year and a half later. If after a year and a half you and your lover really like, understand, and care for one another, you are on to something potentially long-lasting. In the case of death, divorce, or other trauma, expect to grieve for several months. If after a year and a half or two years you feel the pain as intensely as you did during the first few months, you may benefit from psychotherapy or a support group.

Finally, remember that this is a psychological theory that is useful for some people some of the time. Never take any psychological theory too seriously in applying it to your life. It may work for you. It may not.

Which brings us to the issue of personality.

10
The Inhibited Personality

Why is it that two people who face the same trauma can react to it in such different ways? About three years ago, two sisters, Nancy and Alexandra, enrolled in a small advanced class of mine. Because they were fraternal and not identical twins, they looked and behaved quite differently. They even thought differently. Although both performed well on the first exam, their approaches to answering essay questions did not overlap. Nancy tended to rely heavily on facts and specific examples. In answering the same test questions, Alexandra integrated broad theories with her own life experiences.

Midway in the semester, Nancy and Alexandra were stunned to learn that their parents had separated. Their reactions to this news could not have been more different. Nancy showed no signs of being upset. "This is probably a good time for them to get out and meet new people," Nancy calmly explained. Alexandra, on the other hand, was devastated. She started drinking heavily and skipping classes. When I talked with her after she performed poorly on an exam, she tearfully explained that she simply couldn't focus her thoughts.

Nancy and Alexandra had grown up in the same family. They were roommates at college and had the same friends. Nevertheless, they perceived and reacted to their parents' separation in ways that bore no resemblance to each other. In talking with each of them in greater detail, it was clear that the two had always responded differently to upsetting events. When they were seven years old, their baby brother died from a congenital heart problem. Even then, Nancy responded in a fairly matter-of-fact way. Alexandra was plagued by nightmares and fears for years after his death.

More recently, their transition to coming to college was startlingly different. Whereas Nancy fit right into university life, Alexandra experienced a major depression during her first semester.

On the surface, then, Nancy appeared to cope with traumas much better than did Alexandra. The one exception was Nancy's physical health. In the previous year, Nancy had been to a physician four times: twice for strep throat and once each for an ear infection and a urinary-tract infection. In the same time, Alexandra once had the symptoms of the flu but had not gone to a physician.

Every person is unique. All human beings have had different experiences that have shaped the ways they think, feel, and perceive. Despite these differences from person to person, most individuals exhibit fairly stable characteristics over time. The way you may have approached a new situation when you were six years old is probably similar to the way you tackle similar situations now. Your personality, then, is unique, stable over time, and consistent across situations.

The study of personality has been one of the most controversial topics in all of psychology. In many ways, Freud initiated the controversy by claiming that personality resulted from childhood conflicts between people's inborn sexual and aggressive drives and the pressures of society to control these urges. In his view, personality was permanently established by the time a child was around six years old.

Freud's view of personality development produced a violent reaction among American psychologists. Indeed, his stance was decidedly un-American in a young capitalistic society that believed that any person could do anything if given the opportunity. In the early 1900s, America's response to Freud was outlined by John B. Watson, a colorful researcher from the Johns Hopkins University. Watson argued that people's behaviors were shaped by the rewards and punishments they received throughout life. Ten years after being fired from his university position because of a highly publicized sex scandal, Watson boldly claimed:

Give me a dozen healthy infants, well-formed, and my own special world to bring them up in and I'll guarantee to take any one at random and train him to become any type of specialist I might select—doctor, lawyer, artist, merchant-chief, and yes, beggarman and thief. (p. 104)

Although he was then a successful advertising executive for the J. Walter Thompson firm, Watson's vision of personality had struck a responsive chord with other American researchers. By the 1950s, most considered the study of personality an irrelevant endeavor. Since people's actions and thoughts were dictated by the rewards and punishments in their immediate situations, the reasoning went, any differences between people reflected their different environments and not the people themselves. In many ways, this was an optimistic and liberating philosophy. Any flaws or behavioral problems that people manifested could, in theory, be corrected by changing the potential rewards in the environment.

But the behaviorist revolution failed. Maybe the widespread cynicism in the wake of the Vietnam War opened the door to less optimistic "can-do" theories. Perhaps it was inevitable due to other scientific advances. Most psychologists now acknowledge that our behaviors are influenced by thoughts, conflicts, biological activity, and our genes. Stable personality styles do, in fact, exist across situations and over time. Yes, transient rewards and punishments affect us. But they are only part of the human puzzle.

INHIBITION AS A PERSONALITY STYLE

My interests in personality are rather specific. Our early research consistently found that when people did not talk about traumatic experiences, they were more likely to develop health problems. Sometimes, people refused to talk about traumas for clear reasons. They knew that if they disclosed certain socially unacceptable events such as incest, marital infidelity, or embezzlement, they might face severe punishment. Other times, however, people failed to discuss traumas because they simply never talked about their intimate feelings to anyone. This second strategy was candidly revealed by an apparently well-adjusted and introspective woman who participated in one of our studies:

To whomever is running this experiment:
I did not write about my deepest emotions because they are none of your business. They are mine and for me alone. Some things I don't talk about with my parents, my husband, or my best friends. I'm sure not going

to write about them for you. I have had many bad things happen to me and I know how I feel about them. Just because I don't reveal my emotions doesn't mean that I don't feel them. I hope I haven't messed up your experiment. There are just some things in my life that are not for public consumption.

Why do some people habitually avoid disclosing their thoughts and feelings to others? In many cases, it can be traced back to particular childhood experiences. But not always. Several recent studies indicate that inhibition can be an inherited biological trait. That is, some people are apparently born with the proclivity to inhibit their emotional expression. Further, this in-born tendency may be directly implicated in a variety of health problems.

That there are biological bases of inhibition in children is a recent discovery. In 1988, Jerome Kagan and his colleagues at Harvard published the results of a five-year study on inhibition in young children. Drawing from an original group of four hundred two- and five-year-olds, Kagan selected fifty-four inhibited and fifty-three uninhibited children. He defined inhibition by observing the children in social situations with adults and other children. Those classified as inhibited were least likely to initiate an interaction with others. By definition, the inhibited children were consistently shy, quiet, and timid. The uninhibited children, on the other hand, were sociable, talkative, and spontaneous when they met unfamiliar people.

Kagan discovered several important facts. First, most children's degree of inhibition did not change over a five-year period. Those children most timid at age two tended to be timid when they were seven. In addition, by age five, the inhibited children were far more likely than the uninhibited ones to develop unusual fears, such as fear of kidnappers or going to bed alone in the evening. Particularly revealing were the physiological differences between the inhibited and uninhibited children. Overall, the inhibited children exhibited higher heart rates in the laboratory and when asleep. They also had higher levels of urinary norepinephrine and salivary cortisol—both important markers of stress—in comparison with the more outgoing uninhibited participants.

Kagan believes that the differences between inhibited and uninhibited children reflect both genetic and environmental factors. The genetic bases of inhibition may have manifested themselves through early brain development. In a study such as this one, however, the exact genetic mechanisms are impossible to pinpoint. Whatever the genetics, Kagan holds that early family life may also play a key role in the development of inhibition. For example, two thirds of the uninhibited children were firstborns whereas two thirds of the inhibited ones were later borns. Kagan speculates that older siblings may play a key role in the personality development of their younger brothers and sisters. Older children, for example, have been known to tease, threaten, and yell at their siblings. This continued taunting could force the younger children to be constantly wary of others.

Within months of the publication of the Kagan paper, Auke Tellegen and his colleagues at the University of Minnesota surprised the scientific community with new data on the genetic basis of personality. Over several years, the Minnesota group found and tested almost four hundred adult identical and fraternal twin pairs. Particularly impressive was that the researchers were able to track down forty-four identical and twenty-seven fraternal-twin pairs who had been separated, on average, since the time they were three months old. Each participant completed a lengthy personality inventory that tapped, among other things, degree of inhibition. People who scored high on the inhibition or constraint measure described themselves as restrained, cautious, deferential, and avoiding dangerous kinds of excitement or thrills.

I can't emphasize enough how important a study like this can be. Identical twins are genetically identical. Any differences found between them are probably due to their experiences in life. Fraternal twins, on the other hand, share only 50 percent of their genes since they are the product of separate eggs and sperm. The key to interpreting a study such as this is to compare the similarity of identical twins reared together in the same family with identical twins reared apart.

The results? Identical twins, whether they were reared apart or together, were remarkably similar in their degree of inhibition. Fraternal twins were modestly similar if brought up together and were completely unrelated in their degree of inhibition if reared apart. The Tellegen findings strongly implicate genetics as a major determinant of inhibition. Equally striking is that the home environment plays so small a role in determining inhibition.

Researchers are now rethinking the role of genetics in personality development. Since the publication of the Tellegen findings, several laboratories around the world have corroborated their results. In some way, much of our personality is fixed at conception. Unfortunately, it is too early to tell how our genetic code ultimately manifests itself in broad personality traits. Several ideas are currently being offered. One idea is that our genes dictate the size and structure of our brains, along with the biochemical transmitters that allow our brains to work. We know, for example, that certain brain regions are directly linked to inhibition. When these regions are accidentally destroyed, people become much more impulsive and less inhibited. The development of these brain regions is undoubtedly influenced by our genes.

Other factors are also important. Identical twins look and behave alike at birth. Adults and other children may respond similarly to certain body builds, facial configurations, and other distinguishing characteristics in similar ways. For example, exceptionally tall and strong children, no matter what household they grow up in, will probably be encouraged to participate in sports. Children who are overly sensitive to pain may quickly learn to avoid novel situations that may cause injury. In short, subtle genetic differences at birth may inadvertently place many children on a life course from which they will not stray.

Finally, genetics is not everything. From a statistical perspective, genes appear to account for between 30 and 50 percent of what we know about the personality trait of inhibition. In terms of psychological knowledge, this is a huge percentage. In the grand scheme of things, however, unknown or unknowable life experiences are equally powerful in dictating our tendencies to inhibit our thoughts, feelings, and behaviors. Further, we don't yet know the degree to which inhibitory tendencies can be modified. All indications point to the likelihood that the degree to which people constrain themselves can, in fact, be changed. The degree and permanence of change has yet to be tested.

THE INHIBITED PERSONALITY AND DISEASE

What constitutes an inhibited personality? Unfortunately, the answer depends on which researcher asks the question. There are currently several questionnaire scales that tap different dimensions of restraint or inhibition. The following items, however, are fairly common indicators.

* * *

Answer each of the following by responding true or false:

1. Before I make a decision, I usually try to consider all sides of the issue.
2. I believe in playing strictly by the rules.
3. I rarely, if ever, do anything reckless.
4. I am a serious-minded person.
5. I always try to be fully prepared before I begin working on anything.
6. I very much dislike it when someone breaks accepted rules of good conduct.
7. I rely on careful reasoning when making up my mind.'
8. I am a cautious person.
9. Whenever I decide things, I always refer to the basic rules of right and wrong.
10. I am not an "impulse buyer."

These items are drawn from the General Temperament Survey, a much lengthier scale that taps a variety of personality traits including inhibition. According to the authors of the scale, David Watson and Lee Anna Clark, the average college student or adult endorses about five of these items. People who answer true to eight or more are considered to be more inhibited or restrained than those who endorse seven or fewer. As you can see from the items, the trait of inhibition is not inherently bad or unhealthy. Rather, restrained people are often the pillars of society. They do not behave foolishly, are law-abiding, and are downright mannerly. Several studies suggest that extremely inhibited individuals are less likely to complain about their problems to others and to disclose their deepest thoughts and feelings indiscriminately.

In society's eyes, inhibition is a socially desirable trait. Indeed, if all members of society were extremely inhibited, we would have no problems with drug abuse or pornography. The trains would always run on time.

So what's the matter with being inhibited?

The problem is that overly inhibited individuals thrive on predictability in an often unpredictable world. When faced with an emotionally wrenching trauma, it is often essential to remain flexible, to talk to others, and to acknowledge powerful moods.

Extremely rigid people often refuse to discuss traumas because to do so would undermine their conception of an orderly world.

I recently saw a revealing illustration of this problem when I had a long discussion with Jennifer, a friend of mine since grade school. As long as I have known her, Jennifer has always exhibited signs of inhibition. Even in elementary school, she took notes, was polite to everyone, and never took risks. By her own admission, she never had any close friends. About a year ago, she divorced her husband after learning about his having an affair with his secretary. Since the divorce, her twelve-year-old daughter has been expelled from school for alcohol and, possibly, drug use. Two weeks before we met, she learned that she had high blood pressure. When I inquired if I could ask her some rather personal questions, Jennifer politely assented.

ME: I guess the divorce must have been pretty hard for you and your daughter. How did you deal with it?

JENNIFER: I guess it was hard for a little while, but you have to look forward. But [my daughter] and I are doing just great.

ME: Did you talk to anyone about the divorce? Or consider seeing a therapist?

JENNIFER: There wasn't anything to talk about. Therapists are probably good for people who have problems. But I don't see the value of complaining to people.

ME: Did you and your daughter talk in detail about the divorce? You know, really open discussions?

JENNIFER: Oh yes. I told her that I was planning to separate from her father. We have a very open and honest relationship. We haven't needed to talk about it. She knows that she can come to me whenever she has a problem.

ME: It sounds as if her drinking is a problem. Do you think it's related to the divorce?

JENNIFER: She gets that from her father. I think she knows that I don't approve. I'm sure she isn't drinking anymore.

ME: You know me, I've always been nosy. There's a lot of evidence to suggest that high blood pressure can be related to stress. Do you think that may be the case with you?

JENNIFER: Stress? Certainly not. It's just my diet. Too much
             salt. But we are not cooking with salt anymore.
             Besides, if I were under stress, my daughter and
             I wouldn't be doing so well. . . . But enough of
             me, how do you like living in Dallas?

During our entire discussion, Jennifer maintained the same
forced smile on her face. Emotions and feelings were simply inappropriate topics of conversation with friends or family members. Jennifer's rigid style was undoubtedly contributing to her
daughter's behavior and to her own health. There was a psychological monster living in her house, but she was choosing to act
prudently and not acknowledge it.

Is it possible that Jennifer's high blood pressure was linked
to her inhibited personality style? Yes, according to a series of
studies on heart-disease risk and personality. Beginning in the late
1970s at Yale University, Gary Schwartz and his students embarked on a fascinating project to explore repressive coping styles
and health. In their view, a repressive coping style was characterized by high levels of inhibition and the refusal to admit to
feelings of anxiety. In a pioneering project, Daniel Weinberger,
Schwartz, and Richard J. Davidson required forty college students
to call out the first thoughts that came to their mind in response
to phrases they heard over a loudspeaker. Many of the phrases
they heard were sexual and aggressive in content. For example,
students had to respond to phrases such as "the prostitute slept
with the student." During the entire experiment, heart rate and
skin conductance were monitored.

The repressive copers were a unique group. They had the
hardest time coming up with any responses to the phrases. Even
though they claimed that the task did not make them at all nervous,
their physiological levels were much higher than those of any other
group of people. In a psychologically threatening situation, then,
the repressive copers were biologically aroused but denied that
they were upset.

Weinberger, who is now at Case Western Reserve, has extended these findings in several directions. In a recent summary
of the repressive coping work, Weinberger reports that adult repressors have elevated cholesterol levels. Others have found that
adult repressive coping style is associated with higher overall blood
pressure levels both within and outside the laboratory. Indeed,

one recent study found that repressors exhibited greater blood pressure increases in response to challenging tasks than the heart-disease-prone Type As.

Other measures of inhibition are yielding consistent results. Ted Dembroski of the University of Maryland, Baltimore County, and his colleagues find that people who try to inhibit their anger are more prone to heart attacks and other cardiovascular problems than people who express anger. Other measures of suppressed anger have been linked to hypertension across several studies.

And it gets worse. Chronic inhibitors appear to be at risk for a variety of disorders linked to the immune system. Larry Jamner, another of Gary Schwartz's students, recently found that repressive copers had more seriously disturbed white blood cell counts than nonrepressors. According to the researchers, the blood cell counts reflected poorer immune function among the repressors. Similarly, ongoing research by Robert Emmons of the University of California at Davis suggests that people who attempt to inhibit conflicting goals in their lives visit physicians for illness far more frequently than those who have discussed their goals with others.

Other studies now suggest that inhibitors may be at greater risk for early death due to breast cancer. In one study, for example, women who did not openly express negative emotions such as anxiety or anger were more likely to die within the first year of treatment than more expressive women. Other studies indicate that women who openly express joy as well as negative moods have a longer survival time than those who do not express any emotions. These results support an observation made by a group of cancer specialists in 1952 who noted that they were "impressed by the polite, apologetic, almost painful acquiescence of patients with rapidly progressive disease as contrasted to the more expressive and sometimes bizarre personalities" of long-term survivors.

Research on the health hazards of extreme inhibition is growing exponentially. Various studies, many of which are listed in the Chapter Notes section of the book, implicate inhibition in the severity of asthma, diabetes, anorexia nervosa, and even disturbed pain thresholds. Is being an inhibited person really that dangerous?

An uncritical evaluation of the assorted studies would lead to the conclusion that chronic inhibitors are doomed to disease and early death. In fact, there is still controversy about the true mag-

nitude of the health risk of possessing a personality trait of inhibition. In fact, for every two or three studies that show the dangers
of being an inhibited person, at least one study fails to find an
effect. In the grand scheme of things, it is probably more dangerous to smoke, drink excessively, or take up hang gliding than
to be a high inhibitor. Indeed, people who are extremely low in
inhibition are probably more likely to die an early death than high
inhibitors. Very low inhibitors—often referred to as impulsive or
even psychopathic—usually lead strikingly unhealthy lives. They
are more likely to get divorced, have car accidents, engage in poor
health habits, and live dissolute existences than are high inhibitors.

One reason we are unable to determine the exact health risk
of lifelong inhibition is that we are unable to pinpoint the exact
causal links between personality and disease. One problem with
many of the medical studies, for example, is that inhibitors wait
longer to go to a doctor than noninhibitors. By the time they show
up in the physician's office, their disease may have progressed
further than if they had sought medical attention earlier. In many
cases, then, inhibition may be predicting physician use rather than
illness per se. Another unknown is the degree to which an inhibited
personality style might actually cause illness. Kagan's work with
young children hints at the possibility of a fundamental link between long-term inhibition and chronically elevated biological activity. It is entirely possible, however, that physiological arousal
could result in an inhibited personality style rather than vice versa.
A child who is easily startled or who has a low pain threshold
may quickly learn that the safest way to deal with the world is by
being cautious.

My own belief is that there are some real but not overwhelming health risks associated with being an extreme inhibitor. The
major danger the inhibitor faces is in dealing with trauma. When
life is generally predictable and safe, the inhibitor probably fares
extremely well. When flexibility is called for, the overly restrained
person may have the most difficulty in adjusting.

FITTING THE PERSON TO MATCH THE ENVIRONMENT

Recently, a fascinatingly inane debate has been raging on the
editorial pages of our local newspaper. The center of the contro-

versy is a high school football star who was arrested for robbing a video store. One group of letter writers, referred to by their detractors as the "pointy-headed liberals," claim that the football star is merely a product of his background of poverty. According to the pointy-heads, the student has been victimized by his situation. Many of us would have done the same thing in the same situation. On the other side, the "wild-eyed right-wingers" argue that the young man is simply a violent and dangerous criminal. The consensus of the wild-eyed group is that the kid is rotten and should be sent to the penitentiary—the sooner, the better.

The letter writers are playing out the same inane debate that psychologists have been feuding over for several decades. Much like the nature-nurture controversy, one camp asserts that all behavior is dictated by the situation. The other side claims that personality exerts the overriding control over behavior. The reason the personality-situation debate is irrelevant is that the two are inextricably related. To understand any behavior, we must examine people within the context of their environment.

Nowhere is this more evident than in our study of inhibition. Most inhibitors are undoubtedly healthy and happy in predictable and safe environments. Impulsive thrill seekers thrive in exciting and constantly changing settings. Psychological and biological stress results when people are out of their element. That is, optimal health follows from a satisfactory match between the person and the environment.

Beginning in the early 1970s, a group of University of Michigan researchers examined the person-environment fit idea among people in a variety of occupations. They concluded that the more poorly people's abilities fit the demands of their job, the more likely they were to be unhappy and unhealthy. Extrapolating from this work, a thrill-seeking assembly-line worker should be just as stressed as an inhibited ambulance driver. If assembly-line workers and ambulance drivers were forced to completely follow their job descriptions, the person-environment mismatch would be a terrible problem.

But people aren't passive. We are active engineers in our environment. We change the environment to better match our needs. This, of course, is obvious, but it took an experiment for me to appreciate it. Several years ago, I conducted a series of studies on person-environment fit in the laboratory. My goal was to make some people as bored as possible, with the assumption that boredom was stressful. To accomplish this, I required students to slowly stack a bucketful of pennies for an hour. Boring, right? Wrong. Many of the people discovered inventive ways to fill their time. They arranged the pennies by date, by mint, even by color. Some attempted to align the pennies on their edges. I remember one energetic student remarking after the experiment that stacking pennies was a wonderful new experience. In fact, he now planned to make a collage with coins for an art project. Like many others in the study, he had engineered his environment to match his need for creativity.

One secret to understanding the link between inhibition and disease is to consider the degree to which mental effort is implicated. Across the various writing studies, those who have benefited the most were individuals who constantly thought about traumas but did not talk about them with others. A personality style characterized by inhibition is primarily a problem if people have to exert energy to keep their mind, emotions, and behavior under control.

Traumas can pose problems for both inhibited and uninhibited people. Those who are inhibited may choose not to confront their problems because, in their minds, it is not a natural thing to do. Less inhibited people, on the other hand, may elect not to talk about their feelings because they fear possible recrimination for their talking. In many cases, then, the naturally uninhibited individual who can't talk may be under more stress than the naturally inhibited.

We must not lose sight of the fact that people structure their own environment. Some extremely inhibited individuals are able to cope effectively with traumas by maintaining a rigid belief system about the world. For example, an inhibited parent who learns that his son has been arrested for drug smuggling may cope by claiming that his son broke the rules and therefore should be punished. Without reflecting on his son's upbringing or his own feelings about his son's dilemma, the parent's belief system remains intact—no stress, no problem.

The ability to maintain a structured view of the world during times of major trauma is probably rare. One of my graduate students, named Rose, is one of the few I have ever seen. In the space of three months, her son went to college, her husband left her, and her mother died. During this entire period, her physiological levels—which I measured at least once a week—never deviated from normal. In the three years since that time, she has not been sick once, has not been depressed, and has not talked or thought about these traumas in any detail. Her views of life and of herself have not changed, either. "Sure, I've had dozens of traumas in my life. Big deal. Life is unpredictable. I don't think about them, they're history."

By every measure I have ever given her, Rose is an extreme inhibitor. Indeed, a Super Inhibitor. Perhaps it derives from her genes. Or maybe from her extremely traumatic childhood. Whatever the source, Rose is a salient reminder that some inhibitors can thrive in the face of disaster.

CHANGING PERSONALITIES AND ENVIRONMENTS TO PROMOTE HEALTH

Most chronic inhibitors will never achieve Super Inhibitor status. Consequently, they risk a variety of health problems when confronted by a trauma. Can personality be changed? That is, if you are a chronic inhibitor, is there some way to fundamentally alter your approach to life?

The answer to this question is an unqualified maybe. We know, for example, that personality measures of inhibition are moderately stable. Paul Costa and his colleagues at the National Institutes on Aging find that personality-test scores of perhaps 50 percent of adults remain remarkably constant across a twenty-year time span. The remaining 50 percent, however, change. Personality, including measures of inhibition, is not completely static. Unfortunately, studies such as this can't tell us why personality can and does fluctuate on occasion. Probable candidates include traumatic experiences and different life circumstances such as wealth, marriage, or divorce. Some people, however, have undoubtedly made a conscious decision to change and have succeeded.

Unfortunately, very little solid research exists on how to make a chronic inhibitor less inhibited. But that doesn't stop me from speculating. If you are trying to change yourself or are encouraging someone else to change, you should address three questions.

What function is inhibition currently serving? People are often inhibited for a good reason. Freud, for example, believed that rigidity protected people from feelings of anxiety. An inhibited style may be shielding you from dealing with childhood traumas, your own feelings of inadequacy, or your current relationships with other people.

If your inhibited style can be traced back to a specific event in your life, it may be time to directly confront it—either by entering therapy or writing about the event in detail. Many successful therapies assume that traumas can set up lifelong psychological struggles. If one of your parents suddenly died when you were young, for example, you may have dealt with your pain by arbitrarily structuring your world in order to avoid your feelings. If you were victimized by someone close to you, you may have adopted an inhibitory style to defend against others in general.

If you are unable to trace your inhibitory style to any experiences, it is entirely possible that you are biologically and/or genetically predisposed toward inhibition. This does not mean that you can't change. After all, we were not genetically programmed to eat three meals a day or drive automobiles. I recommend reflecting on the behavior patterns you wish to change. If you seek to be more emotionally expressive with others, it could help to write about it first. Don't stop there, however. Practice expressing yourself to people you trust. Any behavior change takes time. Also, don't rule out seeing a psychologist or psychiatrist. Many therapists are specifically trained to deal with emotional expressiveness, assertiveness, and similar issues.

What are your motivations and expectations for change?
Perhaps the best predictor of the success of therapy is the will to change. The more motivated you are, the better chance you have.

You also need to ask yourself why you want to change in the first place. Is it to please someone else or to satisfy yourself? Is it because you are experiencing health problems that may have been exacerbated by inhibition? Whatever the motivation, it is wise to carefully scrutinize your deepest thoughts and feelings about why you think change is necessary. Again, writing can be a powerful tool in exploring yourself and discovering your motives.

Finally, keep your expectations reasonable. Some people can change themselves permanently. Most don't. After successfully changing some aspect of their personality, most people gradually revert back to their old styles of behaving. No big deal. If you can change once, you can change again. Simply monitor what works best for you so that you can marshal the same techniques in the future. Remember that it sometimes takes practice to change behaviors. The more you practice, the better you will become at altering your unwanted behaviors.

What is the nature of your situation? Remember that most behaviors are dictated both by personality and by forces in the environment. People often subtly control their own behavior because of the ways that others treat them. If your spouse hates to see you cry or express yourself, change may be difficult. In cases such as this, both of you need to explore the nature of your interaction. Whatever changes you make must be met with acceptance or understanding.

Also keep in mind that we all tend to structure our own environment. We seek out certain types of friends and occupations that can reinforce our personality style. It can sometimes help to adopt the attitude of a cold and detached scientist who analyzes situations for a living. Be your own environmental engineer by influencing your relationships with friends or the nature of your job. By affecting your situation, you can help change yourself.

11
Inhibited Cities

Inhibited cities? Individual people can be inhibited, certainly. Even uninhibited people can be forced to constrain themselves in talking about events that are psychologically threatening. But entire cities? As I thought about it, however, it was possible. In my research on disclosure and inhibition, I had seen entire families that refused to talk about the death of a family member. I have worked in a company of about fifty people where no one discussed the sudden firing of a popular coworker. Groups, it seems, can foster a conspiracy of silence in which extremely important topics are simply never broached. If families and companies can inhibit disclosure, perhaps similar processes could occur in much larger groups such as communities, countries, perhaps even civilizations.

This is not a new idea. In the early nineteenth century, German philosopher Georg Hegel proposed that over time, cultures were dominated by a set of guiding ideas or beliefs that worked as a divine and absolute Mind. Karl Marx and, later, Freud expanded on the basic view that society evolves a collective consciousness or way of thinking. Indeed, Freud persuasively argued that the roots of psychological problems in a civilization are the result of the suppression of aggressive and sexual drives. Influenced by both Marx and Freud, psychoanalyst Erich Fromm further examined the idea of a shared societal consciousness in *The Sane Society*. Building on his own experiences in Nazi Germany, Fromm suggested that entire countries could evolve seriously disturbed views of the world. During times of economic or cultural upheavals, a society's values could become so distorted as to be certifiably insane.

My interests focus not so much on the development of cultural values but on the forces that lead groups of people to actively avoid discussing psychologically threatening events. Two questions arise from this issue: When and why does it occur? What, if any, are the health implications? As always, I really didn't know about these questions until the answers landed in my lap.

LET'S NOT TALK ABOUT VOLCANOES

It all started in a dingy bar in Charlottesville, Virginia, one Friday afternoon. Darren Newtson, a colleague of mine, and I were having one of our weekly "research meetings" in the late spring of 1980. Our discussion turned to the spectacular eruption of Mount Saint Helens volcano in Washington State earlier in the week. Darren and I share the same ambulance-chasing mentality and had been mesmerized by the news accounts of the eruption. A cubic mile of earth had exploded from the mountain early Sunday morning on May 18. About sixty people had died and much of the surrounding area had been destroyed.

Particularly surprising, however, was that volcanic ash—sand, really—had blanketed cities up to two hundred miles to the west. Because the prevailing westerly winds had been so strong, towns as close as thirty miles to the east of the volcano were virtually untouched. Darren, who had grown up close to Mount Saint Helens, had spoken with several of his relatives who still lived in Oregon and Washington about the eruption. He admitted to being perplexed by what they had said. For some, the eruption was the most excitement they had had in years. Others viewed it as a menace. And one of his relatives simply didn't want to talk about it at all.

Not only was Mount Saint Helens the geological event of the decade, it was also the grist for a fascinating psychological project. Darren and I hastily laid out the plans for a large-scale study on a used paper napkin. A flurry of phone calls followed. Within two weeks, we had scrounged a small grant from the National Science Foundation and were on our way to Washington to study the psychological impact of Mount Saint Helens volcano.

Over the next few weeks, we traveled to several communities, where we interviewed hundreds of people about their perceptions of the volcano. Our most striking findings emerged among the residents of Yakima and Longview, Washington. By way of background, both towns had roughly equivalent populations (between thirty and fifty thousand), median incomes, and ethnic divisions.

Yakima, which is eighty-five miles west of Mount Saint Helens, was covered by almost two inches of sandlike ash. The ashfall brought the city to a halt. During the cleanup, streets were blocked, sewers became clogged, and horrendous bureaucratic problems developed as the city devised plans to dispose of thousands of tons of ash.

Longview, a little over thirty miles east of the volcano, received only about half an inch of talcum-powderlike ash. Although there was little direct damage, the Cowlitz River, which runs through Longview, was choked with ash that had been fed by tributaries from the volcano. Indeed, the river was at flood-stage level even though there was less water than usual in it. People not only feared a severe flood, but the possibility of an even more devastating eruption weighed heavily on their minds. In the months after the initial eruption, Longview residents had watched the volcano spew hot steam and ash on an almost continuous basis.

Psychologically, residents in the two towns were in very different states. By the time we arrived in Yakima, most of the ash deposits had been cleaned up. For them, the volcano episode was over. They were eager to tell us their stories. For both our door-to-door interviews as well as telephone surveys, only 12 percent of the people refused to answer our questions. In fact, once our interviews began, it was often difficult to get the people to stop talking about their experiences. They were exceptionally open and honest. Yes, the volcano scared them and they worried about another eruption. However, when asked if they were glad that the eruption had occurred, over 85 percent said yes. A volcanic eruption, according to Yakima residents, was a once-in-a-lifetime experience. Although they admitted that they wouldn't want to go through it again, the Mount Saint Helens experience had been exciting.

Longview was another matter. The residents didn't want to talk or think about it. In our interviews, 44 percent refused to participate. The nature of the refusals was also revealing. Often, I would knock at someone's door and a person would greet me in a warm and friendly matter. As soon as I mentioned that my interview dealt with the volcano, his or her expression changed to cool politeness. No thank you, I'm not interested. Around my tenth refusal, I asked a man who was in the process of shutting the door in my face why he didn't want to talk. Why, I pleaded, were the people in Longview behaving so differently from people in all the other towns we had visited? The door slowly opened and he spoke in a calm voice, "I've got two suitcases right next to the door in case it blows again. I don't know about other people, but I don't trust that mountain. The last thing I need right now is some kid asking me about it." Kid? Perhaps in the shadow of the volcano I looked younger than my thirty years.

The questionnaire responses of the Longview citizens corroborated what the man had told me. Only about 40 percent of the respondents were glad the volcano had erupted. Ironically, though, most people claimed they weren't anxious, afraid, or angry about the volcano. They couldn't admit to us or to themselves any emotions about the volcano. It was an object to be watched, to be on guard against.

The Longview residents reminded me of an interview I conducted a year earlier with a woman who had been robbed at a convenience store. During the robbery, all she could do was keep her eyes on the gun. Time expanded. She felt nothing. As soon as the robber sped off in his car, she became hysterical. The next day, when I saw her, she talked about it incessantly. She was both euphoric to be alive and terrified about what could have happened.

During the time we were in Longview, people were staring down the barrel of a volcano. There was nothing they could do except be vigilant. A parallel phenomenon was discovered in a University of Minnesota psychology laboratory in 1967 by Bill Walster and Elliot Aronson. The researchers required students to participate in three long and fatiguing tasks, each lasting about fifteen minutes. Half of the participants, however, were misled; they were informed that they would be performing five fifteen-minute tasks instead of three. When all of the students had completed the third task, the researchers asked them how fatigued they felt. Those who assumed that the experiment was over reported feeling extremely tired and fatigued. Those who thought they would continue with two more tasks claimed not to feel much fatigue at all.

If we are in the midst of a task or a disaster, we hold our emotions and feelings in abeyance. Such a strategy is quite adaptive if our feelings could interfere with later performance. Once we know the task is over, however, we can let down and reflect on the task and our emotions.

Fortunately for Washington residents, no flooding or further major eruptions occurred. A year after our initial interviews, we conducted another telephone survey of Longview and Yakima citizens. In everyone's mind, the volcano episode was, by then, over. The refusal rates for people in both towns was 20 percent, which is standard for surveys such as this. There were no differences between the communities in terms of moods or attitudes about the volcano. The Longview residents could now openly express their feelings about their experiences. In looking back, they felt they had moved past the volcano episode about ten months after the eruption. People in Yakima estimated that the whole incident had ended within five or six months after the ashfall.

Suppressing feelings and thoughts while in the middle of a task or uncontrollable event is stressful. In the laboratory, it should be associated with increased skin conductance and possibly other physiological levels. When the event is of the magnitude of a sudden eruption, it should have major health consequences for an entire community for the duration of the event. That is, any group of people forced to inhibit thoughts, feelings, or behaviors for several months should be more prone to stress-related diseases.

And that is exactly what happened in Longview. During the year that its residents were dealing with the volcano, death rates due to heart disease were 6 percent higher than for the two years before and after the event. In Yakima, heart-disease deaths remained unchanged. Other indicators of stress showed similar trends. In 1980, suicide and murder rates were 37 percent and 186 percent higher than usual in Longview, compared with a modest 7 percent drop in suicides and a 51 percent increase in murders for Yakima.

I should note that deaths due to heart disease, suicide, and murder are crude measures of a community's stress levels. In addition to the burden of a volcano, they also reflect economic and other stressors. Further, changes in heart-disease deaths are partly a reflection of the quality of medical care and changes in smoking, exercise and diet as well general stress levels. Nevertheless, they can roughly summarize health changes brought about by community-wide events.

Fortunately, most of us don't live with the specter of a volcano erupting in our backyard. However, many parts of the country must contend with occasional floods, tornadoes, hurricanes, or earthquakes. Are all of us under constant stress because of the possibility of these disasters? Of course not. We have learned to suppress the thoughts of environmental disasters quite effectively. For many of us, however, it takes some time.

Earthquakes are a wonderful case in point. When I moved to California for six months prior to the massive 1989 San Francisco earthquake, I thought about the big one several times each day. Every time I entered a new building, I examined its structural integrity. The only other people who shared these concerns were other newcomers. To natives, however, earthquakes were just another part of life. They rarely thought about them and, in my experience, never initiated a conversation about them.

All of this changed in the San Francisco area immediately after the October, 1989, earthquake. According to telephone surveys conducted by Stanford University researcher Kent Harber and my own research team, San Francisco-area residents thought and talked about the earthquake incessantly for approximately a month. As soon as people saw palpable damage, they openly discussed the earthquake many times each day. San Francisco-area residents, then, behaved similarly to the Yakima, Washington, citizens soon after the volcano.

But something odd happened among Bay Area residents by six weeks after the quake. In our periodic surveys of several hundred people, we found that by the six-week mark, people living in San Francisco were no longer talking about the earthquake but were still thinking about it. When we asked our randomly selected participants about this, they told us that they wanted to talk about the earthquake but when push came to shove, they didn't want to hear other people talk about it. Indeed, a little over a month after the earthquake, printed T-shirts appeared in the area that said, "Thank you for not sharing your earthquake experience."

You can appreciate the dilemma in which the Bay Area residents were inadvertently placing themselves. Although they were tired of hearing about the earthquake from others, they still wanted to discuss their own experiences. The residents, then, were living with a socially imposed rule of not talking about a tremendously significant event. As might be predicted, we found that San Francisco residents reported highter rates of physical symptoms and conflict with others from six weeks until about six months after the earthquake. Our surveys indicated that these effects occured only in the Bay Area and not in Sacramento or Los Angeles.

When do earthquake thoughts diminish? Not surprisingly, it depends on whether you have been in a major earthquake. According to informal surveys by Stanford University psychologist Laura Carstensen, newcomers to the Bay Area who have never felt an earthquake initially think about quakes quite frequently. By the middle or the end of their second year, most earthquake thoughts have disappeared. One sprightly 82-year-old woman who had lived in San Francisco since 1933 told Carstensen, "I never think about earthquakes anymore. Not even when they are happening." Following the 1989 earthquake, Carstensen reported that the woman was baffled by all the publicity the country was devoting to the earthquake damage.

As an aside, the evolution of thoughts of earthquakes seems to parallel the changes in thinking that people experience with passionate love and with grief. As discussed in Chapter 9, it takes about a year and a half for people to come to terms with or assimilate overpowering new experiences. Whether the earth moves figuratively or literally, there is a natural progression in adapting to it.

In our volcano study, several participants spontaneously remarked that the eruption was, at least, a natural disaster rather than one resulting from human error. A form of back-to-nature reasoning, I suppose. But there is something important about distinguishing between natural and man-made disasters. Calamities such as Hiroshima, Three Mile Island, or the Bhopal disaster are potentially destructive for years. Not only do the immediate survivors face the stress of the initial disaster, but they can never be certain when the disaster is really over. With the manufacturing of nuclear and chemical toxins comes a new generation of insidious environmental dangers.

About one year before the Mount Saint Helens eruption, one of the nuclear reactors at Three Mile Island accidentally released a cloud of radioactive gas in central Pennsylvania. Because it was the first disaster of its kind in the United States, residents in the area were terrified by its potential effect on their lives. People were confronting a new kind of disaster that had completely unknown effects. Within days of the Three Mile Island accident, Andrew Baum and his colleagues from the Uniformed Services University for the Health Sciences initiated a large-scale project to examine the psychological effects of people who lived in a five-mile radius of the reactor.

Governmental studies quickly learned that the amount of radioactive exposure to the surrounding area was quite small. Nevertheless, Baum and other researchers discovered that the psychological effects were significant and long-lasting. In addition to collecting questionnaire information, the researchers were able to monitor a variety of physiological measures on repeated occasions over the next six years. People's self-reports of distress were extremely high during the first month after the accident. Although anxiety levels dropped thereafter, they have remained higher than normal even six years later. More striking have been the physiological findings. Baum reports that measures of stress-related hormones such as urinary epinephrine and norepinephrine remained elevated six years after the incident, in comparison with people who lived at least eighty miles away from Three Mile Island. Further, those living close to the reactor continue to exhibit higher blood pressure levels, more physician visits, and greater medication use than nonresidents.

In reviewing findings from dozens of both natural and man-made disasters, Baum concludes that catastrophes caused by humans have a much longer and more insidious effect than natural ones. With nuclear or toxic-chemical accidents, people can't evaluate when the episode is over. People know that radioactive and chemical toxins continue to pose possible health hazards for years or even centuries. They fear that the foods they eat, objects they touch, or the air they breathe may harm them. In short, modern man-made disasters are the psychological equivalent of living in a gun barrel.

COMMUNITY SHAME: THE CASE OF DALLAS AND THE ASSASSINATION OF KENNEDY

I was in a physical education class in junior high school when an announcement was made over the loudspeaker that John F. Kennedy had been assassinated. Like most people old enough to remember, I vividly recall the effect the announcement had on me. At the end of class, a group of us were silently standing by the door waiting for the bell to ring. Jan Taylor, a popular cheerleader, was quietly crying in the corner. To no one in particular, she angrily blurted out, "I hate Dallas. I'm ashamed to be a Texan."

Even then, I was startled by what she said. Denouncing Texas, in my book, was a form of heresy. It wasn't the fault of Dallas, I thought to myself. What would prompt someone like Jan—a girl with whom I had grown up in West Texas—to even think such thoughts? It soon became apparent, however, that her views were shared by millions of people across the United States.

Editorials and magazine articles pointed to Dallas's extreme conservatism and its residents' general disdain for Kennedy and his administration. This general climate of anti-federal government, many people reasoned, fostered an atmosphere conducive to the assassination. Indeed, nationwide surveys conducted approximately one week after Kennedy's death indicated that 15 percent of Americans specifically blamed the people of Dallas for the assassination. Dallas had become "the City of Hate."

Residents of Dallas were not blind to America's rage. Many endured humiliating incidents that suggested that the rest of the country held them personally responsible for the assassination. When traveling out of state, some Dallas families were refused service at restaurants and filling stations. Schoolchildren threw rocks at cars with Texas license plates. Long-distance operators disconnected their calls. Dallas students attending out-of-state colleges were hounded by their peers. Lee Harvey Oswald, a relative newcomer to Dallas who had lived in the Soviet Union for over a year, had murdered the president and Dallas was taking the blame.

Collectively, residents of Dallas faced a powerful and unique trauma. Something horrible had happened in their community and there was nothing they could do about it. A group of leading Dallas citizens met soon after the assassination and decided that Dallas must move rapidly ahead. Plans were made to construct an international airport, to build the tallest skyscrapers in the Southwest, and to create a progressive business climate. Dallas was to be the city of the future. And the city without a past.

When our family moved to Dallas in 1983, one of the first things we did was to go see the sixth floor of the Texas School Book Depository, the location from which Oswald shot the president. The building had been purchased by the county and now housed government administrators. The top floors of the building, however, were vacant and sealed from the public. Nowhere was there any indication that the building or surrounding area had any historic significance. Here an event had happened that had changed the course of American history, but the city was pretending that nothing had happened. Not only was Dallas trying to forget the assassination, but there were virtually no reminders of Kennedy anywhere. Unlike in Houston or neighboring Fort Worth, in Dallas there were no schools, streets, or buildings named after Kennedy. This couldn't be attributed to an antiliberal bias because several private and public schools and buildings were named after Martin Luther King.

In 1986, some people placed a log book on the first floor of the School Book Depository for people to sign and make brief remarks. Thousands of visitors had signed it along with statements such as "Open the sixth floor!" Ironically, almost no one from Dallas had signed it. One of the only ones who had done so noted, "Shameful. We would be better off destroying the building." I later learned that several attempts to open the sixth floor had been met with vehement opposition by Dallas citizens.

Not everyone in Dallas avoided discussions of the assassination. Beginning in the early 1980s, two community leaders, Conover Hunt and Lindalyn Adams, began a low-key campaign to construct an exhibit on the sixth floor. In early 1988, twenty-five years after the assassination, they sought the opinions of several academicians about the impact such an exhibit would have on Dallas. It wasn't until our first meeting that I fully appreciated the psychological significance of such a project. To satisfy my curiosity, I eagerly volunteered my services to evaluate the psychological impact of the assassination and of the exhibit on Dallas.

With the aid of Rhonda Polakoff, a graduate student in anthropology and a native of Dallas, we conducted a random telephone survey of over four hundred people in Dallas, Fort Worth, and Houston, Texas, as well as residents of Memphis, Tennessee, and Columbus, Ohio. Among other things, we wanted to know how much people thought and talked about the assassination. We were particularly curious about their attitudes about Dallas and the proposed exhibit. We divided people into five groups: native Dallasites age thirty or over, who were old enough to remember the assassination; Dallas transplants over thirty who moved to Dallas after the assassination; Dallasites under the age of thirty; non–Dallas residents thirty or older; and non–Dallas residents under the age of thirty.

The one group that stood out from all the rest were the Dallas natives who were at least thirty years old. As a group, the natives reported thinking about the assassination over sixteen times during the previous year compared with eight times for everyone else. Although they thought about it the most, they had actually talked about it the same number of times as everyone else—about four times in the previous year. Over 80 percent of the natives felt that the rest of the country still blamed Dallas, compared with 60 percent of the Dallas transplants or those too young to remember it. (In fact, less than 20 percent of all our survey respondents still blamed Dallas to some degree for the assassination.) The natives also reported being the least likely to visit the exhibit or even to watch a television show about the assassination. Interestingly, those most eager to visit the museum were Dallas residents under the age of thirty.

Reflect for a moment on the basic premise of our research. People who are at most risk for illness are those who have experienced a trauma, who continue to think about it, and who do not talk about it—in short, a thumbnail sketch of our Dallas natives. What is most astounding is that these results were collected twenty-five years after the trauma. Imagine what it must have been like in the months and years immediately after the assassination.

If stress-related illnesses follow from inhibition on an individual level, there should be large-scale indicators of disease on a community-wide basis. In the five years following Kennedy's murder, deaths in Dallas due to heart disease averaged over 4 percent higher than they had been in the four years before the assassination. In all of the other cities we studied, as well as across the entire United States, heart-disease deaths actually declined by 3 percent during the same time. In the year after the assassination, murder rates temporarily jumped 25 percent in Dallas, compared with 1 percent nationwide. During 1964, suicide rates in Dallas increased by 20 percent, compared with a 1 percent increase in the rest of the country. These effects are not attributable to economic factors in that Dallas's median income was increasing at exactly the same rate as that in other Texas cities and the country as a whole.

An unexpected finding that grew out of this research concerned the striking parallels between Dallas and Memphis. It was in Memphis that Martin Luther King was murdered in 1968. Residents of Memphis feel that the rest of the country continues to blame them for the assassination of Martin Luther King. As with

Dallas and Kennedy, the city of Memphis has actively avoided dealing with King's memory. In Memphis, for example, there are no streets, schools, or buildings named after King. In the four years following King's murder, Memphis heart-disease deaths increased over 3 percent from the four preceding years. During the same time, deaths due to heart disease in Dallas and the rest of the country dropped by an average of 4 percent.

Since our surveys in mid-1988, there have been some promising signs that Dallas is now beginning to openly acknowledge the assassination of John F. Kennedy. In February 1989, the Sixth Floor Exhibit finally opened. The opening was prominently heralded as a positive move by all the local media. Since its opening, the number of visitors exceeded all projections. Open seven days a week, the exhibit draws over a thousand people each day—about a hundred of whom are Dallas residents.

Surveys of visitors to the exhibit indicate that Dallas natives are moved by the exhibit as much, if not more, than people from other places. Their comments in a log book at the end of the tour also suggest a lingering self-consciousness about the assassination. These three comments were recorded by native Dallasites on the opening day of the exhibit and reflect the general tone of the remarks by Dallas natives:

> I wasn't in favor of this [exhibit] but now, after seeing it and experiencing it, I feel so much better. It's helpful to those who live here to be able to show how much we care.

> This great city has finally recovered from this tragedy by facing up to it. As a native Dallasite who also loved John Kennedy, I hope the world realizes that Dallas did not kill Kennedy.

> This exhibit is years late in opening, but I'm glad it has finally happened. The world changed forever on November 22, 1963. This exhibit finally allows those of us from Texas to look back, to think, and finally to put the events of that tragic day into some perspective.

Another interesting sign that Dallas is coming to terms with Kennedy's death can be seen in television viewership of assassination-related programs. November 22, 1988, marked the twenty-fifth anniversary of the assassination. During the week preceding the anniversary, several television networks broadcast special commemorative programs. The most widely viewed commercial program was *Four Days,* which aired on CBS on November 17. *Four Days* was a moving two-hour documentary that preempted *Paradise* (a modern-day western serial) and *Knots Landing* (a popular evening soap opera). An analysis of the A. H. Nielsen ratings for the Dallas and Houston markets indicated that 14 percent of all Dallas-area residents watched the JFK special compared to 5 percent of the Houston-area market. The most striking difference in viewership was among people between eighteen and thirty-four years of age. In this group, 13 percent of those in Dallas, compared with less than 3 percent in Houston, viewed the special. Normally, about 10 percent of Dallas viewers and 8 percent of Houston viewers watch the regularly scheduled *Paradise* and *Knots Landing.* Unfortunately, the Dallas market includes Fort Worth and cannot be separated by Dallas natives versus transplants.

People avoid discussing upsetting topics for a variety of reasons. In cases of incest or marital infidelity, an overriding motive may be the threat of humiliation or retaliation. In other cases, the topic may simply be too painful or psychologically threatening to broach. In Longview, Washington, citizens avoided reflecting on their feelings because they were facing the possibility of another deadly eruption of Mount Saint Helens. Californians living in the San Francisco Bay area fear a future massive earthquake.

In the case of Dallas, residents undoubtedly felt a vague sense of guilt that the assassination occurred in their city. Logically, they believed that they did not personally encourage Oswald's actions. The collective sense was to move forward and prove to the rest of the world that Dallas was indeed a great and progressive city. The sooner everyone forgot about it, the better for Dallas.

Such a logical strategy was highly successful in boosting the economic and social prospects of the city. But it also produced some unexpected costs. Dallas historians report that the assassination forced the city to become extremely image conscious. Others have noted similar trends in Memphis after the King murder and in Buffalo, New York, following the assassination of President McKinley in 1901. An overconcern with images and appearances comes at the expense of self-reflection. The refusal to acknowledge that a significant trauma has occurred—whether on the individual or community level—is both psychologically and physically unhealthy.

For a community or even an entire country, the building of exhibits, museums, or monuments is undoubtedly a psychologically healthy move. It is ironic that before it was built, the Vietnam Veterans' Memorial in Washington provoked controversies similar to those in Dallas surrounding the Sixth Floor Exhibit. In both cases, however, the subsequent effects were quite positive. Museums and monuments provide a symbolic acknowledgment that a trauma has occurred. For those people reticent to admit to their feelings about the psychological impact of an upheaval, museums and monuments serve to validate their experiences. In visiting both the Vietnam Memorial and the Sixth Floor Exhibit, I have been impressed by the emotional reactions of the visitors and even myself. In leaving both places, I have heard countless people talking in hushed tones about their personal feelings that had been dredged up.

I suspect that the visitors' talking about what they have seen provides a healthy way by which they can now assimilate and understand their complex thoughts and feelings. Memorials such as these tacitly allow people to openly acknowledge meaningful events in a socially acceptable way.

BEYOND COMMUNITIES: THE FAILURE OF NATIONS TO CONFRONT TRAUMAS

The case of Dallas is, in many ways, a microcosm of society in general. Most societies have their own version of the Kennedy assassination. Americans live with Vietnam, Germans with Hitler, Russians with Stalin. Within each culture, citizens are loath to openly discuss their deepest feelings about their nations' humiliations. In the United States, for example, many Vietnam veterans were treated despicably by their countrymen on their return from the war. Unlike those from all previous wars, Vietnam veterans were actively discouraged from disclosing their battle experiences. Germans who fought for their country in World War Two faced similar humiliations. In all such cases, a significant segment of the population was forced to keep overwhelming personal traumas to themselves.

Anytime people are not free to openly discuss important experiences with others, they should be at greater risk for a variety of health problems. This has certainly been true with Vietnam veterans and, I suspect, with World War Two German soldiers. But the problem goes far beyond soldiers. Any segment of society that must perforce inhibit its emotions, thoughts, or behaviors should exhibit increased health problems.

Consider what happens when a subgroup of people is identified as different by the majority. Prejudice and discrimination within any school, business, or community can force members of an outgroup to withhold expressing their feelings of anger and anxiety. In an effort to be accepted by the dominant members of the group, people must closely monitor their own behaviors and put on a false face in social situations.

A black student from a large city in Ohio who participated in one of our writing experiments explained his dilemma:

> At first, the university seemed to welcome me and make me a part of it. People were friendly and kind, and I felt good. Then came the big slap in my face: I was told that there was almost no interracial dating here at all. Sometimes, many times, it hurts. It's like I'm not a part of this society. Whenever I meet a new person, I often think to myself, "Is this person bigoted?" Or whenever I contemplate asking a girl out on a date, I wonder, "Would she like to go out with me, a black man?" . . . At home, I could always be myself. Here, I have to act very humble. I don't need any publicity.
>
> My feelings about this are sadness, disgust, and anger. Sometimes I just want to hit someone or something, or scream, in order to release my frustration. But no matter how hard I may pound my fists or grit my teeth, the situation will not change. But I just have to get through this and do whatever I can to be accepted, and that saddens me.

Across all of our writing studies, I have read strikingly similar essays by other blacks, Hispanics, and foreign students. But not just from minorities. Similar narratives have come from students who were crippled, stuttered, or were obese. At college, as in society in general, being different is a major social stressor.

The dangers of being discriminated against go far beyond psychological stress. In our society, virtually every ethnic group suffers from higher than average rates of heart disease and other health problems. Infant mortality, alcoholism and drug problems, and even deaths due to suicide and murder are much higher than average for blacks, Hispanics, native Americans and, in some cases, Asian Americans. The problems, of course, go far beyond issues of inhibition. Each of these groups is economically disadvantaged, has less access to medical care, and faces a myriad of cultural barriers to being accepted.

Beyond economic and cultural issues, however, any individuals who seek acceptance into a group of people who view them as somehow different or inferior will be prone to stress-related problems. It takes psychological and physiological work to maintain a false front.

12

Confession in Context: Therapy, Religion, and Brainwashing

The admission of our most personal thoughts and feelings is a powerful act. Across our writing studies, we have found that disclosing dark secrets can improve health and reduce stress. That intimate disclosure or confession can affect people's lives is hardly a new idea. Most societies, whether primitive or advanced, have encouraged confession in one form or another.

Consider the circumstances where confession is found. Religion, psychotherapy, and even thought-reform groups encourage people to disclose their intimate secrets. It is not coincidental that each of these institutions is strongly invested in shaping people's fundamental values and beliefs. It is also not surprising that people who confess in one institution are unlikely to confess in another. Consequently, there has long been friction among confession-based religions, political systems, and psychotherapy. The "confession industry" caters to a basic human need on a more or less exclusive basis. Within any given society, whoever controls the confession market has the power to shape the society's belief systems.

William Sargant, in his 1957 book *Battle for the Mind,* was one of the first people to explore the similarities among therapy, thought reform, and religious conversion. In his view, each system was effective in producing emotional exhaustion, which in turn made people more receptive to new ideas. Jerome Frank, a leading psychiatrist at the Johns Hopkins School of Medicine, expanded on this theme in his classic book *Persuasion and Healing.* Frank was particularly impressed by the context in which confession took place. For confession to bring about broad value changes, the confessor(s) had to give the impression of being all-powerful and forgiving. Further, in Frank's view, the confessors had to provide an overarching belief system that could explain previous suffering and sins. For example, when people confessed in a religious context, their transgressions could be attributed to evil spirits. Confession of personal shortcomings in a political thought-reform group in Chinese or North Korean prison camps could be blamed on the inherent problems of capitalism. And, of course, psychotherapists could attribute their patients' problems to early childhood experiences beyond the patients' control.

OUTLETS FOR PEOPLE'S URGE TO CONFESS

Most cultures have evolved some mechanism that allows people to disclose their deepest thoughts and feelings in a relatively safe manner. Anthropologists have been particularly interested in disclosure because rites of confession are closely linked to the prevailing belief systems surrounding religion, authority, and medicine within the group. Indeed, forms of disclosure across very different cultures appear to serve similar mental- and physical-health functions.

In tribes and smaller societies, for example, rites of confession are often associated with the healers or medicine men. In a fascinating overview of American Indian tribes, Duke University anthropologist Weston La Barre reports that virtually all native Americans—from the Eskimos north of Hudson Bay to the Indians indigenous to Chile—use confession as a cathartic therapy. Historical records of confession ceremonies indicate that they occur with equal frequency whether or not the tribes had been touched by early Roman Catholic missionaries.

Among North and South American tribes, a common belief was that strength and physical health were closely tied to honesty and purity. Illness, then, was a punishment for sin. Among the Aurohuaca Indians of Colombia, the shaman or witch doctor refused to treat sick patients until they confessed their sins. Once confessed, the sins were transferred to pieces of shell or stone and exposed to the sunlight, which in essence bleached the sin out. The Incas of Peru confessed to a high priest while bathing in a river with the belief that the river would carry the sins downstream—a primitive version of downriver dumping. Similar confession rites were and in many cases continue to be common in tribes or remote regions of Africa, Burma, India, and other parts of Asia.

Confession ceremonies are not limited to small bands of Indians or other remote tribes. All the major world religions—Christianity, Islam, Hinduism, Judaism, Buddhism—encourage the acknowledgment and/or disclosure of transgressions. The methods and rationales for confessions differ across the religions. Some encourage private forms of confession through prayer, others expect followers to confess to a designated religious leader or to a group of people. These variations on confession can be found within most world religions as well.

Within Christianity, for example, Quakers, Unitarians, and others are expected to confess to sins in prayer or simply to oneself. Catholics, Episcopalians, and the Greek and Russian Orthodox have formal mechanisms whereby followers can confess to their ministers or priests. Mennonites and various denominations of evangelical Christians are encouraged to disclose shortcomings in the presence of the congregation. Many Christian groups believe that the nature of confession depends on what is to be confessed. Among Southern Baptists, for example, people are expected to admit their sins to those who have been aggrieved. If a member of the church has absconded with funds, most congregations would like to see that person confess his embezzlement to the church as a group. Marital infidelity, by this system, should be confessed to the spouse.

Many researchers note that confession is particularly important when people undergo religious conversion experiences. The great evangelists, from John Wesley to Billy Graham, have demanded that their audiences confess their sins, and once this was done, their hearts would be ready to accept the Lord. Particularly cohesive religious groups outside the mainstream, such as Scientology, Reverend Moon's Unification Church, and the Krishna movement, are usually successful in getting their converts to disclose publicly their most personal experiences and feelings to others within the group.

Confession also occurs outside religious institutions. Within political systems that actively discourage religion, such as offshoots of Marxism, forms of confession or self-criticism are fostered. Mao Tse-tung, the revolutionary leader of China, frequently proclaimed that one of the strengths of the Chinese communist movement was in encouraging the open criticism of the party's and the people's problems. As Mao noted in 1943, six years before consolidating his leadership in China, "We should check our complacency and constantly criticize our shortcomings, just as we should wash our faces or sweep the floor every day to remove the dirt and keep them clean." Mao's approach to self-criticism served as the centerpiece for "reeducation programs." That is, when members of the society displayed bad judgment (e.g., disagreeing with the Party), they were strongly urged to criticize their own views publicly.

Other methods of self-criticism or confession were encouraged by followers of by Lenin and Stalin in the Soviet Union. After World War Two, self-criticism groups were an integral part of education in the Soviet-bloc countries. In postwar East Germany, for example, students met in small groups as often as once a week and were expected to disclose many of their private thoughts concerning love, money, freedom, and other values. The group leaders, who attempted to be supportive, often would redefine the students' psychological conflicts in political terms.

Note that confession and self-criticism are an integral part of most democratic judicial systems. One determinant of criminal punishment is the degree to which the defendant openly confesses and is remorseful for his or her actions. An open and sincere confession indicates that the person acknowledges the values of the judicial system and that he or she has strayed from these values. Confession in the courtroom, then, promotes the values of the state over those of the individual.

In modern societies that actively encourage individual freedoms, confession often takes place within psychotherapeutic settings rather than in situations controlled by political or religious groups. Virtually all therapies expect participants to disclose intimate parts of themselves. Indeed, whenever patients or clients enter the office of a therapist they are, by definition, admitting to some shortcomings. Merely acknowledging and discussing their problems can be viewed as a form of confession. With few exceptions, most therapists consider the patients' understanding of their own problems to be important in treatment. To attain this end, disclosure or confession is almost a prerequisite.

Particularly interesting is the popularization of confession in the broad spectrum of self-help groups. Self-improvement groups such as est (now called the Forum), Lifespring, and Zig Ziglar have been phenomenally successful in training thousands of people world-wide to have a more positive view of themselves. The indoctrination process of these groups typically occurs over a three-to-five-day period wherein people's basic view of themselves is challenged. Pivotal in this process is that most participants usually break down and express many of their deepest and most emotional secrets to others in the group.

Less intense but similar techniques are found in most of the currently popular twelve-step programs that focus on alcoholism, drug abuse, codependency, and so forth. In these groups, people are encouraged to tell their personal stories as they relate to the group goals. In Alcoholics Anonymous, for example, participants relive their most painful thoughts and feelings associated with alcohol. Those who disclose their secrets are given a tremendous amount of support by other members, who have often gone through similar experiences.

AN ANALYSIS OF THE CONTEXT OF DISCLOSURE

Christians, communists, therapists, reformed alcoholics, and Chickasaw Indians—a motley group by any standard—all share the use of confession. The rationale for confession may be different for each group, but the function may ultimately be the same. When people divulge the intimate sides of themselves, their psychological and social worlds change. Psychologically, the act of translating private thoughts into language helps people understand and assimilate the thoughts more efficiently. Socially, when people confess to others, they are often forging a social bond. That is, once individuals admit their deepest secrets, they are in essence proclaiming their trust to the people with whom they share their thoughts and feelings.

The potential psychological and social advantages to confession are inescapable. But a nagging question keeps returning. What makes people confess to others in the first place? Why do individuals disclose intimate parts of themselves to religious leaders, thought-reform groups, or even complete strangers in therapy or self-help groups? Clearly, there must be more than some overriding need to divulge our personal side. People, after all, do not confess indiscriminately. Part of the secret that explains when and why people confess lies within the situation.

Certain settings are more conducive to confessions than others. By trial and error, I eventually discovered what professional confession-getters have known for centuries: The more unique the setting, the more likely people will be to disclose intimate parts of themselves. In our writing experiments, for example, people are unlikely to divulge their darkest secrets when writing in a classroom surrounded by their peers. Interestingly, even if the classroom is empty, they are still reticent to disclose their most personal thoughts and feelings.

Perhaps the most dramatic example of the role of context occurred when my students and I first began our spoken-disclosure studies. When we began the project, volunteers sat in a standard laboratory room and spoke quietly into a microphone. Unfortunately, the acoustics in the room were terrible because of noise from the adjacent hallway. To combat this problem, we desperately needed to soundproof the laboratory on a very, very low budget. Cherie Hughes, one of the resourceful graduate students involved in the experiment, assured me that she would solve our sound problem. A few hours later, she returned with hundreds of used egg cartons, which we soon had taped, nailed, or glued to the walls and ceilings of the laboratory. To hide the dried yolks in several of the cartons, we decided to use a dim purple lamp while people disclosed rather than stay with the bright overhead lights.

Our transformed laboratory was like no place you have ever seen. The purple lamp on the floor cast an eerie shadow over the moonlike egg-carton surfaces of the wall. With the "new" room came new levels of disclosure from our participants. People cried more quickly and disclosed their intimate secrets almost as soon as they sat down. After this experience, I became convinced that the more unusual the setting and the more detached it is from the real world, the more likely that people will let go and disclose their secrets.

The real world provides a number of examples to support the power of unique settings in inducing disclosure. People who have not traveled much tend to reveal a great deal about themselves when on airplanes, trains, or buses. I have always been amazed by the degree to which people will confess their humiliating and embarrassing experiences on national television talk shows such as those hosted by Phil Donahue, Geraldo Rivera, or Oprah Winfrey. My guess is that high disclosers have not spent much time in the unique environs of a television studio.

Uniqueness is only one factor that can promote disclosure. The darker the setting, the more uninhibited people become. We are more likely to confess our love to someone in the moonlight than under the bright fluorescent lights of K mart. Darkness makes us partially anonymous, less psychologically connected to the rules that guide our everyday behaviors. Perhaps the most dramatic demonstration of this was in an ingenious experiment by Kenneth and Mary Gergen of Swarthmore College. In their study, they brought unacquainted students in groups of six, one at a time, into a completely dark room. No one ever saw who the other people in the room were. Each person was in the room for about an hour. According to the Gergens:

> For each group that entered the room, explorations of the space and lively chatter dominated the first quarter of the hour, but soon discussion turned to matters that group members later indicated were "extremely important" to them. After approximately 40 minutes, conversation began to fade, and members of the group began to engage in physical interaction. Some 90 percent of the participants indicated that they touched each other on purpose. Almost 50 percent engaged in hugging. . . . Some 80 percent of the subjects indicated that they were sexually aroused. (p. 382).

Not surprisingly, when separate groups of participants were involved in the same study with the overhead lights shining brightly, everyone sat several feet from one another and talked politely for the entire hour. With lights on, people did not disclose the intimate sides of themselves, nor did they even touch one another accidentally.

Within many confession rituals, the disclosure of intimate secrets typically takes place in the dark. For Roman Catholics, confession traditionally occurs in a darkened booth. In most smaller churches and synagogues, the lighting is usually low during prayer services, where private confessions are encouraged. Among the Plains Indians of North America in the nineteenth century, male members of the tribe would disclose their deepest secrets around a campfire on the first night out on a war party. Even within psychotherapy, many therapists dim the lights while talking with patients. Freud, for example, required that patients lie down so that they could not see him, because, in his words, "I cannot bear to be gazed at for eight hours a day (or more). Since, while I listen . . . I do not wish my expression to give the patient indications . . . which may influence him in his communications." (p. 146) Although his room was not completely dark, Freud engineered the setting to accomplish the same ends that darkness allows.

When it's dark, and perhaps a little eerie, we can't see anyone else's facial expressions. And they can't see ours. We don't have to work to hide our expressions and, by extension, our feelings. Darkness allows us to get into a trance state more easily. While talking with someone else, we can stare at the moon, a light in the distance, or nothing at all. It is a process strikingly similar to hypnosis or to a relaxation response. In these trance states, our tendencies to be critical or self-conscious are reduced. We let go and openly disclose our secrets.

Many confession or self-criticism rituals take place when participants are in an altered emotional or biological state. The nature of this altered state, however, is quite different from group to group. In some cases, confession takes place when people are anxious or excited. In others, the individuals are extremely relaxed. And yet others seek to induce confessions while people are under the influence of alcohol or drugs, or when deprived of sleep or food. The commonality of these various procedures is that when people are in confession-related settings, they don't feel the way they normally do.

Among many North and Central American Indian tribes, for example, confession ceremonies often took place while members were under the influence of peyote, a moderately powerful hallucinatory drug derived from the mescal cactus. The Winnebago tribe of modern-day Wisconsin and the Chichimeca of Mexico expected men to consume peyote around sunset. By midnight or the following day, the men were expected to confess their transgressions, especially those related to sex, in order to purify themselves. Other confession rituals occur after participants have fasted for one or more days.

Ever since William James wrote about religious conversion in 1902, observers have noted that emotional excitement and/or exhaustion typically accompanies confession and attitude change. Modern-day self-help groups such as est, political thought-reform camps, and groups dedicated to religious conversion are particularly successful in attaining their goals if their prospective converts are deprived of sleep, are hungry and emotionally drained.

Perhaps the most common form of emotional excitement that accompanies confession surrounds anxiety. Almost by definition, most unique settings arouse a certain degree of nervousness or fear. In many settings, the leaders who hope to induce confessions actively inspire anxiety. Over the years, for example, I have attended dozens of evangelical faith healing and religious conversion meetings in the United States. In most, the ceremony follows a predictable course. After a few hymns, the speakers begin with warmth and humor. Then more hymns. And then, things turn serious.

Most evangelists that I have heard tell a remarkably similar story that always arouses intense fear, anxiety, and sadness. Apparently, most of them knew a beautiful eighteen-year-old high school student who converted her wayward parents to Christianity. On her way to give her valedictory address to her high school class, she stopped and prayed with the evangelist. Tragically, every one of these beautiful eighteen-year-old valedictorians was killed that very evening in a freak car accident. As the story is told, the organist quietly begins playing a hymn in the background. By the time the evangelist gets to the description of the girl's bloodstained white dress, the solemn music is loud and moving. By then, many in the audience are in tears. Everyone is thinking, Life is random, unpredictable. If death can claim such an innocent and good person, it can certainly get me. It is at this point that the speaker asks people to come and confess their sins and dedicate their lives to Jesus. In a roundabout way, confession is offered as a relief from anxiety.

Laboratory studies indicate that people are vulnerable to persuasion when they are given drugs that cause biological changes associated with anxiety (e.g., Adrenalin) or relaxation (sodium pentothal). The assumption of some of this research is that people can easily misattribute the meaning of their arousal. For example, a person who may be aroused because he has not had enough sleep could be induced to think that he felt happy, sad, or anxious because he had not confessed his sins. In other words, when people are in an altered emotional state, they often do not think as critically as usual. Further, changes in physiological arousal from ambiguous sources tends to make people not trust their bodily cues. The net result is that people will place too much trust in the words of their evangelist, witch doctor, or group leader and ignore their own feelings and common sense.

Note that drugs and certain forms of emotional activation do more than make us ignore our own internal signals. Some drugs selectively affect our ability to inhibit our behaviors. Alcohol, for example, results in the temporary breakdown of specific inhibition centers within the brain. It is not surprising that many confessions of love and hate, made under the influence of alcohol at night, are conveniently forgotten or overlooked in the sober morning light.

Confession is also aided by a powerful, all-accepting, and forgiving audience. People are most likely to disclose their deepest secrets if they perceive that their potential listeners will accept them no matter what they say. In many ways, this was the central idea behind Freud's ideas on transference and Carl Rogers's view of the ideal therapist. From pagan confession rituals to confession in most current religions to self-criticism in thought-reform or self-help groups, people are usually expected to disclose to an important and nonpunitive leader.

One of the exceptions to this rule occurs when people disclose their secrets to their peer group—as in Alcoholics Anonymous or among the Cheyenne Indians, who confessed to all other members of the tribe. Ironically, confession to one's peers may be a particularly powerful bonding experience because when it happens, the group norm is that people will not criticize the individuals who confess. In short, the act of confession to a group of equals demands a great deal of honesty and trust among the group members. After all, in groups such as this, the norm is that each person will, in turn, divulge intimate secrets.

A unique setting, darkness, feelings of anxiety, and a powerful and accepting listener. Bringing all of these components together does not mean that you or anyone else will automatically begin disclosing secrets. Rather, these are simply some of the ingredients that are generally used by professional confession-getters to promote intimate disclosure. Unique settings and dark rooms are important in that they make individuals feel less tied to their day-to-day world. Alterations in emotional states often cause people to use and trust their bodily signals less. A powerful leader can further prompt this process by making individuals feel extremely safe and secure in disclosing their secrets.

Keep in mind that the act of confession is one where people

must let down their inhibitions and other defenses. The contextual cues I have mentioned are primarily significant in initiating the confession. That is, people will usually not disclose to others (or even to themselves) if they do not feel secure, detached from everyday life, and so forth. When and where people confess, however, is only the beginning of the story. More important is how the ultimate disclosure is interpreted and used by the person. Indeed, the entire direction of a confession will be dictated by the underlying values of the confessor, the group, or the person doing the confession in the first place.

PERSONAL VALUES EMBEDDED WITHIN THE CONTEXT

Try the following thought experiment. Imagine that I asked you to write down your very deepest thoughts and feelings concerning your personal feelings of sexuality and love. In the first scenario, imagine that you will keep your writing and no one, not even me, will ever see what you have written. Before we change scenes, seriously think to yourself how you would go about writing this particular topic. What secret issues and hidden desires would you bring up?

Scenario two. Imagine this time that I will be giving your writing sample to your parents and will be asking them to evaluate what you have written on sexuality and love. For some people, the writing style for scenario two would be relatively similar to that for scenario one. Most, however, would subtly—or dramatically—change the content and style of what they had written.

Scenarios three, four, etc. Imagine the same writing assignment, but this time I told you that your essay—which, of course, would have your name on it—would be read by your boss. Or your minister or rabbi. Or maybe the sophomore class at the local high school. Or even a convention of psychologists, who would judge your mental health.

You get the idea. We can all honestly divulge our deepest thoughts and feelings to different audiences. However, we change our definition of "deepest" depending on the audience. We also subtly alter our interpretations of identical events from setting to setting.

There are some obvious reasons why people's stories change depending on the audience. If individuals think that the intended audience would disapprove or could, in some way, punish them, they will almost have to reconstruct their stories. Similarly, if the intended audience is personally or professionally important, people will bend their essays to look as good as possible. But the seeking of rewards and the avoidance of punishment are only two types of motivations that guide how we write and talk about our personal experiences.

Within any given social situation, there are a number of unspoken but tacitly agreed upon values. When you enter a religious establishment, for example, no one needs to give you a written list of approved behaviors. Even if you have never been in that particular house of worship, you instantly know that you shouldn't smoke, drink alcohol, laugh boisterously, and so forth. Similarly, if you go to meet with a bank officer in an attempt to get a loan, there are some topics you avoid. Overarching values in the religious establishment may be *respect* and *tradition*. In the bank foyer, the tacit values might be *frugality* and *fiscal responsibility*.

The importance of settings is that they can engage an entire set of implicit values. These values are the ones by which you measure yourself at that particular time. For example, if a college professor versus a bank officer asked you to evaluate your own personality, your thinking about your own intelligence would flow more naturally in front of the professor and your ideas about money management skills would tend to surface in front of the bank officer. The setting or the context, then, is laden with implicit values.

Imagine, now, that I ask you to write about your deepest thoughts and feelings about yourself. Further, you can keep anything you write and never show it to a soul. The only difference this time is that I am a psychologist or a religious leader. My mere presence will alter the implicit values that are prominent in your own mind. Consequently, the way you write will change even though the person giving the instructions will never see your writing sample.

The implicit values for the psychologist might be for you to explore your own thoughts from the perspective of a psychologist—whatever that might be. At the back of your mind, for example, you might ask yourself, Am I sane? Do I get along with people well? Did I have a normal childhood? These can be central questions that, when answered, give us a better understanding of ourselves.

The implicit values associated with the religious leader may be equally central to our being but may be quite different from those linked to the psychologist. If the religious person asked you to explore your own thoughts and feelings, the implicit values of the situation might prompt you to ask yourself, Am I a good person? Do I treat others honestly and fairly? Was I a good child for my parents? Any self-reflective essay, then, would elicit answers to questions that were implicitly aroused by the religious context.

You can see, then, how traumas can be explained by invoking different implicit values. Assume, for example, that you have been raped and are now trying to grapple with this overwhelmingly traumatic experience. Indeed, whether you are a psychologist, minister, or Mao-inspired communist, you will have no ready understanding of such a trauma. In all likelihood, you will obsess about it, dream about it, develop irrational fears about it, and will probably suffer from several physical illnesses in the year after the trauma.

Now imagine being asked to anonymously write about your traumatic experience within the context of either implicit psychological, religious, or political values. From the psychological perspective, many of the issues you would write about would explore why you currently felt the way you did. From the religious value system, you might address issues of acceptance of hardships as in the book of Job. From a political point of view, you would probably explain your and the rapist's behaviors as reflecting the economic or political system. No matter what value system you adopted, however, you would probably benefit from the writing experience. By translating the event into language, you would now have a better understanding of the event and of yourself.

The irony of writing from any of the three perspectives is that your understanding of the rape would be completely different depending on the context in which you wrote. There would also be another important change in your own mind after writing: You would adhere to the implicit value system to a far greater extent than before your writing. Let me explain.

When we write or talk about a trauma, we tend to use whatever implicit and explicit values are available to help us try to understand it. If, for example, we were asked to confide to a respected pastor in the community, we very likely would try to explain our trauma by way of implicit religious values. The mere act of doing this would define the trauma in semireligious terms. The implicit values of religion, in this example, would be used to define a central, important psychological event in our life—the trauma. If this implicit value *can* explain the trauma, we will be likely to invoke the same value system in the future to explain other traumas. The original implicit values aroused by our confiding in a pastor will have now become a central way by which we define ourselves.

Confession, then, becomes a very powerful psychological force. When people disclose deeply personal experiences within a given context, they will be likely to define their personalities, their very selves, in line with the values of the context. Confession is not necessarily dangerous in and of itself. It only has the potential for danger when people start to understand and define themselves using the implicit values surrounding the context of their disclosures.

And this brings us back to thought reform and brainwashing. Brainwashing is a deliciously value-laden term. Despite the vivid images that brainwashing conjures, there is no such thing as a technique that can wipe out your memories and values, thereby replacing them with new thoughts. The judicious use of confession, however, can cause people to reevaluate fundamental parts of themselves with alternative value schemes. Once individuals actively consider traumatic experiences (which are usually fundamental to their conflicts about their self-image) from a new value-based perspective, they will better be able to understand the trauma and to endorse the new value scheme.

It is little wonder, then, that tribal, religious, and political groups that strongly encourage public confession or self-criticism remain so powerful for as long as they do. They virtually guarantee that any new society members who go through their programs—including rites of passage, confirmation, joining the state's party—will enthusiastically endorse their values.

But wait. The use of confession is rarely a conscious conspiracy employed by cynical leaders of powerful institutions. Rather, people have formed social institutions that encourage confession because they have a need to disclose and understand the intimate sides of themselves. When people take the opportunity to confess, their stress levels drop. That this technique can also alter or cement basic human values is an unintended consequence.

THE IMPLICIT VALUES BEHIND WRITING

Psychologists and other therapists are not value free. In therapeutic relationships, the subtle values and goals of therapists can influence the ways in which their patients disclose their own experiences. Jerome Frank and others have long argued that one of the major roadblocks to successful therapy is when the therapist and patient possess fundamentally different value systems. Fortunately, within any given culture, most therapists and patients will share more fundamental values than not.

There are exceptions. For example, if the therapist has recently faced a trauma such as divorce, his or her beliefs about relationships will undoubtedly be affected in a variety of ways. Should the therapist now see a patient who seeks marital counseling, potential value clashes may occur. The problem is typically exacerbated when the therapist and patient are unaware that their values are coloring their judgments of the other. An interesting therapist-training procedure, currently being developed by Nan Pressor of the University of Missouri, attempts to make the therapist constantly aware of his or her own guiding values while therapy is ongoing. According to Pressor, once the therapist's implicit values become explicit, the therapist can more easily set aside the values in helping a given patient.

Given that implicit values can color the therapist-patient relationship, it becomes interesting to speculate on the role that values play when people write about their deepest thoughts and feelings on their own. If you have faced a trauma, for example, and now write about it in the safety of your own home, what implicit values will affect you? On a certain level, it may not matter. You will attempt to explain the trauma using whatever implicit values you normally hold. The one potential danger, however, is that some of your implicit values may not be adaptive or healthy. For example, if you implicitly believe that you are a worthless individual, your writing about a trauma will be colored by your belief. In a case such as this, it could be worthwhile to confront your beliefs concerning your worthlessness as well as the trauma.

In any situation, implicit values are potentially troublesome because we are usually not aware of them. If you disclose your secrets on paper or to other people, it can be beneficial to reflect on the underlying values you are working from. What are your basic beliefs about right and wrong, about life and death, about sex, love, and hate, about the nature of friendship and God, and about yourself? Once you know those basic values that are affecting your thought processes, you can be more informed in evaluating your emotions and life experiences.

13
Beyond Traumas: Writing and Well-being

We don't need to talk to others to tell our untold stories. Nonetheless, our untold thoughts and feelings should, in some way, be verbalized. Whether we talk into a tape recorder or write on a magic pad, translating our thoughts into language is psychologically and physically beneficial. When people write about major upheavals, they begin to organize and understand them. Writing about the thoughts and feelings associated with traumas, then, forces individuals to bring together the many facets of overwhelmingly complicated events. Once people can distill complex experiences into more understandable packages, they can begin to move beyond the trauma.

Writing, then, organizes traumas. What about other complex experiences that are not traumatic? For example, if you were learning about all the factors that led to the Russian Revolution in 1917, would it help you in your studying to write about what you were learning? Or if you were in the process of beginning a new job, would it be beneficial for you to write about your experiences at the end of each day? Learning about and understanding the Russian Revolution or about a new job can be highly complicated tasks. If writing about a trauma helps organize the experience, writing should work in the same way in our dealing with any new tasks.

WRITING AS A TOOL FOR EDUCATION

Earlier in the book a distinction was made between confronting versus being confronted by a trauma. The idea was that when people are confronted by traumas, their world view is shaken and they become anxious, upset, and physiologically harmed. However, when people confront traumas, by talking or writing about them, their mental and physiological stress levels drop. Confronting traumas allows individuals to reorganize and assimilate the events.

Now consider the nature of American education. The primary goal of high schools and colleges is to get students to understand and integrate ideas and facts from a variety of disciplines in order to enrich their lives and prepare them for the real world. Like all teachers, I secretly hope that my eager students will assimilate what I tell them and when I meet them later in life, they will profusely thank me for changing their world view. Why does this so rarely happen? The answer may lie, in part, in the distinction between confronting versus being confronted by events. As a teacher, for example, I lecture, or psychologically confront, a large group of students with a bewildering number of facts, theories, and stories. The role of the students is to be passive recipients of information. I confront them with information; they are confronted by it. In a twisted sort of way, a lecture is like a trauma for the audience. People are passively confronted by a bewildering amount of information over which they have very little control.

If we want students to assimilate the information we give them, we must change our educational strategies. Students should be actively encouraged to write or talk about our facts and theories. Even more powerful would be to have them write about relevant educational material within the context of their own personal experiences. Further, if exams are intended to stimulate learning rather than solely evaluate students' performance, multiple-choice exams should be outlawed. Essay exams, which actively promote the integration of information, should be encouraged.

An in-class writing system.   Over the last few years, Lizabeth McIntire, a psychology graduate student, and I have developed a simple in-class writing strategy that demands that students confront the reading and lecture information to which they are exposed. One of the classes where we have applied this strategy is a team-taught course entitled Social and Political Institutions from 1854 to the Present. This required class attempts to explain selected social, economic, and political institutions that have shaped the twentieth century and have created many of the current problems in the world. Although a potentially fascinating class,

it has traditionally been disliked by students because of the overwhelming reading load and the seemingly unrelated lectures given
in a rotating manner by one of five instructors from different
disciplines.

In addition to two large lectures each week, students attend
one weekly discussion section of about thirty people. In the section, the instructor attempts to generate an exciting intellectual
debate about the topics of the week. I say "attempts" because most
discussion sections don't work. The students have been so inun-
dated with reading and lecture material, they can't sort what is
relevant from irrelevant. It was in the discussion sections that we
introduced the in-class writing system.

At the beginning of each discussion class, students were provided with a very brief overview of the main ideas of the readings
and lectures. They were then told to write continuously for ten
minutes about their deepest thoughts and feelings about the topic.
Although students turned their writing assignments in to the instructor, they were never graded on what they wrote—no matter
how crazy or offensive it was.

In my own discussion section, I was amazed by the trans-
formation in the students. Before writing, it was impossible to
get a discussion going, unless it had nothing to do with the topic.
After writing, however, almost all of the students contributed
interesting and insightful ideas about formerly obscure topics—
such as how the British East India Tea Company promoted the
growth of imperialism in India. Their writing had forced them to
assimilate ideas from a variety of sources as well as from their
own experiences. All of a sudden, topics such as the British East
India Tea Company or the plight of the Mosquito Indians in Central America became relevant to their own lives. Further, once I
had initiated the writing assignments, absentee rates dropped and
performance on exams (essay, of course) improved dramatically.

We have since used the in-class writing system in other classes,
such as introductory psychology, with equal success. Across the
board, students acknowledge that in-class writing forces them to
integrate ideas and to fundamentally know the subject matter.
Their improved exam scores and lower absentee rates validate their
perceptions. And of course, the irony is inescapable. The in-class
writing assignment takes about ten minutes, or 20 percent, of each
class period. Students are being confronted with less information
but are learning more than students in regular classes.

On the training of writing, reading, and thinking skills.

The role of writing in education has been a hotly debated topic for most of the twentieth century. Much of the controversy has grown from the brilliant writings of Lev Vygotsky, a Soviet psychologist who died at the age of thirty-eight in 1934. Vygotsky proposed fascinating new ways to understand language and thought that have challenged several traditional views of education. Children, he argued, used language to sort out their thoughts and to solve real-world problems. In his view, young children naturally progressed through a series of phases that allowed them to communicate with others and, eventually, themselves. This progression began with noises and gestures, to spoken language, to play, to symbolic play in the form of drawing, and finally to written language. Writing, then, meant going from drawing pictures to drawing words.

In a startling experiment with three- and four-year-olds, one of Vygotsky's colleagues, A. R. Luria, demonstrated that children understood the nature of writing even though they couldn't read. For example, Luria told the children to memorize a series of phrases. Once the children realized that there were too many phrases to remember, Luria handed them a pencil and paper and told them to write down what he was saying. Even though none of the children could write, they seemed to mimic writing behaviors that they had seen in adults. Most of the young children, then, would make little scribbles each time Luria called out a phrase. Later, when Luria asked each of the children to recall the words and phrases, a small percentage would look at the marks and squiggles and, according to Vygotsky, "repeatedly indicate, without error, which marks denote which phrase. . . . We are . . . seeing the first precursor of future writing."

The work of Vygotsky and Luria indicates that speaking and writing skills are fundamental to humans and partially dictate how we perceive the world. Vygotsky was adamant that the way children are taught to read and write in Russian and Western society should be changed. Writing, which he viewed as a symbolic form of drawing, was as basic as speaking. Because it was a natural development, children should be given the opportunity to learn to read and write as early as age three. But the method of learning should not be based on the imposed (confronted-by) rote teaching styles that most of us grew up with. Rather, reading and writing skills should be seen as desirable forms of communication by the children. For example, children should be shown that by writing, they can communicate their thoughts in letters or diaries. In short, Vygotsky argued that young children should confront writing skills rather than be confronted by them.

Much of Vygotsky's work has profoundly affected American educators. Particularly exciting are educational projects that encourage children to write in a stream-of-consciousness manner as early as the first grade. These writing techniques, which are variously called freewriting or process writing, have produced impressive gains in students' writing and reading abilities. Since the early 1970s, Donald Graves, of the University of New Hampshire, has been developing a process-writing program for young elementary-school children. He finds that those who are expected to write freely about their personal experiences learn to read more quickly and to perform better on a variety of verbal tests.

A number of secondary and college educators, too, have been successfully exploring the benefits of freewriting. Peter Elbow, at the University of Massachusetts at Amherst, has been at the forefront of this movement in proposing how college students and adults can overcome writer's block and their general fears concerning writing. He finds that having people write continuously for ten minutes a day serves as a mental-conditioning technique. Indeed, for people who often have trouble writing—whether a paper for class or a report for the office—he finds that the ten-minute freewriting exercise can "jumpstart" the brain.

WRITING AS A BOOST TO LEARNING AND CREATIVITY

As long as we are on the topic of writing and education, it makes sense to comment briefly on the art of taking notes. Note taking, whether in the classroom, in a business meeting, or when talking with a client, serves a similar function to writing in general. We usually take notes to help us remember the main points of a lecture or meeting.

Interestingly, notes can reflect either a *being-confronted-by* or a *confronting* strategy. When people are in a being-confronted-by mode, their notes usually focus on detail, including numerous direct quotes. Indeed, notes taken in this mode are almost transcriptions wherein the note taker is not actively thinking during the lecture or talk. Notes taken with a confronting strategy, on the other hand, are much broader and integrative. The note taker, who is actively thinking about the topic, will often write down a brief summary of what the speaker is discussing along with his or her own views on the matter.

Recent research on note-taking strategies by Gillis Einstein and his colleagues at Furman University indicates that students who perform the best on exams tend to adopt confronting methods of taking notes. Those who perform poorly typically focus on details congruent with a being-confronted-by strategy. It is not coincidental that the being-confronted-by approach is a form of low-level thinking that often occurs when people are in uncontrollable or unpredictable situations. Individuals who adopt a low-level thinking style, not unlike those using a being-confronted-by mode of note taking, tend to focus on details, adopt a narrow time perspective, and are unable to self-reflect.

Like drawing, writing is a natural human activity. One of its values is in helping us integrate and organize our complicated lives. Writing accomplishes this less-than-modest goal in a variety of ways:

Writing clears the mind.   Before beginning a complex task, it can be beneficial to write out your thoughts and feelings. Indeed, professional hypnotists often use this technique in order to accelerate the hypnotic procedure. Basically, they ask their clients to jot down their current thoughts and feelings. When their clients finish writing, the hypnotists tell them to tear up the paper and throw it away. This serves as a symbolic form of clearing the mind.

Writing resolves traumas that stand in the way of important tasks.   Following major upheavals, people tend to obsess about them. In thinking about the traumas, and even in trying not to think about them, individuals use a great deal of their thinking capacity. Hence, they become forgetful and cannot sustain their attention on large new tasks. Writing about traumas helps to organize the traumas, thereby freeing the mind to deal with other tasks.

Writing helps in acquiring and remembering new information.   As the note-taking research indicates, writing thoughtful notes or, in the case of young children, squiggles, helps people to take in and recall new ideas. Writing can help provide a framework by which to understand the new and unique perspectives of others. Indeed, writing about them makes the ideas more vivid and memorable.

Writing fosters problem solving.   Because writing promotes the integration of information, it can help solve complex problems. If people write freely about a complicated problem they are dealing with, they can more readily find a solution. There are several reasons for this. One is that writing forces people to sustain their attention on a given topic for a longer period than they normally would do if they were just thinking about it. Because writing is slower than thinking, each idea must be thought about in greater detail. Writing is also more linear than thinking in that writing forces an entire idea to be transcribed before another is entertained.

Freewriting promotes forced writing.   Most people are called on to write something on occasion—whether a legal brief, a medical opinion, or a letter of complaint to the city dog catcher. Formal writing can be a serious drag. Every sentence can sound stilted, every word inappropriate. Freely writing about your thoughts and feelings before beginning any formal writing can loosen your writing skills. Even using freewriting as the basis of a rough draft can be helpful.

There is no need to belabor the point further. Writing can be an invaluable skill in learning about and coping with the world. Under the right circumstances, writing promotes mental and physical health. Although it is not a panacea, the judicious use of writing can improve the quality of life for many of us.

DIARIES AND JOURNALS

Given that writing has so many apparent benefits, you would think that people who keep diaries would be wonderfully happy, healthy, and creative. I'm afraid the world is not so simple and straightforward. There is a good reason for this. The ways people keep and use diaries are amazingly diverse.

In our surveys of several hundred college students, for example, over 50 percent never write in a diary or journal. Another 40 percent or so write in a diary once or twice a week. Only about 3 percent write daily or almost daily. Although women in our samples tend to use diaries more than men, the gender difference is surprisingly small. Of particular importance is that frequent diary writers are no healthier than people who rarely or never use diaries.

One reason it is hard to evaluate the health effects of diary writing is that we don't know what the diary writers' health would be if they didn't write in their diaries. Who knows? Maybe diary writers are staving off a plethora of dreaded diseases by writing. Similarly, we don't know the personality differences between diary and non-diary writers. Perhaps people who don't use diaries are more socially at ease and can talk about their deepest thoughts and feelings to others. Hence, they don't need to rely on a diary. Finally, it is always difficult to sort out the motivations for people keeping diaries. Some may have been inspired by Samuel Pepys and the remarkably detailed confessional and descriptive diaries he kept for ten years of his life in the seventeenth century. Others may be required to maintain a diary because of religious doctrine. Many I have talked with simply want a record of who they have seen and what they have done in their lives.

A more intriguing issue, however, is what people decide to put in their diaries and journals. Mormons, for example, strongly encourage their members to maintain a diary of their lives. Indeed, the Mormons have assembled one of the most impressive genealogical libraries in the Western hemisphere, which houses many of these journals. Interestingly, the journals are typically factual and not emotional. That is, most Mormons who keep diaries do not explore their most secret and perverse thoughts, probably because they know that their diaries may be read for generations after their death.

Among the people I have interviewed who have kept intimate and emotional diaries, two distinctly different patterns have emerged in the ways they maintain their diaries. One group—of which I am a member—only writes during periods of stress or unhappiness. If life is plodding along in a fairly predictable way, people in this group simply have no interest in writing. The second group, which is less than half the size of the first, writes almost daily. That is, until traumas strike. During massive stressors, people in this group stop writing. For example, one well-adjusted woman, who had written almost daily for years, abruptly stopped writing the day she learned of her daughter's unexpected death.

She explained that she could talk about the death but could not yet write about it. In fact, she did not begin exploring her thoughts and feelings on paper until a year and a half after the death. (That magical year and a half, again.)

Oddly, I have not yet met a person who wrote about his or her deepest feelings who did not fall into one of the two writing patterns. I am certain that there are some exceptions. I just haven't met one yet. I think the existence of these two writing patterns suggests the different functions writing can serve for people. For those who only write during or following a trauma, diaries serve as a way to cope—perhaps as a substitute for talking with others about the traumas. Those in the second group who stop writing during times of trauma report that the emotions are too intense to deal with in journal form. As a group, the overwhelming majority of people I have interviewed are quite sociable and have been able to talk to others about their traumas.

Finally, there exists a separate group of letter writers who do not classify themselves as diary or journal writers but who, in their letters, explore their deepest thoughts and feelings on an almost daily basis. The major difference between diary and letter writing is the degree to which the writers feel free to disclose intimate parts of themselves. A particularly novel twist on letter writing occurs when people write to others whom they don't know. In addition to pen-pal systems, various letter exchanges have become popular. For example, Stephen Sikora of Albany, California, initiated in 1983 a magazine, *The Letter Exchange,* dedicated to creating a forum by which letter writers could write to one another about dozens of different topics. In 1989, Sikora reported that almost twenty thousand people wrote to others by way of the magazine.

Perhaps the most interesting development in the letter-writing world has been the computer bulletin board. Individuals can write long letters or short notes proclaiming their views on politics, physics, or love. What makes computer bulletin boards so intriguing is that people's letters can be anonymous. Bulletin boards, then, are a little like talking to someone on an airplane. Consequently, people often disclose some of their very deepest feelings. Unlike in the airplane situations, however, since everyone is invisible, there are often remarkably hostile interchanges. Particularly striking is the phenomenon of flaming, wherein a computer writer will brutally insult another person. Indeed, it is quite common for one person who might disclose a deeply personal experience to be assailed by another for being too sentimental or phony. So far, the psychological and health effects of computer bulletin board use have not been studied.

THE DOWNSIDE OF WRITING

I tend to get a little too enthusiastic at times. In my excitement about our research findings I may have portrayed writing as a cure for everything. An uncritical reading of this book would give the impression that writing about your deepest thoughts and feelings will make you physically healthier, mentally alert, smarter, and the epitome of psychological health. Yes, writing can be quite healthy. But an overreliance on writing can pose some problems—at least in some situations. In evaluating your own writing, be sure and ask yourself the following questions:

Are you using writing as a substitute for action?   Writing is particularly effective in dealing with issues that are uncontrollable. After a death or other trauma, writing helps people sort out complicated feelings and memories. In potentially controllable situations, however, writing may be counterproductive. That is, if we can do something to change an unpleasant situation, we are much better off changing it than merely writing about it.

In a recent writing experiment, for example, one woman wrote during each session about how much she disliked her roommate. Her roommate, according to her essays, was messy, borrowed her clothes without asking, and talked on the phone too much. Gleaning from what she wrote, her strategy in dealing with her roommate's behavior was to stay away from her own room as much as possible. I can't help but wonder what would have happened if the two women had been able to sit down and discuss the nature of their problems with each other.

Is your writing an intellectual rather than a self-reflective exercise?   I recently had the opportunity to read portions of a diary of a gentleman in his forties who was experiencing a tremendous amount of stress from his job and marriage. Both his physical and mental health were suffering even though he had been writing daily for several months. In many ways, I was entranced by his writing style. He was a fluid writer with an impressive vocabulary and a keen eye for nuances in people's behavior. In his writing, he drew heavily from Jung, Spinoza, Aristotle, Lao-tsu, and other luminaries. Despite his insight into other people's behavior and even his own mental processes, he never wrote about his own emotions or why he felt the way he did. He was so concerned with demonstrating his own brilliance that he forgot why he was writing in the first place.

It's grand to be smart. But intelligence and a classical education do not guarantee anyone emotional stability or personal insight. If you find that your writing often moves in a safe and nonpersonal direction wherein you are citing the work of Virginia Woolf to explain the ultimate failure of Napoleon, your writing may be quite interesting and even publishable. But don't expect intellectualization to improve your health.

Are you using writing as a forum for uncensored complaining? Remember that a prime value of writing is that it forces us to ask how and why we feel the ways we do. As a self-reflective exercise, writing is beneficial to acknowledge our deepest emotions and thoughts. If our lover has left us for someone else, it would undoubtedly be helpful to explore why we feel so bereft, so lonely, or so angry. Merely complaining about our cruel ex-lover will not be particularly healing. Indeed, it may be harmful.

Many studies have demonstrated that blindly venting anger often makes us feel angrier. Hitting a pillow, pretending it is someone we would like to slug, usually increases our blood pressure and encourages us to think of alternative acts of vengeance. Talking or writing about the source of our problems without self-reflection merely adds to our distress. If you find that your writing focuses more on another person than on yourself, stop and ask yourself some questions. Why are you writing this way? How do you feel about what you are writing? Why does the other person bother you as he or she does?

And this brings me to a related point: overdisclosing. Over the years I have been struck by a small group of people with whom I have talked who, with no provocation at all, immediately disclose extremely intimate events in their lives. Not only to me, but they confess the same detailed events to virtually all of their friends, coworkers, and even passersby. Although I have interviewed only four people—all women—who fit this category, all have suffered from major health problems, including uterine cancer, ulcers, and glandular imbalances. Indeed, they disclose their health problems with the same relish as they do their traumas. In all cases, their disclosure is automatic, dramatic, and usually shocking for the listener.

Although these overdisclosers appear to be confiding their deepest thoughts and feelings, a closer analysis suggests that they are divulging traumatic events in a repetitive fashion without self-reflecting. Again, they have rehearsed the events in their minds and in conversations thousands of times but have not explored either their emotions or the meanings of the events to their lives. Overdisclosing, then, is much like a verbal form of obsessive thinking. People talk or write about various aspects of a trauma without integrating the pieces.

Is your writing an exercise in self-reflection or in self-absorption? Periodically and following a major upheaval, it is valuable for people to stand back and reflect on who they are, why they behave in the ways they do, and how and why they respond emotionally. Self-reflection provides a form of feedback so that individuals can decide if they need to adjust their life course. Whereas periodic self-reflection is healthy, it can be carried to an extreme.

Let's be honest. We could ponder the meaning of an infinite number of events in our lives. Why, for example, did I just take a sip of coffee? How do I feel about that? What does that say about my childhood? And my feelings of security? Once we begin analyzing our deepest thoughts and feelings about everything, our self-absorption takes over our lives. During periods of self-reflection, we are by definition looking at ourselves to the exclusion of others. If we live in this self-reflective state, we cannot be empathic, a good friend to others, or a useful member of society. To the degree that writing helps us understand and reorient our lives, it is beneficial. When we self-reflect to the point of self-absorption, it becomes maladaptive.

★   ★   ★

There is nothing magical about writing in a self-disclosing manner. It works much the same way as talking to others, but without the social ramifications. Therein are its strength and weakness. You cannot be punished or humiliated by writing per se. But you also cannot get feedback from others. Other people's views and opinions usually ground us in reality. Without consulting others, we can blow many of our thoughts and emotions far out of proportion.

Writing should not serve as a substitute for friends. Many times, you may not be able to talk with others about particularly upsetting experiences. In these cases, writing can be quite helpful. Friends, however, can offer emotional support, advice, and other forms of assistance in ways that writing just can't do. Just because you may not be able to talk to some of your friends about a specific topic, remember that they are available for general advice and friendship. If friends are unavailable, psychotherapists and other people in the helping profession will listen to your problems and help keep your sense of reality intact.

Throughout this book, I have made numerous comparisons between writing and therapy. Both approaches can yield measurable improvements in psychological and physical health. Both encourage self-reflection and the attainment of insight about thoughts and moods. Both promote the acknowledgment and understanding of emotions.

To the degree that writing and therapy are used with basically healthy and well-adjusted people, the two techniques may provide similar advantages. The similarities, however, often stop here. For people who are deeply distressed and who are unable to cope effectively, therapy is often the only realistic alternative. When extremely distraught, individuals are often unable to write or think at all clearly or objectively. Similarly, when individuals suffer from a significant health problem, writing (or therapy) may positively influence their bodies. In most cases, however, they will be much wiser to visit a physician first. Antibiotic medications, for example, work more quickly and efficiently in dealing with infections than do writing sessions.

Writing, then, should be viewed as preventive maintenance. The value of writing or talking about our thoughts and feelings lies in reducing the work of inhibition and in organizing our complicated mental and emotional lives. Writing helps keep our psychological compass oriented. Although not a panacea, writing can be an inexpensive, simple, and sometimes painful way to help maintain our health.

To summarize: If you are mentally distraught, consult a therapist. If you are physically ill, see a physician. When your mental or physical health starts to return to normal, however, turn to your writing tablet.

Notes

Many of the issues raised in the book are far more complex than I have suggested. This section is included to point the interested reader to other reference sources that expand on particular points. Rather than use footnotes, information is provided by page number of the text.

CHAPTER 1

Page

13   Humans, as most mammals, respond to physical and psychological threats by easily measured biological responses. These stress responses can be immediate or, if the threats are long-lasting, can continue for days, weeks, or even years. The best general discussion of stress responses has been offered by the pioneering researcher Hans Selye in his book *The Stress of Life* (New York: McGraw-Hill, 1976).

14–15   I have run the "joy of talking" experiment almost a dozen times. Overall, the larger the group, the more the talkers like the group. In two-person groups, however, the effect is much smaller. In fact, when there are only two people, both the talker and the listener report disliking the group if one person dominates the discussion. Conversational bores, then, are most happy in large groups.

15–16   The use of the polygraph in law enforcement continues to be highly controversial. The results from a variety of studies indicate that it catches truly guilty people about 95 percent of the time. Unfortunately, it falsely labels innocent people as guilty 10–40 percent of the time. Although some important advances are being made by David Raskin and his colleagues at the University of Utah that take advantage of subtle biological patterns that occur during deception, it is unlikely that the polygraph will surpass an overall accuracy rate of 90–95 percent. For an incisive glimpse into the issues and problems of polygraph testing, see David Lykken's *A Tremor in the Blood* (New York: McGraw-Hill, 1981), or an article by William Waid and Martin Orne, "Cognitive, Social, and Personality Processes in the Physiological Detection of Deception," in an edited book by Leonard Berkowitz, *Advances in Experimental Social Psychology*, Vol. 14 (New York: Academic Press, 1981). For the most recent scientifically valid developments in the field, see the journal *Psychophysiology*.

17–18   One of the best summaries of research by Harold G. Wolff and his colleagues is a classic book by Stewart Wolf and Helen Goodell entitled *Harold G. Wolff's Stress and Disease* (Springfield, IL: Charles C. Thomas, 1968). This fascinating book traces the history and primary findings of Wolff's laboratory, including the nature of the stress interview.

17–18   A recurring debate among researchers interested in psychosomatics and emotion concerns whether specific emotions or situations can bring about specific biological changes. The specificity hypothesis states that an emotion such as guilt is biologically distinct from another emotion such as anger. The alternative hypothesis assumes that people respond in a general biological way to all situations and emotions. My bias is that most emotions do, in fact, have unique biological substrates. However, particularly powerful situations can "fool" people into thinking that they are feeling an emotion that is not biologically present. Robert Gatchel, Andrew Baum, and David Krantz provide a nice overview of this issue in *An Introduction to Health Psychology*, 2nd ed. (New York: Random House, 1989).

18–19   The role of defense mechanisms was discussed at length by Sigmund Freud in, among other places, his *Introductory Lectures on Psychoanalysis* (New York: Norton, 1966 [originally published in 1920]). For an excellent overview of the current thinking about defense mechanisms, see George E. Vaillant's *Adaptation to Life* (Boston: Little, Brown, 1977) and an article by Norma Haan, "A Tripartite Model of Ego Functioning: Values and Clinical-Research Applications," *Journal of Nervous and Mental Disease*, Vol. 148 (1969), pp. 14–30.

One of the more important issues related to defense mechanisms concerns the role of self-deception. People often fail to see a cause-effect relation between a psychological event and illness because they do not want to see it. You can appreciate the paradox. To not see something that is threatening requires some degree of awareness that the threatening event or relation exists. The various dimensions of self-deception have been expertly discussed by Daniel Goleman in his book *Vital Lies, Simple Truths: The Psychology of Self-Deception and Shared Illusions* (New York: Simon & Schuster, 1985). See also Matthew H. Erdelyi's *Psychoanalysis: Freud's Cognitive Psychology* (New York: Freeman, 1985).

19–20   For a remarkably sane approach to psychosomatics and health, I strongly recommend a book by Robert Ornstein and David Sobel, *Healthy Pleasures* (Reading, MA: Addison-Wesley, 1989).

21   For a more detailed account of this theory, see my article "Confession, Inhibition, and Disease," in Leonard Berkowitz's *Advances in Experimental Social Psychology*, Vol. 22 (New York: Academic Press, 1989).

CHAPTER 2

Page

23   The concept of inhibition has been used in a variety of ways by psychologists. It is beyond scope of this book to delve into the distinctions and subtleties of the types of inhibition. See the edited book by R. R. Miller and N. S. Spear, *Information Processing in Animals: Conditioned Inhibition* (Hillsdale, NJ: Erlbaum Publishers, 1985) for a discussion of the current uses of the term *inhibition* in behavioral research.

23–24   For a summary of Schachter's arguments, see his article "Recidivism and the Self-Cure of Smoking and Obesity," in the journal *American Psychologist*, Vol. 37 (4) (1982), pp. 436–444, and a related article, "More on Recidivism," in the same journal in Vol. 38 (7) (1983), pp. 854–855. Note that Schachter does not directly test or prove that the self-cure rates for smoking and weight loss are caused by practice alone. Rather, he views this explanation as a strong candidate. For a discussion of a similar process in the elimination of unwanted thoughts, see Dan Wegner's book *White Bears and Other Unwanted Thoughts: Suppression, Obsession, and the Psychology of Mental Control* (New York: Viking, 1989).

24–26   Bulimia clearly reflects society's value of thinness. Indeed, at both the University of Virginia and Southern Methodist University, we have found that among women, the higher the status of the various sororities (as rated by the students' themselves), the greater the bulimia rate in the sororities. In the last few years, a number of superb research projects on bulimia have pointed to the dangers of social pressure to be thin. See *The Etiology and Treatment of Bulimia Nervosa* by Craig Johnson and Mary Connors (New York: Basic Books, 1987).

27–28   Rubenstein's article that summarizes these findings was published in *Psychology Today,* Vol. 16 (1982), pp. 28–37. More detailed analyses of these data are reported by Claudia Hoover and me in an edited book by Richard J. Davidson and his colleagues, *Consciousness and Self-Regulation,* Vol. 4 (New York: Plenum Press, 1985).

28   Virtually all of Freud's students and most of today's psychoanalysts agree that Freud placed too much emphasis on sexuality in his work. Several scholars argue that many of the neuroses that Freud investigated in the late 1800s and early 1900s reflected the Victorian values of the time. Now, the argument goes, since we live in a more open sexual environment, many of the basic sexual conflicts that Freud witnessed are less striking. This line of reasoning may portend a new wave of creative neuroses in our society over the next several years due to the retrenchment of sexual values wrought by the AIDs epidemic. For a nice examination of Freud within the context of his society, see Peter Gay's book *Freud: A Life for our Time* (New York: Norton, 1988).

29–30   From a journal article with Joan R. Susman, "Disclosure of Traumas and Psychosomatic Processes," in *Social Science and Medicine,* Vol. 26 (1988), pp. 327–332. See also a more sociological investigation of individuals who must constantly portray a false public face in *The Managed Heart,* a book by A. R. Hochschild (Berkeley: University of California Press, 1983). I also recommend an important philosophical discussion associated with deception by Sissela Bok, *Secrets: On the Ethics of Concealment and Revelation* (New York: Vintage, 1983).

31–35   From a journal article with Robin O'Heeron, "Confiding in Others and Illness Rates Among Spouses of Suicide and Accidental Death Victims," in *Journal of Abnormal Psychology,* Vol. 93 (1984), pp. 473–476.

33–34   Other researchers have corroborated these general findings with much larger samples of people. Particularly impressive has been an ongoing project in West Germany that has interviewed hundreds of people whose spouses have died from a variety of causes. I strongly recommend a book by the primary investigators of this project, Wolfgang and Margaret S. Stroebe, entitled *Bereavement and Health: The Psychological and Physical Consequences of Partner Loss* (New York: Cambridge University Press, 1988).

34   Many of those people who appear to be the healthiest freely talk about the death, acknowledge their emotions, and insist on looking ahead to the future. I think all three dimensions are important. Merely wallowing in misery and self-pity for months or years cannot be beneficial—no matter how much you talk to others. By the same token, looking to the future without talking about the death is also unhealthy. For an excellent discussion of the value of an optimistic and yet open approach to coping, see Bernie S. Siegel's *Love, Medicine, and Miracles* (New York: Harper & Row, 1986).

34–35   The link between obsessive thoughts and talking is not entirely clear-cut. There is good evidence that actively inhibiting a given behavior increases thoughts about the behavior. If you have ever started to diet or tried to stop smoking, you probably remember thinking about food or cigarettes an inordinate amount of time. Further, if you actively hold back in talking to others about a trauma, you probably ruminate more about the trauma.

But the link between talking and not ruminating is not always there. Several studies by Camille Wortman and Roxanne Silver suggest that many people who constantly talk about the death of their child or other overwhelming tragedies also report thinking about the child a great deal as well. Similarly, recent work by Susan Nolen-Hoeksema points out that people most prone to depression ruminate and, often, talk about their miserable situations in an unhealthy way. Interestingly, there are gender differences, such as that women ruminate more than men, according to Nolen-Hoeksema in her book *Sex Differences in Depression* (Stanford, CA: Stanford University Press, 1990). As I discuss in greater detail in Chapter 5, many of the problems of these excessive ruminators is that they are not thinking about their situations in a self-reflective way and, rather, are often attempting to control their thoughts.

CHAPTER 3

Page

38–39   Breuer and Freud's work is summarized in their book *Studies in Hysteria* (New York: Avon Press, 1966 [originally published in 1895]). The case of Anna O. is unique along several dimensions. Over the two years of treatment, Anna O. (actually Bertha Pappenheim, who later became a major figure in the field of social work) exhibited a common psychological tendency of falling in love with her therapist, Josef Breuer. This phenomenon, called transference, was later identified by Freud as an essential ingredient for successful psychotherapy. Breuer, who was married, demonstrated signs of countertransference by becoming engrossed with Anna O. Unfortunately, toward the end of treatment, Anna O. developed the psychological symptoms of a hysterical pregnancy and phantom birth, claiming, "Dr. Breuer's child is coming!" This so shocked Breuer that he transferred the care of Anna O. to another physician and left Venice on a second honeymoon with his wife, never to practice psychotherapy again.

39–40   One of the more interesting discussions of the possible value of catharsis is provided by T. J. Scheff in his book *Catharsis in Healing, Ritual, and Drama* (Berkeley: University of California Press, 1979). For a summary of relevant experiments and therapies that employ catharsis, see *Catharsis in Psychotherapy* (New York: Gardiner Press, 1977), by M. P. Nichols and M. Zax.

40   The value of insight is acknowledged by therapists from several competing perspectives. Among current psychoanalysts, see *States of Mind* (New York: Plenum, 1987), by Mardi J. Horowitz; among humanistic therapists, see Carl Rogers's classic book *Client-Centered Therapy* (Boston: Houghton Mifflin, 1951); among cognitive therapists, excellent books are available by Aaron T. Beck, *Cognitive Therapy and the Emotional Disorders* (New York: NAL, 1979), or Donald Meichenbaum, *Stress Innoculation Training* (New York: Pergamon, 1985).

41–46   From J. W. Pennebaker and S. K. Beall, "Confronting a Traumatic Event: Toward an Understanding of Inhibition and Disease," *Journal of Abnormal Psychology*, Vol. 95 (1986), pp. 274–281.

46   For a nice summary of the work by Janice K. Kiecolt-Glaser and Ronald Glaser, see their chapter on the behavioral influences and immune function in a book edited by Tiffany Field and her colleagues, *Stress and Coping*, Vol. 2 (Hillsdale, NJ: Erlbaum Press, 1989).

46–48   From J. W. Pennebaker, J. K. Kiecolt-Glaser, and R. Glaser, "Disclosure of Traumas and Immune Function: Health Implications for Psychotherapy," *Journal of Consulting and Clinical Psychology*, Vol. 56 (1988), pp. 239–245.

47   Research in the area of psychology and immunology—or as it is now called, psychoimmunology—is a relatively new and rapidly changing area. Two excellent accounts of the developments in this field have recently been published: by Joan Borysenko, *Minding the Body, Mending the Mind* (Reading, MA: Addison-Wesley, 1987); and by Steven Locke and Douglas Colligan, *The Healer Within: The New Medicine of Mind and Body* (New York: Dutton, 1986).

48–49   A recent experiment by Ed Murray, Alicia Lamnin, and Chuck Carver, "Psychotherapy versus Written Confession: A Study of Cathartic Phenomena," *Journal of Social and Clinical Psychology*, in press, finds the same health patterns of writing that we have. See also a groundbreaking study by David Spiegel, J. R. Bloom, H. C. Kraemer, and E. Gottheil, "Effects of Psychosocial Treatment of Patients with Metastatic Breast Cancer," *Lancet*, ii: (1989), pp. 888–891. In the experiment, half of eighty-six patients with advanced breast cancer were randomly assigned to receive weekly psychotherapy. Those receiving psychotherapy lived, on average, one and a half years longer than controls.

50–51   Writing as a form of therapy has long been recommended by a number of therapists. Ira Progoff, for example, has strongly emphasized the value of writing in journals—see Progoff's book *At a Journal Workshop* (New York: Dialogue House Library, 1975). Others, such as Tristine Rainer [*The New Diary* (New York: St. Martin's Press, 1978)] and Arnold Lazarus [*The Practice of Multimodal Therapy*, (New York: McGraw-Hill, 1980)] have recommended that writing be used as one of several techniques by therapists.

The value of talking per se as a form of communication and insight therapy has recently been discussed by Gerald Goodman and Glenn Esterly in *Talk Book*. (Emmaus, PA: Rodale Press, 1988).

CHAPTER 4

Page
52–53   Joey's diagnosis was posttraumatic stress disorder, or PTSD. Although PTSD has only recently been defined as a separate disorder by the American Psychiatric Association, it commonly occurs with people who have experienced any type of massive trauma. An excellent overview of PTSD has been written by H. Hendin and A. P. Hass: "Posttraumatic Stress Disorder," in a book edited by C. G. Last and M. Herson, *Handbook of Anxiety Disorders* (New York: Pergamon, 1988).

53–57   The letting-go experience is closely linked to a variety of altered states of consciousness. The nature of a trancelike state in psychotherapy, for example, has been discussed by Milton H. Erickson and his colleagues in their book *Hypnotic Realities: Induction of Clinical Hypnosis and Forms of Indirect Suggestion* (New York: Irvington, 1976). Other techniques to help people get into these relaxed states have been discussed by Herbert Benson in *The Maximum Mind* (New York: Avon, 1987). Basically, any technique that induces a state of relaxation while maintaining mental alertness will promote the letting-go experience.

56   A wonderful and understandable summary of the history and thinking of the autonomic nervous system is Richard A.

Sternbach's *Principles of Psychophysiology* (New York: Academic, 1966).

56–57   Donald C. Fowles, "The Three Arousal Model: Implications of Gray's Two-Factor Theory for Heart Rate, Electrodermal Activity, and Psychopathy," *Psychophysiology,* Vol. 17 (1980), pp. 87–104. Fowles's approach was built on the original theorizing of Oxford University psychologist Jeffrey Gray, who has long distinguished between the behavioral inhibition system (BIS) and the behavioral activation system (BAS). According to Gray, the BIS and BAS are organized in fundamentally different ways in the brain. Evidence for BIS brain structures has focused most closely on the hippocampus and septum (in the emotional parts of the brain) and the frontal cortex. For a summary of these ideas, see Jeffrey Gray's *Elements of a Two-Factor Theory in Learning* (New York: Academic, 1975).

58–61   From J. W. Pennebaker, C. Hughes, and Robin C. O'Heeron, "The Psychophysiology of Confession: Linking Inhibitory and Psychosomatic Processes," *Journal of Personality and Social Psychology,* Vol. 52 (1987), pp. 781–793.

62–65   I am deeply indebted to Tyler Lorig for helping me set up our EEG laboratory and to Scott Cain, who spent hundreds of hours programming our computer to accomplish the brain-wave experiments. A summary of the brain-wave work is reported in my chapter in the book edited by Leonard Berkowitz, *Advances in Experimental Social Psychology,* Vol. 22 (New York: Academic, 1989).

63–64   Other work on brain activity is consistent with the cortical-congruence idea. I particularly recommend a popular book by Michael Gazzaniga, *The Social Brain* (New York: Plenum, 1986). Also, see work by University of Wisconsin researcher Richard J. Davidson, such as his chapter, "Affect, Cognition, and Hemispheric Specialization," in a book edited by C. E. Izard and colleagues, *Emotion, Cognition, and Behavior* (New York: Cambridge University Press, 1984).

CHAPTER 5

Page
68–70   The research on the suppression of thoughts is best summarized in Daniel M. Wegner's enchanting book *White Bears*

and Other Unwanted Thoughts: Suppression, Obsession, and the Psychology of Mental Control (New York: Viking, 1989). For an understanding of the clinical problems of obsessions and compulsions, see Judith Rappaport's *The Boy Who Couldn't Stop Washing* (New York: Dutton, 1988). A general professional overview of obsessions can be seen in a book by S. J. Rachman and R. J. Hodgson, *Obsessions and Compulsions* (Englewood Cliffs, NJ: Prentice-Hall, 1980).

69–70   Victor Frankl was one of the first people to note that one of the best ways to overcome unwanted thoughts was to stop trying to inhibit thoughts. In fact, he encouraged patients to actively try to think about their unwanted thoughts. His technique, called paradoxical intention, has been found to be quite effective in the treatment of obsessions. Frankl's original article, "Paradoxical Intention: A Logotherapeutic Technique," was published in the *American Journal of Psychotherapy*, Vol. 14 (1960), pp. 520–525. For a more recent approach to paradoxical intention and the treatment of worries, see work by Tom Borkovec and colleagues, "Stimulus Control Applications to the Treatment of Worry," *Behavioural Research and Therapy*, Vol. 21 (1983), pp. 247–251.

70–71   William James, *The Principles of Psychology* (New York: Jason Aronson, 1890). For a more recent summary of work on the stream of thought, see an edited book by K. S. Pope and J. L. Singer, *The Stream of Consciousness* (New York: Plenum, 1978).

71–75   For a report on the levels of thinking project, see J. W. Pennebaker, Jeanne Czajka, Russell Cropanzano, Brad Richards, Sondra Brumbelow, Kathleen Ferrara, Ron Thompson, and Toosje Thyssen, "Levels of Thinking," *Personality and Social Psychology Bulletin*, Vol. 16 (1990). A general summary of this work is reported in a book chapter by me, "Stream of Consciousness and Stress: Levels of Thinking," in an edited book coauthored by James Uleman and John Bargh, *The Direction of Thought: Limits of Awareness, Intention, and Control* (New York: Guilford, 1989). I should note that the Uleman and Bargh volume is an excellent compendium of recent work on the control of thoughts.

73–74   The perceived-control technique is reported in detail in an excellent book by David C. Glass and Jerome E. Singer, *Urban Stress* (New York: Academic, 1972).

76   A discussion of Israeli women whose spouses were listed
        as missing in action was conducted by Y. Tiechman, "The
        Stress of Coping with the Unknown Regarding a Signifi-
        cant Family Member," in a book edited by I. G. Sarason
        and C. D. Spielberger, *Stress and Anxiety*, Vol. 2 (New
        York: Wiley, 1966).

76–77   The best summary of defense mechanisms can be found in
        George E. Vaillant's *Adaptation to Life* (Boston: Little,
        Brown, 1977).

76–78   A good summary of the mindlessness research can be found
        in Ellen J. Langer's recent book, *Mindfulness* (Reading, MA:
        Addison-Wesley, 1989).

79   Various forms of implosive therapy encourage people to
        relive their most traumatic experiences as vividly as pos-
        sible. For example, people with claustrophobia may be
        placed in a dark closet until their panic subsides. Although
        implosive therapy has been found to be effective in treating
        various fears, it has been particularly valuable in the treat-
        ment of posttraumatic stress disorder (PTSD). For a dis-
        cussion of implosive therapies in general, see D. H. Barlow,
        Anxiety and Its Disorders (New York: Guilford, 1988). Both
        the Barlow book and one by J. H. Griest, J. W. Jefferson,
        and I. M. Marks, *Anxiety and Its Treatment: Help Is Available*
        (Washington, DC: American Psychiatric Association,
        1986), detail the use of implosion and related methods in
        treating PTSD with Vietnam veterans.

80–82   The thought-extraction project is reported in Holly Wil-
        liams's unpublished master's thesis, *The Effect of Thought
        Vocalization on Sleep Latency* (Dallas: Southern Methodist
        University, 1987). Two excellent books on sleep and sleep
        problems are by W. C. Dement, *Some Must Watch While
        Some Must Sleep* (San Francisco: W. H. Freeman, 1974) and
        by Richard M. Coleman, *Wide Awake at 3:00 AM* (New
        York: W. H. Freeman, 1986).

81–82   On the nature of dreaming, see the work of Stephen
        LaBerge, such as his book *Lucid Dreaming* (New York: Bal-
        lantine, 1985).

CHAPTER 6

Page

85   Elisabeth Kübler-Ross, *On Death and Dying* (New York: Macmillan, 1969).

85–87   There are many stage models other than the one first posited by Kübler-Ross. A good overview and comparison of models is covered by J. Schneider, *Stress, Loss, Grief* (Baltimore: University Park Press, 1984).

86   Mardi Horowitz, *Stress Response Syndromes* (New York: Jason Aronson, 1976).

87–88   Roxane Silver and Camille Wortman, "Coping with Undesirable Life Events," in an edited book by Judy Garber and Martin Seligman, *Human Helplessness: Theory and Applications* (New York: Academic, 1980). Other articles by Wortman and Silver include, "The Myths of Coping with Loss," *Journal of Consulting and Clinical Psychology*, Vol. 57 (1989), pp. 349–357, and a book chapter, "Effective Mastery of Bereavement and Widowhood: Longitudinal Research," in a book edited by P. B. Baltes and M. M. Baltes, *Successful Aging: Research and Theory* (London: Cambridge, in press).

90–91   Excellent summaries concerning the stress of attending college have been written by Shirley Fisher, *Homesickness and the Psychological Effects of Transition and Change* (London: Erlbaum, 1988).

91–94   James W. Pennebaker, Michelle Colder, and Lisa K. Sharp, "Accelerating the Coping Process," *Journal of Personality and Social Psychology*, Vol. 58 (1990), pp. 528–537.

94–96   Dozens of superb books have been written on the psychological effects of the Holocaust. Particularly striking is by Terrence Des Pres, *The Survivor* (New York: Simon & Schuster, 1983). A compilation of studies that have examined long-term health problems of Holocaust survivors can be found in an edited book by Paul Matussek, *Internment in Concentration Camps and Its Consequences* (New York: Springer-Verlag, 1975).

95–96   James W. Pennebaker, Steven D. Barger, and John Tiebout, "Disclosure of Traumas and Health among Holocaust Survivors," *Psychosomatic Medicine*, Vol. 51 (1989). pp. 577–589.

CHAPTER 7

Page

100–102   B. W. Zeigarnik, "Über das Behalten von erledigten und unerledigten Handlungen," *Psychologische Forschung* (1927), pp. 1–85. See also, Kurt Lewin's *A Dynamic Theory of Personality* (New York: McGraw-Hill, 1935).

101–102   The idea that thoughts reflect a failure to reach some kind of psychological completion of a task has been put forward in several guises over the years since Zeigarnik and Lewin. Two particularly interesting developments related to the completion tendency have been reported by Robert A. Wicklund and Peter M. Gollwitzer, *Symbolic Self-Completion* (Hillsdale, NJ: Erlbaum, 1983). See also a book chapter by Len Martin and Abe Tesser, "Toward a General Model of Ruminative Thought," in a book edited by J. Uleman and J. Bargh, *Unintended Thought: Limits of Awareness, Intention, and Control* (New York: Guilford, 1989).

102   Sigmund Freud, *The Interpretation of Dreams* (New York: Avon, 1965).

102–104   The need to understand our world is a central tenet of most current social and cognitive theories. For a discussion of the thought processes related to this need or expectation, see Richard E. Nisbett and Lee Ross, *Human Inference: Strategies and Shortcomings of Social Judgement* (Englewood Cliffs, NJ: Prentice-Hall, 1980). For a developmental perspective, see Jean Piaget, *The Construction of Reality in the Child* (New York: Basic Books, 1971).

103   Blaming the victim is most likely to occur among people who believe that the world is fundamentally just and fair. The more you think the world is just, the more invested you are in rationalizing unfair occurrences to others. See M. J. Lerner, "The Desire for Justice and Reactions to Victims," in a book edited by J. R. Macaulay and L. Berkowitz, *Altruism and Helping Behavior* (New York: Academic, 1970).

104   The incest quotations come from R. L. Silver, C. Boon, and M. H. Stones, "Searching for Meaning in Misfortune: Making Sense of Incest," *Journal of Social Issues,* Vol. 39 (1983), pp. 81–102.

104–105   Ronnie Janoff-Bulman, "Victims of Violence," in an edited book by Shirley Fisher and James Reason, *Handbook of Life Stress, Cognition, and Health* (Chichester: John Wiley, 1988).

107–108   David Spiegel, T. Hunt, and H. E. Dondershine, "Dissociation and Hypnotizability in Posttraumatic Stress Disorder," *American Journal of Psychiatry*, Vol. 145 (1988), pp. 301–305.

109–110   Daniel M. Wegner, Toni Guiliano, and Paula T. Hertel, "Cognitive Interdependence in Close Relationships," an edited chapter in a book by William Ickes, *Compatible and Incompatible Relationships* (New York: Springer-Verlag, 1985).

110   Abraham Maslow, *Toward a Psychology of Being,* 2nd ed. (Princeton, NJ: Van Nostrand Reinhold, 1968).

110–112   There are a number of interesting ways that therapists have used drawing and other art forms to tap self-expressiveness. For practical exercises, see the books of Lucia Capacchione, including *The Power of Your Other Hand* (North Hollywood, CA: Newcastle Publishing, 1988).

CHAPTER 8

Page
113–115   I am indebted to the Dallas-area Bereaved Parents groups whose members shared their stories with me about the deaths of their children.

114–116   The confronting/confronted-by distinction explains why traumatized people prefer to talk about threatening topics rather than hear about them. UCLA psychologist Shelley Taylor has found that women in various stages of breast cancer often talk to others about how poorly other cancer patients were faring. The women, for example, often mentioned how others were depressed, gravely ill, or had recently died. In contrast, when given the option, cancer patients want to hear about success stories. In other words, people with cancer talk about tragedies but want to hear about triumphs. For a discussion of these issues, I particularly recommend Taylor's book, *Positive Illusions: Creative*

Self-Deception and the Healthy Mind (New York: Basic, 1989), and a recent journal article: S. E. Taylor and M. Lobel, "Social Comparison Activity Under Threat: Downward Evaluation and Upward Contacts," *Psychological Review,* in press.

116–118   An interesting discussion of some of the dynamics that can occur in a relationship when the members are under stress can be seen in a book by Steve Duck, *Relating to Others* (Chicago: Dorsey, 1988).

117–119   Since the original publication of Stanley Cobb's paper on social support, "Social Support as a Moderator of Life Stress," *Psychosomatic Medicine,* Vol. 38 (1976), pp. 300–314, hundreds of research reports have bolstered his basic arguments. For recent developments on the nature of social support, see S. Cohen and S. L. Syme, *Social Support and Health* (New York: Academic, 1985), and a recent article by J. S. House, K. R. Landis, and D. Umberson, "Social Relationships and Health," *Science,* Vol. 241 (1988), pp. 540–545.

118   For a summary of the work by both William B. Swann and Jonathon D. Brown, see their coauthored chapter, "From Self to Health: Self-Verification and Identity Disruption," which will soon appear in an edited book by I. Sarason, B. Sarason, and G. Pierce, *Social Support: An Interactional View* (New York: Wiley, in press). For those people who may be trying to understand the possible meaning of a personal trauma, I recommend an insightful book by Harold Kushner, *When Bad Things Happen to Good People* (New York: Avon, 1983).

119–120   From the J. W. Pennebaker, C. Hughes, and R. C. O'Heeron paper cited earlier.

120   The work of Carl Rogers speaks directly to the social factors linked to the expression of thoughts and feelings. His analysis of the social dynamics in therapy is discussed in his classic book *Client-Centered Therapy: Its Current Practices, Implications, and Theory* (Boston: Houghton Mifflin, 1951).

121   A particularly cogent book on the links between the development of identity and society has been written by Roy F. Baumeister, *Identity: Cultural Change and the Struggle for Self* (New York: Oxford University Press, 1986).

121–122   Georg Simmel, *The Sociology of Georg Simmel* (New York: Free Press, 1950).

122   The confession hotline trade has now expanded to most major cities in the United States. For basic information on its development, see Jeanne McDowell, "True Confessions by Telephone," *Time*, October 3, 1988.

122   The data on the rapid increase of doctoral degrees granted in clinical and counseling psychology were furnished by Dr. Jessica Kohout of the American Psychological Association.

123   The experiment by E. Murray, A. Lamnin, and C. Carver, "Psychotherapy Versus Written Confession: A Study of Cathartic Phenomena," *Journal of Social and Clinical Psychology*, in press, compares writing and talking about upsetting experiences. What is most striking, however, is that both forms of expression—which were done over two thirty-minute sessions separated by a week—produced health improvements. Overall moods following writing or therapy were unrelated to long-term health improvements.

123–124   The transference issue has recently been discussed in detail in a fascinating chapter by Jerome L. Singer in a book edited by Dennis C. Turk and Peter Salovey, *Reasoning, Inference, and Judgment in Clinical Psychology* (New York: Free Press, 1988).

124–125   A research literature that is particularly germane to this chapter deals with self-disclosure. The first serious observations on how and when people disclosed to others were discussed by Sidney M. Jourard, *The Transparent Self* (New York: Van Nostrand Reinhold, 1971). Since that time, a number of researchers in the fields of social and clinical psychology have mapped out the dimensions of self-disclosure in much finer detail. An excellent compilation of research can be seen in the edited book of Valerian J. Derlega and John H. Berg, *Self-Disclosure: Theory, Research, and Therapy* (New York: Plenum, 1987). See also the fascinating analysis of social penetration theory as it relates to the disclosure of two people at the beginning of a relationship, in Irwin Altman and Dalmas A. Taylor, *Social Penetration: the Development of Interpersonal Relationships* (New York: Holt, 1973).

126   This experiment is described in Joanne Shortt's unpublished

master's thesis, *The Autonomic Effects of Listening to Another's Trauma* (Dallas: Southern Methodist University, 1989).

126–127   For a good general discussion of burnout, see Christina Maslach's book *Burnout: The Cost of Caring* (Englewood Cliffs, NJ: Prentice-Hall, 1982).

CHAPTER 9

Page

130–132   The physiological effects of expressing different emotions is far more complicated than I allude to in this section. There has been a long and fascinating debate about whether different emotions are associated with unique physiological patterns—the specificity debate. Recent evidence suggests that there probably is a modest specificity relationship between emotions and autonomic nervous system activity. A series of important articles and books address this issue: Robert W. Levenson, "Emotion and the Autonomic Nervous System: A Prospectus for Research on Autonomic Specificity," in a book edited by H. L. Wagner, *Social Psychophysiology and Emotion* (New York: John Wiley, 1988). See also Paul Ekman, Robert W. Levenson, and W. V. Friesen, "Autonomic Nervous System Activity Distinguishes Among Emotions," *Science,* Vol. 221 (1983), pp. 1208–1210. Also, Howard S. Friedman and Stephanie Booth-Kewley, "The 'Disease-Prone Personality': A Meta-analytic View of the Construct," *American Psychologist,* Vol. 47 (1987), pp. 539–555. Finally, for a general overview of emotions, see Nico H. Frijda, *The Emotions* (Cambridge: Cambridge University Press, 1986).

It is important to note that the physiological similarity among emotions to which I am referring is only relevant along the continuum of inhibition. We get the same autonomic effects when people inhibit (versus express) positive or negative emotions. Physiological indices that tap other psychological processes may differ from specific emotion to specific emotion.

130–131   This experiment is the unpublished master's thesis of Jeanne A. Czajka, *Behavioral Inhibition and Short-Term Physiological Responses* (Dallas: Southern Methodist University, 1987).

132   A particularly well-written overview of who gets sick and
       when is a book by Blair Justice, *Who Gets Sick: How Beliefs,
       Moods, and Thoughts Affect Your Health* (Los Angeles: Jer-
       emy P. Tarcher, 1987). See also, D. P. Phillips and K. A.
       Feldman, "A Dip in Deaths Before Ceremonial Occasions:
       Some New Relationships Between Social Integration and
       Mortality," *American Sociological Review*, Vol. 38 (1973),
       pp. 678–696.

133   For a summary of research findings on laughter and health,
       see *Humor and Life Stress* (New York: Springer-Verlag,
       1986) by Herbert Lefcourt.

134–135 A lively discussion of issues surrounding pornography and
       other sexual issues is available in an edited book by Mary
       Roth Walsh, *The Psychology of Women: Ongoing Debates*
       (New Haven: Yale University Press, 1987).

135   Cross-cultural data are reported by C. S. Ford and F. A.
       Beach, *Patterns of Sexual Behavior* (New York: Harper and
       Row, 1951). Current estimates of homosexuality are re-
       ported in H. A. Katchadourian and D. T. Lunde, *Biological
       Aspects of Human Sexuality* (New York: Holt, Rinehart and
       Winston, 1980).

136–138 Current estimates on the number of married adults who
       have had affairs are quite variable. Averaging across studies,
       it appears as if 50 percent of males and 30 percent of females
       have engaged in affairs. These numbers vary tremendously
       as a function of age, social class, and other factors. For a
       review, see A. P. Thompson, "Extramarital Sex: A Review
       of the Literature," *Journal of Sex Research*, Vol. 19 (1983),
       pp. 1–22.

137–138 An increasing number of studies point to the importance
       of interpersonal trust in maintaining physical health. A
       particularly impressive account can be seen in a book by
       James J. Lynch, *The Broken Heart* (New York: Basic, 1977).
       A more recent analysis suggests that a lack of trust, or
       cynicism, is particularly threatening to the cardiovascular
       system, according to Redford Williams, *The Trusting Heart*
       (New York: Random, 1989). See also, M. Ueno, "The So-
       called Coition Death," *Japanese Journal of Legal Medicine*,
       Vol. 17 (1963), p. 330.

138–139 Several recent books have analyzed the nature of passion
       and intimacy in relationships. I strongly recommend an

insightful and popular book by Maggie Scarf, *Intimate Partners* (New York: Ballantine, 1988), as well as Dan P. McAdams, *Intimacy: The Need to Be Close* (New York: Doubleday, 1989).

139   The Anaïs Nin quotation comes from a volume edited by Gunther Stuhlmann, *The Diary of Anaïs Nin, Vol. 5, 1947–1955* (New York: Harcourt Brace Jovanovich, 1974).

139–140   The Grinch project is based on unpublished data by J. W. Pennebaker, J. A. Czajka, H. Patel, and K. Ferrara, 1986. For more information on passionate love among adolescents, see Elaine Hatfield and Susan Sprecher, "Measuring Passionate Love in Intimate Relationships," *Journal of Adolescence,* Vol. 9 (1986), pp. 383–410.

CHAPTER 10

Page
146   Freud's view of personality is particularly well summarized in Peter Gay's *Freud: A Life for Our Time* (New York: Norton, 1988).

John B. Watson, *Behaviorism* (New York: Norton, 1930).

148–149   Jerome Kagan, J. Steven Reznick, and Nancy Snidman, "Biological Bases of Childhood Shyness," *Science,* Vol. 240 (1988), pp. 167–171. See also a paper by Rebecca A. Eder, "Uncovering Young Children's Psychological Selves: Individual and Developmental Differences," *Child Development,* 1990, in press.

149–150   Auke Tellegen, David T. Lykken, Thomas J. Bouchard, Kimerly J. Wilcox, Nancy L. Segal, and Stephen Rich, "Personality Similarity in Twins Reared Apart and Together," *Journal of Personality and Social Psychology,* Vol. 54 (1988), pp. 1031–1039. For the statistically inclined, the intraclass Pearson correlations for scores on the constraint measures are as follows: identical twins reared together = .58, identical twins reared apart = .57, fraternal twins reared together = .25, fraternal twins reared apart = .04.

These general patterns have now been replicated by R. J. Rose, "Genetic and Environmental Variance in Content Dimensions of the MMPI," *Journal of Personality and*

Social Psychology, Vol. 55 (1988), pp. 302–311. See also, N. L. Pederson, R. Plomin, G. E. McClearn, and L. Friberg, "Neuroticism, Extraversion, and Related Traits in Adult Twins Reared Apart and Reared Together," *Journal of Personality and Social Psychology*, Vol. 55 (1988), pp. 950–957.

151   The inhibition questionnaire items come from the Disinhibition (vs. Constraint) Scale of the General Temperament Survey developed by Lee Anna Clark and David Watson, Department of Psychology, Southern Methodist University. I am indebted to them for allowing me to reproduce the items.

153–155   The repressive coping style has traditionally been measured by selecting individuals who have high scores on scales that tap inhibition (the Marlowe-Crowne Social Desirability Scale) and who have low scores on anxiety measures (the Taylor Manifest Anxiety Scale). The original repressive coping style study was published by Daniel A. Weinberger, Gary E. Schwartz, and Richard J. Davidson, "Low-Anxious, High-Anxious, and Repressive Coping Styles: Psychometric Patterns and Behavioral and Physiological Responses to Stress," *Journal of Abnormal Psychology*, Vol. 88 (1979), pp. 369–380. Weinberger's more recent work is summarized in his paper "The Construct Validity of the Repressive Coping Style," which will soon appear in an edited book by Jerome L. Singer, *Repression and Dissociation: Defense Mechanisms and Personality Styles* (Chicago: University of Chicago Press, 1990). Note that in the Weinberger research, cholesterol levels are most likely to be elevated when adults are habitually repressing anger.

154   The work on repressed or suppressed anger and heart disease is somewhat controversial. As of this writing, there are several studies pointing to the probable links between repressed anger and various cardiovascular risk factors. See, for example, T. M. Dembroski, J. M. MacDougall, R. B. Williams, T. Haney, and J. A. Blumenthal, "Components of Type A, Hostility, and Anger-in: Relationship to Angiographic Findings," *Psychosomatic Medicine*, Vol. 47 (1985), pp. 219–233; H. S. Goldstein and colleagues, "Relationship of Blood Pressure and Heart Rate to Experienced Anger and Expressed Anger," *Psychosomatic Medicine*, Vol. 50 (1988), pp. 321–329; M. Koskenvuo and colleagues, "Hostility as a Risk Factor for Mortality and Ischemic Heart

Disease in Men," *Psychosomatic Medicine,* Vol. 50 (1988), pp. 330–340; Joel E. Dimsdale and colleagues, "Suppressed Anger and Blood Pressure: The Effects of Race, Sex, Social Class, Obesity, and Age," *Psychosomatic Medicine,* Vol. 48 (1986), pp. 430–436.

Without doubt, the best summary of research on the emotion of anger—whether suppressed or expressed—is a book by Carol Tavris, *Anger: the Misunderstood Emotion* (New York: Simon & Schuster, 1982). In her book, she calls into question many of the commonsense views that suppressed anger leads to heart disease. Her argument is that it is not anger per se that leads to heart problems but rather conflict. When a person is conflicted about expressing an emotion, such as anger, the person should manifest more biological signs of stress. Conflict, in Tavris's terms, is much like inhibition in mine—if not identical.

154–155   The jury is still out on the overall links between measures of the inhibited personality and immune problems such as cancer. Those studies that have found links with immune and allied health measures include: Larry D. Jamner, Gary E. Schwartz, and Hoyle Leigh, "The Relationship Between Repressive and Defensive Coping Styles and Monocyte, Eosinophile, and Serum Glucose Levels: Support for the Opioid Peptide Hypothesis of Repression," *Psychosomatic Medicine,* Vol. 50 (1988), pp. 567–575; Robert A. Emmons and Laura A. King, "Conflict Among Personal Strivings: Implications for Psychological and Physical Well-Being," *Journal of Personality and Social Psychology,* Vol. 54 (1988), pp. 1040–1048.

The original cancer work was quite promising, especially after the publication of a study by Leonard R. Derogatis and his colleagues, "Psychological Coping Mechanisms and Survival Time in Metastatic Breast Cancer," *Journal of the American Medical Association,* Vol. 242 (1979), pp. 1504–1508. See also, M. R. Jensen, "Psychobiological Factors Predicting the Course of Breast Cancer," *Journal of Personality,* Vol. 55 (1987), pp. 317–342. The failure to find any links between inhibition and cancer has been reported by Victoria W. Persky and her colleagues, "Personality and Risk of Cancer: 20-year Follow-up of the Western Electric Study," *Psychosomatic Medicine,* Vol. 49 (1987), pp. 435–449. An interesting new twist on this line of research is the finding by Sandra M. Levy and her colleagues that the expression of joy is associated with better prognosis once breast cancer is diagnosed than if the person does not express joy, see "Survival Hazards Analysis in First Recurrent Breast Cancer Patients: Seven-Year Follow-up," *Psychosomatic Medicine,* Vol. 50 (1988), pp. 520–528.

Besides cancer and heart disease, measures of inhibition have been linked to other health problems, including pain endurance—see Larry D. Jamner and Gary E. Schwartz, "Self-Deception Predicts Self-Report and Endurance of Pain," *Psychosomatic Medicine,* Vol. 48 (1986), pp. 211–223—and bronchial asthma in children, see Irmela Florin and colleagues, "Facial Expressions of Emotion and Physiologic Reactions in Children with Bronchial Asthma," *Psychosomatic Medicine,* Vol. 47 (1985), pp. 382–393. For a historical view of this approach, see the work of Franz Alexander, *Psychosomatic Medicine* (New York: Norton, 1950).

154–158   In reviewing the links between personality and disease, it is critical to distinguish those studies that rely on self-reports of stress and health from those that hinge on objective measures. David Watson, Lee Anna Clark, and others have identified a general personality style called Negative Affectivity, or NA. Individuals high in NA tend to be chronically anxious and emotionally distraught. They also complain about their health frequently even though they are no different biologically than those low in NA. For summaries of this research, see David Watson and Lee Anna Clark, "Negative Affectivity: The Disposition to Experience Aversive Emotional States," *Psychological Bulletin,* Vol. 96 (1984), pp. 465–460. Also, D. Watson and J. W. Pennebaker, "Health Complaints, Stress, and Distress: Exploring the Central Role of Negative Affectivity," *Psychological Review,* Vol. 96 (1989), pp. 234–254.

155–157   The person-environment-fit research has examined the links between individuals' abilities and the demands of their jobs in a variety of settings, ranging from factories to more controlled laboratory tests. See, for example, a book by Robert D. Caplan and his colleagues, *Job Demands and Worker Health* (Washington, DC: Government Printing Office, 1975). For a brief summary of this work, see Chapter 2 of my book *The Psychology of Physical Symptoms* (New York: Springer-Verlag, 1982).

158   The work by Paul T. Costa, Robert R. McCrae, and David Arenberg find that the twelve-year test-retest of the Re-

straint scale of the Guilford-Zimmerman Temperament Survey was .71 using a sample of 418 adults. Although it is impossible to estimate precisely what percentage of people would be defined as stable or unstable based on correlation coefficients, it is not unreasonable to assume that approximately 50 percent of the sample changes appreciably over the twenty-year interval.

CHAPTER 11

Page

161 Perhaps the best discussions of the evolution of a collective consciousness can be found in Sigmund Freud's *Civilization and Its Discontents* (London: Hogarth Press, 1961), and Erich Fromm's *The Sane Society* (New York: Holt, Rinehart and Winston, 1955).

162–165 The volcano research is summarized in a chapter by J. W. Pennebaker and Darren Newtson,"Observation of a Unique Event: the Psychological Impact of Mount Saint Helens Volcano," in a book edited by Harry T. Reis, *Naturalistic Approaches to Studying Social Interaction* (San Francisco: Jossey-Bass, 1983).

164 Bill Walster and Elliot Aronson, "Effect of Expectancy of Task Duration on the Experience of Fatigue," *Journal of Experimental Social Psychology*, Vol. 3 (1967), pp. 41–46.

166–167 Within a week of the October 17, 1989, Bay Area earthquake, a group of volunteers, under the direction of Kent Harber and me, began a series of random phone calls to residents of San Francisco, Sacramento, Claremont/Los Angeles, and Dallas. In the first three months after the quake, almost one thousand residents have been surveyed on at least one occasion. We are deeply indebted to Joann Shortt at SMU, Lewis Ellenhorn at Pitzer College, and the many students who have helped with this project. The project would not have been possible without an emergency grant from the National Science Foundation. For a summary of the findings, see J. W. Pennebaker and K. Harber, *The Psychological and Health Effects of the Loma Prieta Earthquake* (Dallas: Southern Methodist University, 1990).

 Laura Carstensen's unpublished observations are congruent with the denial patterns reported by others. For example, E. L. Jackson and T. Mukerjee report that people in areas most prone to earthquakes least want to talk about them, according to their chapter, "Human Adjustment to the Earthquake Hazard of San Francisco, California," in a book edited by G. F. White, *Natural Hazards: Local, National, Global* (New York: Oxford, 1974). See also an intriguing report by Darrin R. Lehman and Shelley E. Taylor that indicates that the more seismically unsafe people's houses in earthquake areas are, the more likely they are to deny the seriousness of earthquakes, as reported in the article "Date with an Earthquake: Coping with a Probable, Unpredictable Disaster," *Personality and Social Psychology Bulletin,* Vol. 13 (1988), pp. 546–555.

167–168   One of the best summaries of the Three Mile Island disaster is by Andrew Baum, "Toxins, Technology, and Natural Disasters," in a book edited by G. R. VandenBos and B. K. Bryant, *Cataclysms, Crises, and Catastrophes: Psychology in Action* (Washington, DC: American Psychological Association, 1987). Some interesting social parallels between natural and manmade disasters were seen in the aftermath of the Great Chicago Fire of 1871. Immediately after the fire, people were drawn together. However, within a few weeks, increased social and ethnic tensions became apparent. For an interesting review of these effects, see an article by Karen Sawislak, "Smoldering City," *Chicago History* (Fall/Winter 1988–1989), Vol. 17, pp. 70–101.

168–173   For a discussion of the Kennedy assassination project, see J. W. Pennebaker and Rhonda Polakoff, "The Effects of the John F. Kennedy Assassination on Dallas," *Psychological Science,* in press (pending revision).

169–170   An original nationwide survey as well as a survey of Dallas residents was conducted several days after the assassination and again one month later. The survey results are reported by B. S. Greenberg and E. B. Parker in their edited book *The Kennedy Assassination and the American Public* (Stanford, CA: Stanford University Press, 1965).

173   An interesting personal account of the assassination and its effects on Dallas is recounted by Dallas historian A. C. Greene, *Dallas USA* (Austin: Texas Monthly Press, 1984).

173–174   For a discussion of demographics and health, see David Mechanic's *Medical Sociology* (New York: Free Press, 1978).

CHAPTER 12

Page
177–178   William Sargant, *Battle for the Mind: A Physiology of Con-
           version and Brainwashing* (London: William Heinemann,
           1957). Also, I strongly recommend the seminal book by
           Jerome D. Frank, *Persuasion and Healing* (New York:
           Schocken, 1973). Both books point to the close parallels
           among religious conversion, thought reform, and psycho-
           therapy.

178–179   Much of the information concerning disclosure in the West-
           ern hemisphere has been drawn from the fascinating chapter
           by Weston La Barre, "Confession as Cathartic Therapy in
           American Indian Tribes," in the book edited by Ari Kiev,
           *Magic, Faith, and Healing: Studies in Primitive Psychiatry To-
           day* (New York: Free Press, 1964). Indeed, Kiev's edited
           book contains several interesting chapters for anyone in-
           terested in cross-cultural comparisons of healing rituals. I
           am indebted to Nia Georges of Rice University for intro-
           ducing me to this literature.

179–180   Mao Tse-tung, "Get Organized!" (November 29, 1943),
           Selected Works of Mao Tse-tung, Vol. III (Peking: Foreign
           Language Press, 1977). Although Mao attributed self-
           criticism to Marx and Lenin, there is very little evidence
           that either Marx or Lenin endorsed the idea. Lenin, ac-
           cording to Alfred G. Meyer, who authored *Leninism* (New
           York: Praeger, 1957), believed that there should be open
           debate within the Communist party as long as there was
           unanimity in the final decision. Criticism was not self-crit-
           icism so much as a logical critique of ideas or strategies.
           Accordingly, the growth and use of self-criticism tech-
           niques in the Soviet Union and its satellite countries are
           usually associated with Stalin.

183   The best summary of the Gergen experiment can be found
           in their book: Kenneth J. Gergen and Mary M. Gergen,
           Social Psychology, 2nd ed. (New York: Springer-Verlag,
           1986). The Freud quotation is from: Sigmund Freud, "Fur-
           ther Recommendations in the Technique of Psychoanaly-
           sis," *Therapy and Technique* (New York: Collier, 1963).

184–185   William James, *Varieties of Religious Experience* (New York:
           Collier, 1961).

187–190   The entire argument concerning the nature of implicit values within a confession setting has been made by other authors using different terminology. For example, Jerome Frank points out the importance of the confessor and confessee sharing the same assumptive worlds.

191–192   For an interesting discussion of the underlying values and dynamics of the interchange between client and therapist, I recommend a superb book edited by Dennis C. Turk and Peter Salovey, *Reasoning, Inference, and Judgment in Clinical Psychology* (New York: Free Press, 1988).

CHAPTER 13

Page
194–195   For a more general discussion of the in-class writing work, see my chapter, "Self-Expressive Writing: Implications for Health, Education, and Welfare," in a book edited by S. I. Fontaine, P. Belanoff, and P. Elbow, *Nothing Begins with N* (New York: Boynton-Cook, 1990). In addition, see Lizabeth McIntire's master's thesis, *The Effects of Writing Exercises on Student Performance* (Dallas: Southern Methodist University, 1989).

196–197   I particularly recommend two books by Lev S. Vygotsky: *Thought and Language*, edited by Alex Kozulin (Cambridge, MA: MIT Press, 1986), and *Mind in Society*, edited by Michael Cole and colleagues (Cambridge, MA: Harvard University Press, 1978). Note that the description of the Luria experiment came from *Mind in Society*. For additional reading, see A. R. Luria's superb book *Language and Cognition* (New York: John Wiley, 1981).

197   D. Graves and V. Stuart, *Write from the Start: Tapping Your Child's Natural Writing Ability* (New York: New American Library, 1985). Peter Elbow, *Writing with Power* (New York: Oxford University Press, 1981). I also recommend an enjoyable book by Natalie Goldberg that may help to get one's creative juices flowing through writing, *Writing Down the Bones* (Boston: Shambhala, 1986).

197–198   The research by Gillis O. Einstein and colleagues distinguishes between information that is high versus low in importance. Good note takers are adept at pulling out information that is highly important and also broad and integrative. Both good and poor note takers perform equally well on exam questions that ask low-level facts (i.e., low-importance information). For a description of this research, see: G. O. Einstein, Joy Morris, and Susan Smith, "Note-taking, Individual Differences, and Memory for Lecture Information," *Journal of Educational Psychology*, Vol. 77 (1985), pp. 522–532. See also, R. Peper and R. E. Mayer, "Note Taking as a Generative Activity," *Journal of Educational Psychology*, Vol. 70 (1978), pp. 514–522.

201   For more information on *The Letter Exchange*, write to Steve Sikora, editor, The Letter Exchange, Box 6218, Albany, CA 94706. I am indebted to Jannay Morrow, Caroline Collins, and Delia Cioffi for introducing me to the secret worlds of computer bulletin boards.

Index